Measuring Pupil Achievement and Aptitude

Second Edition

Measuring Pupil Achievement and Aptitude

Second Edition

C. Mauritz Lindvall and Anthony J. Nitko

Learning Research and Development Center
University of Pittsburgh

Harcourt Brace Jovanovich, Inc.
New York   Chicago   San Francisco   Atlanta

ISBN: 0-15-557792-1

Library of Congress Catalog Card Number: 74-29370

Printed in the United States of America

Preface

The second edition of *Measuring Pupil Achievement and Aptitude,* though revised and expanded throughout, has the same purpose as the original edition —to provide a brief introduction to the basic principles of testing and evaluation.

Since the turn of the century, psychologists, psychometricians, and educators have developed an extensive technical body of measurement theory and practice, including test development procedures and statistical techniques for the detailed analysis of tests and test results. To master this body of knowledge requires several courses in mathematics and statistics, followed by a considerable number of courses in the content itself. Because of the limited time usually allotted to fundamental training in testing, many students will receive only an introduction to educational measurement. Others, because of particular interest, will go on to do advanced course work in the field. This book is directed at both categories of student; it can be used as a brief core text or as a supplement in various courses in the field of education. Those who wish to undertake a more intensive study while using this book can consult the suggestions for further reading that appear at the end of each chapter. The sources mentioned range from the basic to the complex and are designed to enrich the material of the text.

As in the first edition, this book discusses the role of tests in education, the need for specific objectives, and the considerations that should determine the choice of tests. It describes different types of test items and gives instructions for their preparation and use; it includes separate chapters on standardized achievement and aptitude tests; and it presents statistical information essential to understanding scoring. The final chapter gives advice for the integration of a comprehensive classroom program of testing and evaluation.

New to this edition are discussions of major advances in the field; for example, criterion-referenced testing, the use of structured hierarchies of objectives as a basis for monitoring pupil progress, and techniques for examining such important test characteristics as validity, reliability, and standardization. Throughout, the book reflects the recent trends of increased attention to the role of testing in planning and guiding instruction, and of greater emphasis on adapting instruction to differences among individual students. Specifically, we have added a new chapter, Testing and Evaluation in the Individualization of Instruction.

As must be the case for anyone writing a textbook, especially in the area of testing and evaluation, the authors are indebted not only to their colleagues but to their teachers and their students, from whom they have learned most of what is presented in this book. These persons are too numerous to name here, but many of them are mentioned in footnotes and in the suggestions for further reading. For their valuable comments on the manuscript we would like to thank: Lois E. Burrill and Gary J. Robertson of the Test Department at Harcourt Brace Jovanovich; Professor Robert A. Forsyth, University of Iowa; and Professor Darrell L. Sabers, University of Arizona. We would also like to extend thanks to Pat Graw, Kathryn Pikula, and Alma Johnson, who worked tirelessly in helping us prepare the manuscript. Finally, we express our gratitude to our wives, Marian and Veronica, to whom we dedicate this book.

C. M. L.
A. J. N.

Contents

Measuring Pupil Achievement and Aptitude

Second Edition

1

The Role of Testing and Evaluation in Education

Jan Miller was preparing for her first day of teaching. When she graduated from State University last spring and obtained her beginning teacher's certificate, she took a position as a third-grade teacher in one of the city's large elementary schools. Now, since school was starting this coming Monday, she had all the concerns of a teacher about to start a first job. What would her pupils be like? Would she be able to hold their attention? What kinds of learning activities would be of real interest to them? How could she fit her teaching to their needs and abilities? How would she know if her teaching was effective? Would she have any problem learners? She realized that she probably would. She would have to try, as quickly as possible, to learn something about the unique abilities and aptitudes of each pupil. Certainly they would vary greatly in what they had learned in first and second grade. Some would probably be very good readers, others, nonreaders. Also, some would undoubtedly have gone farther than others in beginning arithmetic. Jan recognized that if she was going to be successful in her new job, one of the things she would have to do would be to obtain a great deal of information on her pupils. Only then would she be able to make valid decisions about how to plan her teaching.

The need for extensive information about pupils, cited here as a basic concern of the new teacher, must be a major concern of all persons in teaching positions. The essential purpose of teaching is to produce changes in pupils. Any program of instruction must be based upon and be guided by information on pupil aptitude, interest, and achievement. A father who is teaching his son how to swim plans his teaching steps on the basis of what he knows about the child. These steps will follow one pattern if the son seems to love to be in the water, has no fear of it, and has a close friend who is already able to swim. The steps will probably be quite different if the son really fears the water and has no desire whatsoever to learn how to swim. The son's present abilities and aptitudes will also influence his father s decision about how to proceed. A child who has shown a capacity for learning physical tasks quickly and easily may not have to be taken through all the steps that would be necessary for a child with less aptitude. Also, as the instruction progresses, the achievement that the child has displayed in mastering previous steps will determine what will be done next. Throughout, the father's instruction will be guided by his perceptions of his son's attitude, aptitude, and achievement.

In a similar fashion, the work of the classroom teacher should be guided by continuous information about pupil aptitude, interest, and progress. It may be possible for a teacher with only one student to obtain most of the necessary information concerning that student through intensive informal observation. However, since the typical teacher must collect such information on a large number of students in a limited period of time, this type of intensive personal observation is not possible. What is required is a more efficient method for securing this necessary knowledge.

To return to our swimming analogy, it will be impossible for a swimming instructor teaching a whole class of nonswimmers rather than a single individual to learn everything necessary concerning each student merely by observing the general behavior of each as the class splashes around in the pool. It will be essential to develop some regular procedure for observing students while they perform certain standard tasks. For example, to learn something about pupil readiness and aptitude, the instructor might ask all pupils to jump into the water from the edge of the pool, to walk out into the deeper water until it reached waistline depth, and to lift their feet from the bottom so as to float in a face-down, prone position. By asking each student to perform simple standard tasks of this type, the instructor can obtain a record of what each student can and will do.

In the same way, every classroom teacher, while employing as much informal observation as possible as a means of acquiring information about pupils, will also find it necessary to use more formal procedures such as testing. Some of these procedures may be quite similar to those used by our hypothetical swimming instructor. Pupils may be asked to carry out certain set tasks while the teacher observes the quality of each performance. In this case the teacher is using performance-type tests. Other procedures may involve paper-and-pencil tasks such as are found in a typical essay or objective-type examination. All these procedures receive major emphasis in the study of theory and technique in testing and evaluation. However, it is essential to remember that the procedures are of no educational value in and of themselves; they are merely refined techniques that are used to obtain necessary information about pupils. Tests are of value only if they yield information that is used to improve the total teaching-learning process. This must be the basic consideration for any teacher attempting to determine which of the many available types of measuring instruments will be of use in the classroom.

Areas of Pupil Evaluation

The major pupil variables in educational testing and evaluation are typically grouped into four broad categories: (1) achievement, (2) aptitude, (3) interest, and (4) personality. The following sections provide an overview of the problems and procedures in each of these categories and indicate the extent to which each will be explored in this text.

ASSESSING PUPIL ACHIEVEMENT

Quite obviously the classroom teacher must frequently assess the level of pupil achievement. The teacher's major "business" is to produce changes in pupils, and the degree of teacher success can be determined only through regular assessments of what the pupils have learned.

1. *Nontesting procedures*—All teachers make some use of relatively informal procedures for determining what pupils have learned. They watch pupils perform in class; they listen to them recite; and they grade homework assignments. Although most teachers choose to supplement such techniques with more reliable and objective procedures, the obvious validity of many nontesting procedures makes them important tools for the teacher. Therefore, this text will devote some attention to suggestions for the improved use of these techniques.

2. *Teacher-made tests*—A traditional and essential tool of the classroom teacher is the teacher-made test, undoubtedly the most widely used procedure for assessing pupil achievement. Although many teachers produce excellent tests, most readers probably would agree on the basis of their own experience as students that there is much room for improvement. Because of the important role of teacher-made tests, this textbook devotes considerable attention to the construction of such examinations and the use of their results.

3. *Published achievement tests*—Although classroom achievement is most frequently evaluated through the use of teacher-devised procedures, good standardized achievement tests can be valuable for certain purposes. How-

ever, a teacher should be able to judge the worth of any such tests and know something about how the results should and should not be used. In order to choose the best published tests, a teacher should be familiar with the recommended steps to be followed in constructing a standardized test and should understand the statistical procedures used in deriving scores and in assessing the reliability and validity of the instrument. Since the classroom teacher must be prepared both to make proper use of such devices and to avoid common misuses, these tests are an important topic in this text.

DETERMINING PUPIL APTITUDE

Teacher planning of any instructional activity must take into account pupil aptitude for that type of learning. A teacher obtains much information on pupil aptitude through procedures other than tests. Certainly one of the best indicators of aptitude for study in a given subject is past performance in that subject. A teacher planning arithmetic instruction for sixth-grade students will want to know how these students did in arithmetic in fifth grade. A chemistry teacher at the end of the first month of instruction learns quite a bit about the students' aptitudes by noting their achievement up to that point. Also, teachers discover much about pupil aptitude by observing and listening to students as they work and perform in class.

But nontesting procedures, although they must be used by all teachers, are not always sufficient, nor are they in many cases the most efficient or the most valid sources of information. For some students, true aptitude for a given subject may not manifest itself in classroom performance; a student may have a latent aptitude that is not being aroused by a certain type of instruction. Also, letting a group of students proceed through much of a course together before testing their individual aptitudes will be an inefficient use of both pupil and teacher time. For such reasons as these, good aptitude tests can result in more effective instruction.

1. *General scholastic aptitude*—All students take a number of scholastic aptitude tests at selected stages in their school careers. If the results from these tests are used with care and with an understanding of what they do and do not measure, they can be a real help to guidance counselors, to school administrators, and to the classroom teacher. On the other hand, if the results of scholastic aptitude tests are improperly interpreted, it is quite easy to make incorrect and even harmful decisions on the basis of scores from them. Certain basic understandings are necessary if teachers are to use these tests to serve the important and useful purposes for which they are intended and if they are to avoid the all-too-common misuses.

2. *Readiness tests*—One special type of aptitude test, used principally in kindergarten and first grade, is the readiness test. This test is designed specifically to determine a pupil's readiness or aptitude for beginning formal

school instruction. Since the principal subject to which a student is exposed in the first year or two of school is reading, many of these tests measure aptitude for this one subject only and are appropriately called reading-readiness tests. Other instruments measure readiness in several areas at once, for example, reading, arithmetic, and writing. In general, kindergarten and first-grade teachers have found readiness tests to be a useful supplement to both scholastic aptitude tests and informal procedures in deciding when a pupil is ready to profit from formal instruction.

3. *Tests of aptitude for specific subjects or vocations*—At certain times in a pupil's school career, decisions must be made as to what type of course he or she should take or what would represent a meaningful career goal. Of course, such decisions are made on the basis of a variety of types of information, and it is doubtful that any one test score should be a major determining factor. However, tests have been developed that measure aptitude for a given subject or for a given line of work, and the results of these tests may be of some value in such decision-making. But, since the validity of aptitude tests varies greatly from test to test and from subject to subject, and since data on validity are generally presented in a somewhat technical form, all educators should know how to evaluate specific aptitude tests.

DETERMINING PUPIL INTEREST

Of considerable importance in educational and vocational planning is knowledge of a pupil's interests. Again, much information will be obtained by the teachers and parents as well as the pupil through informal assessments. However, there are a number of tests or inventories that provide relatively objective procedures for determining interest. Such instruments, typically described as measuring *interest* or *preference,* can be used as aids to further exploration of pupil interests through personal counseling sessions. The publishers of these devices usually caution the user not to take the results as an absolute measure of interest that can be used for making arbitrary decisions about areas in which pupils could be expected to find satisfaction and success. The beginning teacher should be warned to use the test results only under the direction of a guidance counselor or some other person with considerable training and experience in their interpretation. Since interest inventories are not an essential tool of the typical classroom teacher and should be used only with the qualifications described above, they are not discussed in any detail in this text.

ASSESSING PUPIL PERSONALITY

There are many published instruments for assessing personality. They are variously described as inventories, schedules, records, profiles, checklists, surveys, and tests, and their titles suggest that they measure such things as temperament, personality problems, preferences, values, and attitudes. Many of these devices can be quite helpful when used judiciously by a trained psychologist or counselor. However, indiscriminate use of such instruments by a teacher without special training may actually aggravate the problems they are intended to help solve. It is the authors' judgment that these instruments should not be used by the classroom teacher but, rather, should be left to the clinical psychologist and the researcher. Therefore they are not dealt with in this text.

The Focus of This Textbook

The foregoing sections have provided a general survey of the field of testing and evaluation. Obviously a brief textbook such as this one can only cover certain topics within the field. In the present case the authors have chosen to concentrate on those topics that they feel should be of most practical value to the classroom teacher.

If we reexamine the concerns of the hypothetical third-grade teacher introduced at the beginning of this chapter, we can see that most of them involve the basic problem of getting the information about students that should be used for guiding instruction. Much of a teacher's task involves making decisions: What should I teach next? Is my teaching effective? Have my pupils mastered this unit? Answering such questions and making the related decisions requires information. Providing the necessary information is the role of testing and evaluation. This, then, is the focus of this textbook: *The use of testing and evaluation in instructional decision-making.*

Teachers should find it useful to keep this focus in mind in planning and assessing a program of testing for use in the classroom. Concerning each test, the following question should be raised: "Can I use the results for making important instructional decisions?" If the answer is "no," the test probably should not be given. The question "What tests should I use?" must be preceded by the question "What instructional decisions do I need to make?" In this book the effort will be to concentrate on such questions and to offer specific suggestions about how to answer them.

Summary

Teachers and other educators are quite familiar with the precept "Tests are of no value unless the results are used." This statement almost seems to imply that it is a teacher's responsibility to be prepared to make some valid use of any type of test results. The authors of this text propose that a more reasonable and valid maxim would be "No tests or other evaluation procedures should be administered unless careful plans have been developed that specify exactly how the results are to be used for making important instructional decisions." The following chapters will discuss how to develop such plans for the classroom use of tests and how to employ the necessary instruments in carrying out the plans.

SUGGESTIONS FOR CLASS DISCUSSION
AND FURTHER INVESTIGATION

1. Assume that you are a teacher in a classroom situation in which you are not able to use any written tests, either essay or objective-type, but must rely solely on class discussion and on informal observation of pupil performance to evaluate pupil achievement. What are some of the difficulties you would face?

2. Assume that you are a pupil in the classroom described in Suggestion 1 and that the teacher is going to determine your course grade solely on the basis of how you answer questions during class discussion. List some of the objections you might have to this procedure.

3. As a pupil you have taken many teacher-made achievement tests. List some of your most common complaints about these tests and the ways in which they were used. As you proceed through this text, develop a list of suggestions that you might follow to avoid similar student complaints about your own tests.

4. Imagine that you are assigned to teach a subject in which you are competent to a student who is a complete stranger to you. What types of information about this student would you want before you started teaching? What information could be secured through a test? What information could not be secured through a test?

SUGGESTIONS FOR FURTHER READING

To understand present practices in testing and evaluation it is important to know something about the historical development of this field. The following sources give brief but informative descriptions of this history: Anne Anastasi, *Psychological Testing,* 3rd ed. (New York: Macmillan, 1968), chapter 1; Leonard P. Ayres, "History and Present Status of Educational Measurements," *The Measurement of Educational Products, 19th Yearbook of the National Society for the Study of Education* (Bloomington, Ill.: Public School Publishing Co., 1922); Julian C. Stanley and Kenneth D. Hopkins, *Educational and Psychological Measurement and Evaluation* (Englewood Cliffs, N.J.: Prentice-Hall, 1972), chapter 7.

For an extended discussion of interest inventories and personality tests, instruments that will not be dealt with in this text, the following sources should be consulted: Anne Anastasi, *Psychological Testing,* 3rd ed.; Lee J. Cronbach, *Essentials of Psychological Testing,* 3rd ed. (New York: Harper & Row, 1970).

2

Planning for Instruction and Evaluation

Jan Miller, the third-grade teacher introduced in Chapter 1, was pictured as being concerned about planning for her first year of teaching. The chapter went on to suggest that one of her needs was for information about her pupils, information that could be used to guide instruction. But how is such information to be obtained and how should it be used? This might well be the query of Jan or of any classroom teacher. The purpose of Chapter 2 is to provide a start toward answering this question.

The Basic Nature of Instruction and Evaluation

In general terms, instruction may be considered a process for producing planned changes in the behavior of students. A father teaching his son how to swim directs his instruction toward changing the son's behavior from that of a nonswimmer to that of one who is able to swim. A first-grade teacher teaching pupils to say "cat," "sat," and "rat" when they see the words in print is interested in producing a change in behavior that results in the ability to read. The process of instruction involves three basic steps:

1. Determining what the pupil is to learn.
2. Carrying out the actual instruction.
3. Evaluating the change in pupil behavior.

Each of these steps would seem to be essential if instruction is really to take place. Step 1 provides direction for the teaching effort and also specifies the criterion for determining if the planned change has been produced. Learning can take place randomly without a prior specification of the desired outcome, but *instruction* in a given area, as a process for producing planned change, requires prespecification of what the pupil is to learn. Step 2, carrying out activities to produce the change, is obviously the heart of the instructional process. Step 3, evaluation, is equally essential to the total process because until we have information as to whether or not change in behavior has been produced, we have no way of knowing that instruction has indeed taken place. In practice, of course, these steps follow each other in a repeating cycle: Evaluation (Step 3) will identify outcomes that have not been achieved and will thus indicate what still needs to be learned (Step 1), and the necessary remedial instruction will then be carried out (Step 2).

This simple three-step outline of the instructional process makes it clear that the step of evaluation is an integral and essential part of the total process. It should also serve to emphasize that both the actual teaching and the evaluation are based on the careful specification of the new abilities the pupil is expected to acquire. This means that the starting point for the relating of instruction and evaluation must be careful attention to goals and objectives.

THE NEED FOR CLARIFYING
WHAT PUPILS ARE TO LEARN

If instructional objectives are to serve their purpose of providing the basis for teaching and evaluation, they should be clear and specific. Unfortunately, although all teaching is directed toward some goal (even though it may be merely "covering chapter three in the textbook"), objectives are not always spelled out in such a way that they provide definite direction for instruction and evaluation.

In mentioning objectives, we are not talking about the general purposes of education as they might be found in statements outlining the philosophy of a school system or in reports of persons or groups commissioned to define the "goals of education."[1] Nor are we speaking of the overall goals for a given

---

[1] Examples of broad goals of this type may be found in: Educational Policies Commission, "The Purposes of Education in American Democracy" (Washington, D.C.: American Council on Education, 1938); Will French and Associates, *Behavioral Goals of General Education in High School* (New York: Russell Sage Foundation, 1957); Harvard Committee on the Objectives of Education in a Free Society, *General Education in a Free Society* (Cambridge, Mass.: Harvard University Press, 1945).

course. Such general and comprehensive statements are important in developing a total school program, but they must be broken down into more detail if they are to be used in determining pupil achievement. In order to evaluate what a pupil has learned in a given unit or an entire course, we need to know the specific ways in which one should be able to exhibit that achievement. We must have statements of objectives describing what a pupil should have learned in specific and limited units of instruction. We need statements that answer such questions as: "What should the pupil be able to do as a result of the instruction received this week (or this month, or this day)?" The answers to such questions become statements that suggest the necessary evaluation procedures. Statements of instructional goals are sometimes referred to as "terminal behaviors" because they describe the behavior that a pupil should be able to exhibit at the termination of some period of instruction. Here they will be referred to as *specific behavioral objectives* or merely as *specific objectives*.

Deriving Specific Objectives

Ideally, specific objectives will be spelled out in the course outlines or curriculum guides followed by the teacher. In order to produce changes in pupils, day-by-day instruction should be guided by a knowledge of the nature of these desired changes. Unfortunately, the instructional objectives usually found in curriculum plans are neither specific nor behavioral. Even the better listings of objectives will include such statements as "Pupils will understand _____" or "They will have command of _____" without specifying exactly what the students should be able to do to show that they "understand" or "have command of" the concept in question. The first step in planning instruction and evaluation is to translate the broad goals or objectives that have served as general guides for teaching into a list of specific desired outcomes that can direct instruction and evaluation.

If statements of specific objectives are to be of maximum utility in evaluation, they should meet the following criteria.

1. *Objectives should be worded in terms of the pupil*—Because the evaluation is to determine what the pupil has achieved, objectives worded in terms of what the teacher does are of little value. Teacher-oriented objectives may cause the teacher to feel that instruction is completed when a lecture has been presented, whether or not it can be shown that the lecture has actually taught the students something. Objectives must be pupil-oriented.

2. *Objectives should be worded in terms of observable behavior*—Objectives specified in such words as "understand," "know," "appreciate," or "have command of" must be defined further if they are to provide a basis for instruction and evaluation. The teacher needs to know what behavior a student should be able to exhibit if he or she "understands," "knows," or "appreci-

ates." "Understand" may be translated into such behavioral terms as being able "to explain," "to give examples," or "to put in one's own words." "Knowing" implies being able "to list," "to supply terms," or "to associate events with persons."

3. *Objectives should refer to the specific content to which the behavior is to apply*—For example, the objective "the pupil will be able to spell correctly" makes no mention of the level of difficulty of the words to be spelled; therefore, it would have different meanings for different grade levels. If this objective is to provide a basis for instruction and evaluation, it must delineate its content either by specifying the exact words to be spelled correctly or by describing their level of difficulty.

The task of defining specific behavioral objectives can be illustrated with examples taken from a typical curriculum development effort.[2] In developing a seventh-grade social studies unit on Africa, the curriculum committee started with such general goals as: The pupils should (1) determine how geography has affected the politico-socioeconomic development, (2) understand the ever-increasing importance of Africa in the world community. To make such goals meaningful for both teaching and evaluation, it was necessary to decide what specific behavior the pupils should be able to exhibit if they had acquired the general abilities suggested by these statements. Therefore, the question that the curriculum developer or teacher raised at this point was: "What should I expect the pupils to be able to do if they have successfully determined how geography has affected the politico-socioeconomic development of Africa?" Answering this question resulted in such specific behavioral objectives as: The pupils should be able to (1) describe the geography of the various regions of Africa, (2) explain how geography has affected the economic development of at least one country from each major geographic division of Africa, and (3) explain how geography has affected the social and political development of those selected countries.

A similar question was raised concerning what the pupils should be able to do to show that they understood the ever-increasing importance of Africa in the world community. The resulting specific objectives included such statements as: The pupils should be able to (1) list the contributions that African countries make to the world community, (2) describe some current world problems resulting from recent political changes in Africa, and (3) compare the influence that certain African nations had in the world community twenty-five years ago with their present influence.

Note that each of these specific objectives is behavioral, that it includes an action verb—*describe, explain, list, compare*—rather than a verb refer-

---

[2] C. M. Lindvall, "The Importance of Specific Objectives in Curriculum Development," *Defining Educational Objectives* (Pittsburgh: University of Pittsburgh Press, 1964), pp. 14–16.

ring to a mental state—*understand, know, appreciate.* Stressing the need to translate general abstract goals into specific behavioral terms does not mean that less importance is attached to an appreciation and deep understanding of what has been learned. It only means that this appreciation and understanding will be fully defined by the terms that tell what specific behavior a pupil should be able to exhibit when each goal has been achieved.

FLEXIBILITY IN THE DEVELOPMENT AND USE OF SPECIFIC OBJECTIVES

The emphasis in this textbook upon the use of behavioral objectives is intended to aid the teacher (1) in planning instructional activities that are directed toward important outcomes and (2) in carrying out a valid and meaningful evaluation of pupil progress. Rather specific suggestions about the wording of objectives, represented by the three criteria discussed in the preceding section, are presented as guidelines for achieving maximum clarity in describing desired outcomes. As indicated in the examples above, phrasing statements in terms of a desired "behavior" does not place any narrow limit on the types of outcomes that can be specified. It merely aids one in answering the question "How can I tell when the student has acquired this knowledge or ability?" Also, employing such statements of clearly defined objectives does not restrict the methods of instruction that can be used. Any of a number of procedures—lecture, study of a textbook, independent activities, discovery, and so on—might be used to enable a student to master a given specific objective. The authors recognize that the process of defining specific objectives could be carried to such lengths that the resulting objectives would be absurd both in minuteness of detail and in the number of them used to describe the outcomes for a given unit of study. Certainly this degree of detail is not advocated here. It is also recognized that in some situations the teacher may not have the time or the opportunity to set down the objectives that would guide instruction. But even in this case, just thinking about the specific behaviors that a given instructional session is designed to produce should serve to provide clearer direction for teaching and a sounder basis for evaluation.

Organizing and Sequencing Objectives

Instruction in school subjects is almost necessarily a sequential process. What students study in second grade builds on what they studied in first grade. Similarly, within any given grade, learning usually progresses from day to day and from week to week as a cumulative process. If this process is to be effective, what is to be learned must be organized in meaningful sequences. This is essential both for planning instruction and for making decisions about pupil progress. To take a simple example, if a mathematics textbook is organized in such a way that students are to work through it chapter by chapter, the fact that a pupil has mastered one chapter will warrant the decision that he or she is ready to move on to the next. Within the chapter itself, similar information will be used in determining when a student should progress from one section

Figure 2.1

SEQUENCE OF UNITS AND OBJECTIVES FOR THREE UNITS
IN BEGINNING MULTIPLICATION

UNIT 1

Relating Simple Multiplication Sentences to Representations
of Several Sets of the Same Size

1. Given a picture of several sets of the same size, the pupil is able to write the repeated addition sentence that the picture represents. (Limit: no more than 5 sets per picture, 5 elements per set)
2. Given a picture of several sets of the same size, the pupil is able to write the multiplication sentence that the picture represents. (Limit: same as in 1, above)
3. Given an incomplete multiplication sentence (A $\times$ B = _____), the pupil can draw a picture of sets to illustrate the sentence and use this to find the product. (Limit: factors of 5 or less)

UNIT 2

Mastery of Multiplication Facts with Factors of 5 or Less
(relating to arrays)

1. Given a picture of arrays of objects in a certain number of rows and columns, the pupil can write 2 multiplication sentences for the picture. (Limit: factors of 5 or less)
2. Given an incomplete multiplication sentence, the pupil can draw arrays of rows and columns to illustrate the problem and use this to find the product. (Limit: factors of 5 or less)
3. Given any "multiplication fact" problem, the pupil can give the answer from memory. (Limit: factors of 5 or less)

UNIT 3

Mastery of Multiplication Facts with Factors of 9 or Less
(relating to arrays)

1. Given an incomplete multiplication sentence, the pupil can draw arrays of rows and columns to illustrate the problem and use this to find the product. (Limit: factors of 7 or less)
2. Given any "multiplication fact" problem, the pupil can give the answer from memory. (Limit: factors of 7 or less)
3. Given an incomplete multiplication sentence, the pupil can draw arrays of rows and columns to illustrate the problem and use this to find the product. (Limit: factors of 9 or less)
4. Given any "multiplication fact" problem, the pupil can give the answer from memory. (Limit: factors of 9 or less)

to the next. In cases where instruction is organized on some basis other than the sequence in a textbook, comparable information must be obtained. Basic questions that teachers need to answer in guiding instruction include "Has the student mastered the lesson on which he or she is currently working?" and "What should the student study next?" Answers to such questions will be clear if objectives and units of instruction are organized in a sequence such that mastering one unit gives the student the abilities prerequisite for studying the next. Figure 2.1 provides an example of such an organization for three units in arithmetic covering beginning multiplication. Here we will assume that the teacher or other person who listed the objectives in this order plans to teach them in this sequence because achieving each successive objective provides the student with the needed capability for moving on to the next. Students would move from objective to objective within each unit and would master Unit 1 before moving on to Unit 2 and would go on to Unit 3 only after mastering both of the first two units.

The reader will note that the objectives listed in Figure 2.1 are specific and detailed. As such, they may be more representative of the objectives found in a course prepared by a curriculum development agency than those found in a teacher-prepared course. It is likely that most teachers would not have the time or resources to prepare an outline in this detail. However, as we have said, being able at least to think about objectives with this degree of specificity will be important in planning diagnostic evaluation procedures.

USE OF TESTS WITH SEQUENCED OBJECTIVES

The sequence of units and objectives in Figure 2.1 provides the basis for a simple illustration of the use of tests in instructional decision-making. Figure 2.2 suggests the types of tests needed. Here we have three short tests, each covering one of the three objectives included in Unit 1. Note that provision is made for a score for each objective. Each of these short tests could be used independently. After the pupils had completed the necessary study and practice on Objective 1, they would be given the test for it. Those students who passed the test would be judged ready to move on to Objective 2. Here the study and testing process would be repeated. The decision as to when a pupil had mastered one objective and should move on to the next could be based largely on how well he or she did on the short test covering that objective.

It might also be useful to have a unit test covering all the objectives in a unit. For Unit 1 such a test might look like the test shown in Figure 2.2. Obviously, such a unit test should not contain exactly the same items as the tests given on completion of each objective but should include different set sizes and different numbers of sets. The unit test should provide for a score on each objective. In this way it can serve not only as a test of the pupil's overall mastery of the unit but also as a type of simple diagnostic instrument. For example, it might tell us that a given student had retained the skills of Objectives 1 and 2 but had forgotten the skill of Objective 3. This might

Figure 2.2

UNIT TEST FOR TESTING PUPIL MASTERY OF EACH
OBJECTIVE IN UNIT 1 IN BEGINNING MULTIPLICATION

Write a repeated addition sentence for each picture.

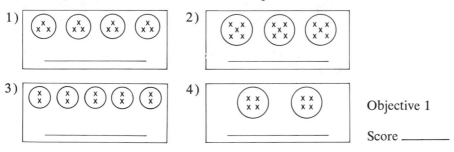

Objective 1

Score _____

Write a multiplication sentence for each picture.

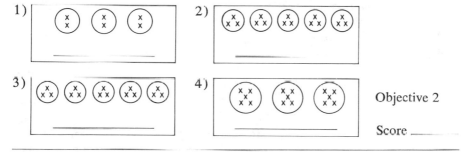

Objective 2

Score _____

Draw a picture for each multiplication sentence. Use it to find the answer.

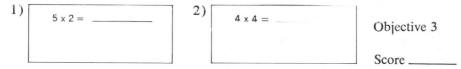

1) $5 \times 2 =$ _____

2) $4 \times 4 =$ _____

Objective 3

Score _____

cause the teacher to decide that this pupil should do further work on Objective 3 before moving on to Unit 2. Students who showed mastery of all three objectives on the unit test would be ready to go directly to Unit 2. Of course, a comparable unit test could also be developed to serve as a pretest for helping to plan the pupil's initial study in the unit.

This simple illustration using three units in beginning multiplication is intended to show how an organization based on objectives and units of instruction can be useful in providing information for instructional decision-making. More complete illustrations are provided in Chapter 9.

Of course, it should be added that decisions about pupils ought to be based on more than test scores. For example, how the pupils have done in carrying out lesson activities for a given objective is also an important consideration. In some cases formal tests may, in fact, not be appropriate. Earlier in this chapter a description was given of steps followed in developing a unit of study on Africa. Two of the objectives defined for that unit were that the pupil should be able to (a) *describe* some current world problems resulting from recent political changes in Africa and (b) *compare* the influence that certain African nations had in the world community twenty-five years ago with their present influence. Achievement of such objectives might be evaluated through an essay examination, an oral quiz, or a term paper. The evaluation procedures that will be of value must be determined on the basis of the type of ability that the pupil is to display.

Planning for Instructional Decision-Making

The preceding section provided a highly specific example of a way in which objectives and units of instruction could be organized to serve as a basis for teaching, for testing, and for making decisions about pupil progress. Obviously, there are other ways of organizing a curriculum. A traditional course outline or the sequence of topics found in a comprehensive textbook could also provide a framework for structuring a course. The important point is that there must be some type of organization and that it must be one that aids systematic diagnosis of pupil abilities and therefore is helpful in guiding progress.

In planning a program of testing and evaluation the basic consideration is determining what kinds of decisions will have to be made in guiding pupils through the given curriculum. It should be added here that not all these decisions will necessarily be made by the teacher. Certainly, in many situations they will be. However, the same kinds of decisions and the same types of information are important in programs that rely heavily upon independent study and upon pupil decision and self-direction. It should also be pointed out that instructional decisions are often unique with respect to each individual pupil. This is the essence of individualized instruction (see Chapter 9) and it has been kept in mind in the outlining of desirable procedures in this chapter. However, the same information and the same decisions are essential in guiding group instruction. In the latter case, instead of looking at individual performances, one would have to look at group averages.

INSTRUCTIONAL DECISION-MAKING

As we have said, the planning of classroom teaching activities and the day-by-day work of carrying out these activities require the teacher to make a number of decisions. What should I teach today? How can pupils best pursue their study of this? Are the pupils really mastering this content? When are the pupils ready to move on to a new unit or a different topic? Answering these questions and countless similar ones requires the teacher to make decisions. As indicated in Chapter 1, the authors feel that a program of testing and evaluation will be most useful if it is structured in a way that will help the teacher make these important daily and weekly decisions. This is what is meant by "using test results for some purpose." Quite obviously, test scores or data obtained from some other formal method of evaluation are only *aids* to teacher decision-making. We have emphasized that any actual decision will be based on a variety of information available to the teacher. At times, test scores will be most important; at other times, some other type of information will be given the greatest weight. In the examples of decision situations used in this chapter test results will be used to illustrate the decision process. This is done mainly for simplicity of presentation, and the reader should recognize that many procedures and types of data might be used in any such process.

DECISIONS TO BE MADE

In identifying the types of instructional decisions that must be made, then, one starts with some type of curriculum structure. It may be a system of units and objectives. It may be a more traditional course outline. Or it may be the organization provided by a good textbook or workbook. Within any of these structures, the specific kinds of decisions to be made should be identified. This might result in a list such as the following:

1. What a pupil is prepared to study next.
2. How a pupil's study of a given objective, topic, or unit might best be carried out.
3. When a pupil has mastered a specific instructional objective (or some limited specific skill).
4. When a pupil has mastered a unit of instruction (or some larger body of skills such as those found in one textbook chapter).
5. When a pupil has achieved a major composite goal (such as the ability to prepare a certain kind of report, conduct a particular kind of study, achieve a given level in some physical performance).
6. When a review of past learnings or an integration of such learnings is needed.

OBTAINING THE NEEDED INFORMATION

When the decisions that must be made have been specified, the information required for making each decision should be identified, and the appropriate means for obtaining it should be chosen. The nature of some of this information is rather obvious. In many situations, such as those suggested by the first five types of decisions listed above, test scores will be useful. However, these must be test scores that tell exactly what one needs to know to make the specific decision. Consider the example (Figure 2.2), presented in the preceding section of this chapter, of tests covering each of the three objectives in a unit on multiplication. Each short test provided a score that indicated the pupil's mastery or lack of mastery of a limited skill. This is the type of information needed for making decisions concerning pupil mastery of each objective and of the unit as a whole. A general test of assorted multiplication exercises would be of no real use here. What is needed is a short, specific test dealing in sequence with the single abilities defined by each objective in the unit. Of course, under certain conditions it may not be necessary to develop a test in order to evaluate what the pupils have learned. It may be possible, or even essential, to obtain the needed information by observing the students, by examining their daily work, by talking with them, or by using some other informal procedure. Also, in decisions dealing with how a pupil's study can best be carried out, a teacher's general knowledge of the pupil's attitudes, interests, typical style of study, and need for personal attention may represent the critical data. The important thing is to use every means available for getting information pertinent to making a specific instructional decision.

MAKING DECISIONS

Using evaluation results to make decisions concerning what pupils are to study requires that alternatives be available and that specific criteria be established for choosing the proper alternative. Here we might turn again to the example of the tests of the three objectives in the first unit on multiplication. A teacher might feel that the criterion for mastery of the first objective is passing all four test items. The decision would be made that students receiving a score of 4 on this test should move on to study Objective 2. Here we assume that a pupil scoring 3 or less will be required to do further work on Objective 1. Some procedure for carrying out this further study must be available. The student could simply restudy the same lesson. On the other hand, the teacher might either explain again the process involved and then assign the student further practice exercises, or ask the student to study the same objective using a different workbook or textbook. What is important is that there be some type of remedial activity available for students who fail to show mastery of a given ability the first time they are tested on it. Using tests for this form of diagnosis and decision-making demands that there be a ready answer to the question "What should I do with the pupil who fails?"

This same concern for remedial treatments or for alternate forms of instruction must be present in other evaluation-decision situations. Can we make specific provisions for review in the case of the pupil who fails a midterm test designed to measure pupil retention? Such an exam is of little value if it results only in the recording of a grade in the teacher's roll book. It is really worthwhile only if it results in review activities designed to help each student with those topics in which lack of retention was evidenced. Making an instructional decision—for example, that a student is not ready to move ahead —is meaningful only if the teacher takes some action on the basis of what is decided. Of course, not all such teacher actions involve assignment to alternative lesson materials or activities. Certain types of useful evaluative information have a bearing on such things as how the teacher should interact with a pupil, the length of assignments, the physical setting for study. For example, a teacher may know that certain students need frequent personal encouragement if they are to persevere and succeed in their study. This type of information, obtained from daily observation of the pupils rather than from any test, represents evaluation data that is useful for making decisions about instruction. Here the suggested instructional treatment is for the teacher to provide the necessary personal attention to each of these students. Obviously, what is known about other pupils may indicate that their progress will be best if they are left free from the interference involved in frequent teacher contacts. Similar personal knowledge about pupils may result in the decision to give one pupil much more drill than another, to check a certain student's work on a page-by-page basis rather than waiting until a lesson is completed, and so on.

Although the use of test results to aid instructional decisions lends itself to the most specific examples of how the process can be carried out, this should not be permitted to obscure the fact that much subjective information obtained through informal procedures can be of equal value in identifying the desirable instructional treatment. However, it may well be that the relatively formal decision point represented by the student's taking a unit posttest, for example, should be the occasion for considering as well the various non-test data available.

Choosing the Evaluation Procedure

When a teacher has defined the goals and objectives of instruction and has determined what kinds of decisions will require evaluation information, that teacher is then in a position to select the most appropriate methods of evaluation. The teacher should be guided by certain criteria that define the important qualities in any evaluation procedure. These criteria will be introduced and discussed in relatively nontechnical terms in this chapter. The discussion will be sufficient to enable the teacher to decide what is the best procedure for assessing classroom achievement. Some of these criteria will be presented in greater depth later in the text, with a more technical discussion.

VALIDITY

Any procedure for obtaining information about students is valid to the extent that it actually provides the desired information. In the evaluation of pupil achievement, the information desired is the degree to which pupils have achieved the specified instructional objectives. The important question to ask in determining the validity of any procedure for evaluating pupil achievement is, then, whether or not it provides evidence of the extent to which pupils can exhibit the specific behavior described in the objectives. If it does not provide this, it will be of little value.

Validity, then, is the first consideration in the selection of an appropriate procedure—a procedure designed to permit the students to exhibit the behavior described in the objective. If the objective states that the pupils should be able to list, name, or define, we should give them an opportunity to do this, either orally or in writing. If they are expected to explain, describe, translate, or interpret, they should have a chance to do these things. In all these instances the evaluation procedure could be an oral quiz, an essay examination, or, in some instances, an objective-type test. If a specific objective states that the pupils should be able to perform certain feats or demonstrate certain skills, evaluation could be made through observation of pupil performance. The important point is that we must give the pupils the opportunity to display the ability described in the specific objective so that we can assess the extent to which they have mastered it.

Another point to emphasize is that no instrument or procedure is valid in and of itself. A procedure may be valid in one situation and for one purpose and quite invalid in another situation or for another purpose. Validity also depends on how a procedure is applied and how the resulting pupil performance is assessed. We are concerned with the results, and in selecting an appropriate procedure we are taking only the first step toward validity.

In most situations the teacher will employ the single most direct and valid procedure for assessing a particular type of pupil achievement; however, the teacher may often wish to supplement this evaluation by using another procedure that is less obviously valid but that has certain qualities lacking in the first procedure. For example, assume an objective states that pupils should, after reading data presented in the form of graphs, be able to explain how several countries differ in such characteristics as population, amount of rainfall, agricultural exports, and per capita wealth. The most direct way to evaluate this objective would be to give the pupils graphic data on the given countries and ask them to write an explanation of how they differ. This is a valuable procedure and would usually be used. However, if reliance were placed solely on this procedure, the teacher might be troubled by the fact that the entire assessment of the pupils' achievement of this objective depended upon the teacher's own subjective judgment of each pupil's written explanation. The teacher might, therefore, choose to supplement the evaluation obtained through this essay examination by making use of some objective-type test items as well. For example, the students might be presented with appropriate tabular data and with multiple-choice questions requiring them to select the best explanations of what the tables show. Here the objective would not be evaluated directly because the students would not be required "to explain" but only "to select the best explanation." However, there is a close connection between these two abilities, and the greater objectivity and reliability of the second procedure could make the information it provided a very useful supplement to that yielded by the more direct procedure.

There are additional reasons why the problem of selecting an evaluation procedure is not always settled by a choice of the most obvious method suggested by the behavioral objective. In some situations this obvious method may not produce a comprehensive assessment. Let us assume that an objective states that a pupil will use correct punctuation in writing. The direct and most obviously valid procedure for evaluating this ability is to require the student to submit a number of written assignments and to grade each of these for punctuation. However, a given pupil may turn in a number of such assignments yet never need to use several kinds of punctuation that he or she is supposed to have mastered. To overcome this difficulty the teacher might employ as a supplementary evaluation procedure a test requiring the pupil to punctuate correctly a number of given sentences and paragraphs. This second procedure could be made comprehensive enough to cover all types of punctuation that had been studied, and it would thus be a useful and necessary supplement to the more direct procedure.

These examples of situations where the single most valid evaluation procedure is not necessarily entirely sufficient for determining pupil achievement suggest that although validity is the most important quality to be sought, additional qualities must be considered in planning evaluation. We will now turn to a consideration of some of the other criteria.

RELIABILITY

A data-gathering procedure is reliable to the extent that it will produce consistent results in assessing the same thing. If we use a reading-readiness test to help us decide whether a first-grade pupil is ready for formal reading instruction, we must know that, no matter whether we administer the test in the morning, in the afternoon, or tomorrow, we will get essentially the same results. If the test cannot produce results that are consistent in this sense, we will not have confidence in the measurement we obtain on any one occasion. It is obvious that reliability is important in any procedure for obtaining information about pupils.

As with validity, the reliability of a procedure is dependent on things other than just the particular test or device being used. It depends on the conditions under which it is administered, on the nature of the quality being measured, on certain characteristics of the group of students involved, and on the way in which results are scored or assessed. All these things must be taken into account in the effort to ensure adequate reliability.

Reliability is also a matter of degree. No procedure is absolutely reliable. If we use a weight scale to measure the weights of pupils, there is a certain degree of unreliability because of the improbability of perfect accuracy in reading the dial, differences in the weights of clothing worn by the pupils, and minor inconsistencies in the operation of the scale itself. Similarly, with tests and other evaluation procedures we recognize that the results will not be perfectly reliable; our goal is to secure the most reliable results possible.

Among various evaluation procedures, some are generally more reliable than others. If, for example, we use oral quizzing of the class as a method of assessing achievement, we should recognize certain sources of unreliability. Typically, we cannot ask many questions of any one student, so we are forced to evaluate each student on the basis of a very limited sample of responses. It is quite possible that if given students had been asked to respond to different questions, the adequacy of the answers might have been quite different. Thus, results from the oral quiz are generally unreliable. A written examination in which each student responds to a relatively large number of questions should produce more reliable results. Another reason for the unreliability of the oral quiz is that all responses are subjectively graded by the teacher. To the extent that a teacher's moods and perceptions change, a given response might be graded one way at one time and quite differently at another. This same subjectivity in grading also means that use of essay examinations and homework assignments as a basis for evaluation produces results less reliable than those obtained through more objective procedures.

Of course, the fact that these subjective procedures are somewhat less reliable than one would wish does not mean that they should not be used. In many cases they are necessary because they are highly appropriate for a specific purpose. However, it is a good idea to check the results of subjective evaluation through the supplementary use of more objective procedures.

OBJECTIVITY
Objectivity, in connection with evaluation devices, may be defined as the extent to which an assessment is independent of the subjective judgment of the evaluator. In the discussion of reliability, it was pointed out that a lack of objectivity in scoring could produce inconsistent and unreliable results. For this reason objectivity is often sought as a means for improving the reliability of an evaluation.

Objectivity is desirable also for another reason. An objective assessment is more likely to be acceptable to the person whose work is being evaluated. Results from subjective procedures may be taken by students as merely representing the biased opinion of the teacher and therefore as something to be rejected. Results from the use of objective methods may be taken less as personal judgments and more as independent and unbiased evaluations.

On the other hand, many pupils are interested in the subjective judgment of the teacher. They feel that teachers are experts in their field and that their judgment, based on a comprehensive understanding of the subject, may be more meaningful than the result produced by an objective device. Objectivity can be of considerable importance and should be sought in many types of evaluation; but some types of performance are so complex that they can be evaluated only through subjective procedures.

Of course, it should be realized that objectivity is only a relative quality and that no tests or other evaluation procedures are completely objective. For example, when objective tests containing multiple-choice questions are used, the "objectivity" that is obtained is in the scoring. With a scoring key, the students' responses are scored in the same way from student to student. However, the particular questions that appear on the test, the format and verbal style of these questions, and, sometimes, the particular alternative that is chosen as "the" correct answer, are most often under the control of the teacher. Thus, the teacher's subjective judgment influences the construction of the so-called objective tests as well as that of essay tests and other less formal procedures for assessment. The teacher should realize that subjectivity enters into all assessment and evaluation procedures. It is the professional responsibility of the teacher to be aware of personal biases and subjectivity that influence the judging of pupils and to be prudent and fair in making judgments.

COMPREHENSIVENESS

Most of us have been students in classroom situations where the teacher was quizzing students orally and we fervently hoped we would be asked questions to which we knew the answers. We recognized that there were certain aspects of the lesson we had not mastered but knew that if we could make a good showing in our responses to the few questions we were given, we might convince the teacher that we were "A" students. Unfortunately, however, we were sometimes asked questions we could not answer and, hence, gave the teacher the opposite impression.

When we look at this situation from the teacher's point of view, we can understand how this lack of comprehensiveness in assessing the achievement of any one pupil can yield misleading information. As we mentioned previously, the assumption by the teacher that a pupil's responses to one or a few questions represent the pupil's command of all questions will produce results of low reliability. It is easy to see that if this assumption is not made and the teacher takes a pupil's answer to a particular question as an indication only of his or her command of that particular point, then the information obtained concerning any particular student by such oral quizzing is extremely limited.

A concern for comprehensiveness should be a part of the planning for any evaluation. The oral quiz is not the only type of test that is limited in this respect; a written test may be very limited in its comprehensiveness in that it is confined to topics that can be tested most easily. Teachers frequently fall into a habit of continually asking the same types of essay questions or habitually using objective items that measure only one type of ability.

The carefully planned evaluation program will start with a detailed outline of all of the major objectives to be covered and then will ensure that all students are evaluated accordingly. Comprehensiveness should be a very conscious goal, and it can be achieved only through careful planning.

OTHER CONSIDERATIONS

The four criteria discussed in the preceding sections are basic to the planning of any pupil evaluation process. Certainly the validity and reliability of the results must be uppermost in the mind of the teacher as procedures for assessing achievement are planned and the needed instruments are developed. Objectivity and comprehensiveness also merit attention.

In addition to these basic criteria, several other considerations, although of relatively minor importance, will play a part in determining which evaluation procedures will be used.

1. *Ease of Construction and Scoring*—Some instruments, such as check lists, rating scales, and objective-type tests, may be more difficult to construct than less formal procedures. However, this difficulty may be balanced by greater ease in scoring.

2. *Economy of Class Time*—Certain techniques of evaluation may require considerable class time. For example, personal interviews can be quite time-consuming. In considering the use of interviews, the teacher must decide whether it would represent the most efficient use of class time. Other procedures, such as written tests, are generally more efficient because with them all pupils can be examined at the same time.

3. *Economy of Teacher Time*—Different evaluation procedures will take different amounts of a teacher's time. If lengthy term papers are used as a major means of assessing achievement, careful checking of these papers should take considerable time. Another time-consuming procedure is the compiling and analyzing of anecdotal records on each student. In many cases the investment of major blocks of a teacher's time in these types of evaluation procedures may represent the very best use of time. However, the teacher must always exercise professional judgment to decide how his or her time can best be spent.

Summary

Education is a process of producing desired changes in the behavior of the learner. If education is to be effective, frequent assessments must be made of the extent to which the desired behavioral changes have been produced. This evaluation of pupil achievement is based on clearly defined instructional objectives. These instructional objectives will be most helpful in guiding both evaluation and instruction if they (1) are worded in terms of the pupil, (2) are worded in terms of observable behavior, and (3) refer to the specific content of the behavior. Wording the objectives with this degree of specificity should clarify their exact meaning and in this way serve to make instruction more effective and evaluation more useful. The content and objectives of any course of instruction should be so organized as to indicate the order in which most students can best proceed to mastery. This organization provides the framework within which decisions regarding pupil progress and type of instruction can be made. If such decisions are to be meaningful, the alternative instructional procedures to which they point must be carefully specified. If the instructional decisions are to be valid, the information on which they are based must be obtained through procedures possessing the necessary degree of reliability, validity, comprehensiveness, and certain other essential qualities.

SUGGESTIONS FOR CLASS DISCUSSION AND FURTHER INVESTIGATION

1. Obtain the outline for a course or part of a course that is of interest to you. (If no other resource is available, you could outline a course based on the table of contents of this textbook or some other textbook.) Identify the important instructional decisions (such as those listed on page 19) that should be made in teaching this course. Outline a program of evaluation for obtaining information that would be useful in making each of these decisions.

2. Select a unit of study from the course outlined in Suggestion 1 or from some other course. Define the general goal(s) of this unit. Write the specific behavioral objectives that would be derived from each general goal.

3. Suggestions 1 and 2 in Chapter 1 asked you to list the weaknesses of an evaluation procedure that relies solely on class discussion and observation. Reexamine each such objection or weakness and determine if it is a weakness in validity, reliability, objectivity, or another criterion considered desirable in an evaluation procedure or instrument.

SUGGESTIONS FOR FURTHER READING

Further clarification of procedures for deriving specific instructional objectives from broader statements of educational goals is provided in: Norman E. Gronlund, *Stating Behavioral Objectives for Classroom Instruction* (New York: Macmillan, 1970); Julie S. Vargas, *Writing Worthwhile Behavioral Objectives* (New York: Harper & Row, 1972).

Detailed explanations of what is involved in stating objectives in behavioral terms is found in the two publications listed above and also in: Robert F. Mager, *Preparing Instructional Objectives* (Palo Alto: Fearon Publishers, 1962); W. James Popham and Eva L. Baker, *Establishing Instructional Goals* (Englewood Cliffs, N.J.: Prentice-Hall, 1970).

Rather detailed listings of objectives for most subject matter areas are published by: The Instructional Objectives Exchange, P.O. Box 24095, Los Angeles, California.

An analysis of the task involved in developing sequences and hierarchies of instructional objectives is provided in Robert M. Gagné, *The Conditions of Learning* (New York: Holt, Rinehart & Winston, 1970).

3

Emphasizing Important Learning Outcomes

Jim Briggs was thinking about the type of learning that was taking place in his seventh-grade social studies class. He knew, from what had been emphasized in his teacher training courses, that he should avoid placing emphasis merely on the learning of facts; that applications, interpretations, and other aspects of understanding should be stressed. However, in social studies it was so easy to ask pupils questions concerning facts—divisions of the government, elective offices, responsibilities of various officials, etc.—that he knew he had a tendency to concentrate on this during class discussions and in his weekly quizzes. Jim was worried that his pupils were concentrating their study on acquiring more and more information and were not being forced to think about the applications of what they were learning.

The concern expressed here by Jim Briggs should be a concern of every teacher. We all like to feel that our instruction is helping pupils to understand and to be able to apply what they are learning. But if outcomes of this type are to be achieved, teaching and evaluation must be planned and carried out with great care. Some persons criticize the use of paper-and-pencil tests, stating that it can result in too much emphasis on certain limited types of outcomes. However, the exclusive use of very informal methods of evaluation can also lead to limited emphasis: Jim felt that his class discussions and oral quizzes were centered too much on the pupils' knowledge of facts. In fact, if informal evaluation procedures are not carefully planned, they are less likely to sample a variety of types of abilities than are paper-and-pencil tests, which, of necessity, require some degree of planning. The point here is that if classroom instruction is to be directed toward all the important types of outcomes, both the teaching activities and the evaluation procedures must be carefully planned so as to emphasize such outcomes. This chapter will offer suggestions for this planning.

Planning for the Achievement and Evaluation of Important Types of Outcomes

Chapter 2 described procedures for planning an evaluation program that could be of value in guiding classroom instruction. It emphasized the importance of defining specific instructional objectives and of organizing these objectives into sequences and units to provide a structure for planning instruction and for identifying points where evaluation data can aid instructional decision-making. This planning and specification of objectives also provides a means whereby attention can be given to the problem of making certain that students are achieving a proper variety of important learning outcomes. When objectives are specified in written form and are stated in terms of the specific abilities the student is to acquire, it is possible to make a critical examination of the list of objectives to determine what types of outcomes are being emphasized. Such an examination could result in a realization of the fact that certain types of abilities were being neglected and that additional objectives were needed. Suggestions for carrying out this process are presented in the following sections.

USING THE TAXONOMY

In planning a list of objectives that will cover all the desired abilities, a teacher might obtain considerable help by consulting a listing of abilities such as the one found in *Taxonomy of Educational Objectives*.[1] This taxon-

---

[1] Benjamin S. Bloom, ed., *Taxonomy of Educational Objectives, Handbook I: Cognitive Domain* (New York: David McKay Co., 1956).

In discussions of the taxonomy in this text, the reference will always be to *Handbook I: Cognitive Domain*. However, the reader should be aware of a companion volume, *Taxonomy of Educational Objectives, Handbook II: Affective Domain*, by David Krathwohl, Benjamin S. Bloom, and Bertram B. Masia (New York: David McKay Co.,

omy, developed by a group of university examiners, tries to construct a comprehensive outline of the cognitive abilities as they might be acquired from instruction in a given subject area. The outline, which consists of six major categories, starts with the simplest ability, knowledge (defined as the ability to recall information), and builds up to abilities of much greater complexity. The taxonomy is outlined and described in great detail in Bloom's handbook, but the following major categories will illustrate its scope:

1.00 *Knowledge*
  1.10 Knowledge of Specifics.
      1.11 Knowledge of Terminology. Knowledge of the referents for specific symbols (verbal and nonverbal).
      1.12 Knowledge of Specific Facts. Knowledge of dates, events, persons, places, etc.
  1.20 Knowledge of Ways and Means of Dealing with Specifics.
      1.21 Knowledge of Conventions. Knowledge of characteristic ways of treating and presenting ideas and phenomena.
      1.22 Knowledge of Trends and Sequences. Knowledge of the processes, directions, and movements of phenomena with respect to time.
      1.23 Knowledge of Classifications and Categories. Knowledge of the classes, sets, divisions, and arrangements that are regarded as fundamental for a given subject field, purpose, argument, or problem.
      1.24 Knowledge of Criteria. Knowledge of the criteria by which facts, principles, and conduct are tested or judged.
      1.25 Knowledge of Methodology. Knowledge of the methods of inquiry, techniques, and procedures employed in a particular subject field as well as those employed in investigating particular problems and phenomena.
  1.30 Knowledge of the Universals and Abstractions in a Field.
      1.31 Knowledge of Principles and Generalizations. Knowledge of particular abstractions that summarize observations of phenomena.
      1.32 Knowledge of Theories and Structures. Knowledge of the body of principles and generalizations together with their interrelations which present a clear, rounded, and systematic view of a complex phenomenon, problem, or field.

2.00 *Comprehension*
  2.10 Translation. Comprehension as evidenced by the care and accuracy with which the communication is paraphrased or rendered from one language or form of communication to another.
  2.20 Interpretation. The explanation or summarization of a communication.
  2.30 Extrapolation. The extension of trends or tendencies beyond the given data to determine implications, consequences, corollaries, effects, etc., that are in accordance with the conditions described in the original communication.

1964). The second handbook deals with objectives in the general realm of interests, attitudes, and other personality variables; because we will not be concerned with techniques for assessing such variables, it is not treated here.

3.00 *Application* The use of abstractions in particular and concrete situations. The abstractions may be in the form of general ideas, rules of procedure, or generalized methods.

4.00 *Analysis*

    4.10 Analysis of Elements. Identification of the elements included in a communication.

    4.20 Analysis of Relationships. The connections and interactions between elements and parts of a communication.

    4.30 Analysis of Organized Principles. The organization, systematic arrangement, and structure that hold the communication together.

5.00 *Synthesis*

    5.10 Production of a Unique Communication. The development of a communication in which the writer or speaker attempts to convey ideas, feelings, or experiences to others.

    5.20 Production of a Plan or Proposed Set of Operations. The development of a plan of work or the proposal of a plan of operations.

    5.30 Derivation of a Set of Abstract Relations. The development of a set of abstract relations either to classify or to explain particular data or phenomena, or the deduction of propositions and relations from a set of basic propositions or symbolic representations.

6.00 *Evaluation*

    6.10 Judgments in Terms of Internal Evidence. Evaluation of the accuracy of a communication from such evidence as logical accuracy, consistency, and other internal criteria.

    6.20 Judgments in Terms of External Criteria. Evaluation of material with reference to selected or remembered criteria.[2]

The handbook, in describing the various categories of the taxonomy, gives examples of objectives and specimen test items for each category to clarify the various parts of the outline. However, the usefulness of the taxonomy does not depend on a complete understanding of every category and subcategory, nor does it depend on a capacity to make a definitive categorization of any given objective or test item (which has proved to be quite difficult even for those who have worked extensively with it). For the majority of teachers, its most useful function is to call attention to all the abilities that should be considered in assessing pupil achievement.

In outlining material for a test, we have found the first three categories —knowledge, comprehension, and application—to be the most useful.

Knowledge involves recalling terms, facts, rules, and principles and other generalizations. Objectives in this category include the ability to name, list, state, describe, or define.

Comprehension involves understanding a given content well enough to put it into other words, summarize it, or explain it. Objectives in this cate-

---

gory include the ability to translate, give examples, illustrate, interpret, summarize, or explain.

Application involves the use of rules, methods, procedures, principles, and other types of generalizations to produce or give reasons for certain consequences or to predict the result of some described situation. Objectives here would include the ability to solve, give reasons for, prove, put into practice, or predict.

Objectives that fall into the first three major categories of the taxonomy can be evaluated through objective-type tests, as well as a variety of other procedures.

Synthesis is another category that should be given considerable attention in most instructional programs. The achievement of objectives in this category cannot be well measured with objective-type tests and must be assessed through essay testing, assignment of homework, observation of pupil performance, and other procedures that require the pupil actually to develop, create, or produce something. Specific objectives here are phrased in terms of the pupil's ability to develop a plan, write a paper, produce or demonstrate something, or show one of a number of other behaviors requiring the creation of something original.

Teachers and teacher-trainees can greatly improve the comprehensiveness of their lesson plans and their evaluation procedures by checking them to be sure they include the objectives in these four categories.

USING A MATRIX

One useful way of outlining an instructional unit in order to reduce the possibility of overlooking the important goals of any particular subject content is to draw up a matrix—a table with content categories on one axis and ability categories on the other. An example is shown in Table 3.1, where a matrix is used to outline three units in a course in testing and evaluation such as the one being presented in this text. Four of the categories from the taxonomy, presented as sideheads, specify which abilities are of concern. This scheme will help a teacher consider whether the objectives that have been defined for each content area cover the four cognitive abilities described above.

The teacher should ask: "What facts or generalizations should pupils know or remember from this unit? What should they comprehend? What are the principles or procedures they should be able to apply? What types of plans or products should they be able to develop or synthesize?" This questioning should lead to greater comprehensiveness both in teaching and in evaluation of pupil achievement; however, it should not force the teacher to insert objectives in every cell of the matrix. The lack of objectives in some cells in Table 3.1 suggests that there may be certain content units for which a given type of ability may be neither important nor appropriate. The matrix requires the teacher to consider whether a particular type of ability is important in a given unit.

Table 3.1

A MATRIX SHOWING INSTRUCTIONAL OBJECTIVES FOR THREE
UNITS IN A COURSE IN TESTING AND EVALUATION

Cognitive abilities involved	Content units		
	Specifying objectives	Criteria for evaluation instruments	Constructing tests
Knowledge	Can list sources of objectives	Can list criteria used in judging evaluation instruments	Can list various types of tests
	Can state criteria for specific objectives		Can state rules and suggestions for constructing tests and test items
Comprehension	Can state criteria in own words	Can state criteria in own words	
		Can give examples of criteria	
Application	Can use criteria to state specific objectives	Can use criteria to select best procedure for a given purpose	
Synthesis	Can develop an outline of overall goals and specific objectives for a unit		Can use suggestions to construct test items Can develop valid and effective tests

Developing Tests to Evaluate a Variety of Important Learning Outcomes

The preceding sections of this chapter have suggested procedures for specifying objectives that cover a broad range of important types of abilities. Outlining the abilities in this rather formal way should help to ensure that they will all be emphasized in classroom instruction. And it follows that pupil achievement of all of these types of learning outcomes must be assessed as a part of the teacher's program of testing and evaluation. Pupils will become serious in attempting to acquire these varied abilities only when they realize that they are the abilities upon which they will be evaluated. The answer to the criticism that many paper-and-pencil testing programs cause pupils to concentrate too much on the acquisition of facts lies in making certain that the total testing and evaluation program does not concentrate only on such limited abilities. The following sections of this chapter offer some specific suggestions as to how tests and other procedures can be designed to test a variety of types of learning outcomes.

Objective-Type Tests

Objective-type tests can be used to evaluate a variety of abilities. Many of the better published achievement tests contain items that require the examinee to interpret data, use generalizations to explain or predict results, apply procedures in order to arrive at answers, and demonstrate similar complex abilities. Also, many skilled teachers develop tests that measure some rather complex types of learning. The following sections will explain how objective-type test items can be used to measure several of the types of abilities discussed in the *Taxonomy of Educational Objectives, Handbook I: Cognitive Domain*[3] and will provide examples of items that measure each of those abilities.[4] To show how all these abilities might be measured in a single subject area, the first illustrative item for each ability deals with science content. The other illustrations are drawn from a variety of subject areas.

TESTING FOR KNOWLEDGE

Although many tests can justifiably be criticized for consisting largely of items that measure only recognition or recall of information, this criticism does not imply that tests should contain *no* items at the knowledge level of the taxonomy. Although the ultimate goal in most areas of study is the development of more complex abilities, the achievement of these abilities depends in part on the pupil's ability to recall or recognize principles, rules, procedures, and specific facts. Therefore, any comprehensive and diagnostic evaluation of a pupil's strengths and weaknesses must devote some attention to the behaviors outlined in the knowledge category of the taxonomy.

The development of test items to measure knowledge of specifics—of persons, places, terminology, dates, sources, and similar information—is a rather straightforward task. One simple and effective procedure is to have the student choose the correct words to complete a statement, as in the middle two items in Figure 3.1. A variation of this procedure is shown in the first and last items where a question is used as the item stem. Although these

---

[3] Bloom, op. cit.

[4] A much more complete discussion of what is involved in developing tests for each taxonomy category and examples of items in many content areas is presented in Benjamin S. Bloom, J. Thomas Hastings, and George F. Madaus, *Handbook on Formative and Summative Evaluation of Student Learning* (New York: McGraw-Hill, 1971).

Figure 3.1

TEST ITEMS MEASURING KNOWLEDGE OF SPECIFICS

SCIENCE: **10** Which cells carry oxygen to the muscles?

    5 nerve cells   7 skin cells

    6 heart cells   8 red blood cells

SOCIAL STUDIES: **41** The "Forty-niners" were seeking —

    Ⓐ oil   Ⓒ diamonds

    Ⓑ furs   Ⓓ gold

                     ⓄⓀ

    42 The place where a river flows into a larger body of water is called its —

    Ⓔ mouth   Ⓖ bed

    Ⓕ source   Ⓗ banks

                     ⓄⓀ

LANGUAGE: **2** Where is the best place to find a synonym for the word "parade"?

    Ⓔ dictionary

    Ⓕ encyclopedia

    Ⓖ *The World Almanac*

    Ⓗ world atlas

Item 10 reproduced from the Stanford Achievement Test, Advanced Battery, Form A, Test 9, Science, copyright © 1972, by Harcourt Brace Jovanovich, Inc. Reproduced by special permission of the publisher.

Items 41 and 42 reproduced from the Metropolitan Achievement Test, Intermediate F, Test 9, Social Studies, copyright © 1970, by Harcourt Brace Jovanovich, Inc. Reproduced by special permission of the publisher.

Item 2 reproduced from the Metropolitan Achievement Test, Intermediate F, Language, Part A, copyright © 1970, by Harcourt Brace Jovanovich, Inc. Reproduced by special permission of the publisher.

items are in multiple-choice form, it is obvious that with minor modifications the same questions could be made into completion or supply-type items.

The beginning writer of objective-type test items is likely to rely rather exclusively on items that demand only a one- or two-word response, whether the items are multiple-choice, matching, or completion. This is a satisfactory and desirable practice as long as the writer is concerned only with measuring knowledge of specifics. However, most tests should include as well some items evaluating the examinee's knowledge of principles, procedures, laws, and similar generalizations. The most effective objective-type item for this purpose is the multiple-choice item.

The first item in Figure 3.2 uses a question as the item stem and possible sentence answers as responses. The second item uses an incomplete statement as the item stem and possible completing phrases as responses. In items

Figure 3.2

TEST ITEMS MEASURING KNOWLEDGE OF PRINCIPLES

SCIENCE: 2 What happens when an electric bulb lights?
   5 Electrical energy is transformed into heat and light energy.
   6 Heat energy is transformed into electrical energy.
   7 Heat energy is transformed into physical energy.
   8 Physical energy is transformed into chemical energy.

SOCIAL STUDIES: 1 In general, the better educated a person is, the more likely he is to —
   1 be active in church organizations
   2 live in the inner city
   3 have a large family
   4 be adaptable to new job requirements

measuring knowledge of generalizations, it is necessary that the responses consist of something more than one or two words. Since this is the case, the use of completion-type items would lead to considerable subjectivity in scoring and a consequent reduction in reliability and validity. (For a discussion of the subjectivity of completion-type items, see Chapter 4.)

TESTING FOR COMPREHENSION

The second major category in the taxonomy is comprehension. The abilities involved in this category are frequently considered aspects of "understanding." In helping teachers to develop tests that measure a variety of these abilities, the authors have found it useful to give some attention to two subcategories of comprehension—*translation* and *interpretation*.

Translation is the expression of a communication in words or symbols different from those given. This may mean "putting something in your own words," changing an expression from mathematical symbols to words or vice versa, or giving an example or an illustration. Although the ability to translate represents a minimal level of understanding, it is an essential ability in almost any area of study.

Figure 3.3

TEST ITEMS MEASURING ABILITY IN TRANSLATION

SCIENCE: The chart shows the data recorded from observations of a stone falling under the action of its weight alone.

Time (sec.)	Distance (ft.)	Speed (ft./sec.)
0	0	0
1	16	32
2	64	64
3	144	96
4	256	128
5	400	?

6 At the end of 1 second, how many feet had the stone fallen?
5 64   6 0   7 16   8 32

7 When the stone had fallen a distance of 144 feet, at how many feet per second was it falling?
1 144   2 96   3 128   4 160

SOCIAL STUDIES:

Ⓐ MUNICIPAL JUDGE

Ⓑ NON-PARTISAN ELECTION

Ⓒ **VOTE FOR JOHN MURPHY**

Ⓓ 4-YEAR TERM

Ⓔ LICENSED ATTORNEY

Ⓕ FORMER DISTRICT ATTORNEY—8 YEARS

Ⓖ FAMILY MAN

Ⓗ HELP FIGHT CORRUPTION

Ⓘ REGISTER AND VOTE

32 Which one of the following shows that Murphy has legal training?
5 H   6 E   7 A   8 G

33 The poster announces an election for —
1 a representative   3 an attorney
2 a judge   4 a mayor

One can measure the ability to translate by presenting examinees with some type of communication and asking them either to construct a translation of it or to identify the correct translation from several given choices. The first item shown in Figure 3.3 requires the student to translate tabled information by answering a prose question. Understanding the question requires the student to convert information from symbols to words. In the second item the student must translate specific information contained in a political poster in the same way. Of course, a very common type of item for measuring translation is one in which the examinee reads a paragraph and then answers factual questions about the content. Items of this type are typically used in evaluating reading comprehension but are also useful in assessing the ability to translate material in specific subject areas, such as the sciences, social studies, and foreign languages. In the area of mathematics, some typical translation items would require the student to write the fraction represented by the shaded portion of some whole area, to write the proper number sentence for a simple statement in a story problem, or write the addition fact for a picture showing the union of two sets.

Interpretation refers to a slightly more complex form of comprehension than that involved in translation. It includes making comparisons between or summaries of separate elements of a communication. The test items in Figure 3.4 illustrate this. In Item 43, the science item, the examinee must analyze data from all four bars in the graph to answer the item correctly. In Item 56 the student must compare population entries for all six regions to be able to determine the correct answer.

The items in Figure 3.4 measure the pupil's ability to interpret information presented in tables and diagrams. Perhaps an even more common test of interpretation is that based on the reading of paragraphs or of longer written passages. This type of interpretation can be assessed through items quite similar to those involving tables. The essential step is to present the examinees with some reading material new to them (so that they cannot answer the items by simple recall) and then prepare questions that they can answer only if they relate ideas from several different parts of the communication. An efficient procedure, and one that is followed with most reading-comprehension tests, is to base some translation and some interpretation items on the same reading passage.

TESTING FOR APPLICATION

Most teachers probably like to feel that pupils in their classes are learning to apply what they know. If application is to be a realistic goal in any particular instructional situation, then the tests that are used to evaluate achievement must include items that measure the pupil's ability to make applications.

The taxonomy suggests that application means

the use of abstractions in particular and concrete situations. The abstractions may be in the form of general ideas, rules of procedures, or general-

Figure 3.4

TEST ITEMS MEASURING ABILITY IN INTERPRETATION

SCIENCE: A class studied right-handed and left-handed children. They used the results to make the graph below.

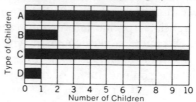

A. right-handed boys   C. right-handed girls
B. left-handed boys   D. left-handed girls

43 The characteristic common to most of the children is that they are —

1 boys   3 left-handed
2 girls   4 right-handed

SOCIAL STUDIES:

Area and Estimated Population, 1950–1990 of Selected Regions of the World

Region	Area (Millions of sq. miles)	Population (Millions)		
		1950	1970	1990
Africa	11.7	191	346	588
Asia (not incl. U.S.S.R.)	10.6	1,274	2,017	2,850
Europe	1.9	391	454	504
North America	9.4	217	318	471
South America	6.9	108	193	333
U.S.S.R.	8.6	193	246	316

56. Of the six regions of the world given in the table, how many had a larger population than the U.S.S.R. in 1950?

1) 2   2) 3   3) 4   4) 5

Item 43 reproduced from the Stanford Achievement Test, Intermediate 1, Form A, Test 10, Science, copyright © 1972, by Harcourt Brace Jovanovich, Inc. Reproduced by special permission of the publisher.

Item 56 reproduced from Iowa Tests of Basic Skills, Levels Edition, Form 5, Test W, Work-Study Skills, W-2: Reading Graphs and Tables, copyright © 1971 by University of Iowa, Houghton Mifflin Co., Boston.

ized methods. The abstractions may also be technical principles, ideas, and theories which must be remembered and applied.[5]

This makes it clear that what is applied in any situation is not facts or data but rules or principles that describe the relationships between facts or that

---

[5] Ibid., p. 205.

spell out methods or procedures. The first task of the teacher, then, in developing test materials to measure the ability "to apply" is to identify exactly what the pupil is expected to be able to apply. The teacher should ask: "What are the principles, rules, or procedures that have been studied in this unit?" The second step is to determine exactly what should result from the application of these rules or principles. A pupil may apply given principles or procedures to

1. produce an outcome.
2. explain an outcome.
3. predict an outcome.

Some procedures for evaluating these types of application are suggested below. Of course, in developing items to measure application it is important to make sure that the situation described is new to the student so that the answer can be obtained only through application of the principle and not merely from memory.

1. *Application to produce an outcome*—This ability is involved in such tasks as applying principles and procedures to arrive at an answer to a "story problem" in arithmetic, following rules of punctuation and capitalization to produce a correctly written paragraph, or applying certain principles to produce a desired result in a science laboratory demonstration. The evaluation of abilities of this type frequently can best be made by the inspection of student work products or by an essay examination. However, objective-type items can also be of some use. Figure 3.5 shows this; it provides examples of items that test the pupil's ability to apply procedures to produce results in science and mathematics. Of course, the application of certain principles or procedures may involve tasks of such magnitude and complexity that it is unrealistic to have the pupil actually carry them out. In such cases it may be meaningful to ask the student to explain what should be done to achieve a desired outcome, and perhaps to devise a plan of action. A modified approach to the evaluation of this ability is to use objective-type test items in which the examinee is asked to identify the essential element or essential step in a plan for attaining a desired goal.
2. *Application to explain an outcome*—The ability to tell why a given situation exists by applying the pertinent principle can be measured directly through the use of multiple-choice items. The general procedure is to describe a particular situation and the expected outcome and then ask the examinee to choose the principle that best explains it. Figure 3.6 provides examples of items of this type.
3. *Application to predict an outcome*—This is another important way in which principles may be applied—particularly in the physical and social sciences. Figure 3.7 presents items measuring this ability. Here in the science item, the pupil has to apply certain principles of energy and motion in order to predict what will happen in an experiment. In Item 34 the task is to apply

Figure 3.5

TEST ITEMS MEASURING APPLICATION OF PRINCIPLES OR PROCEDURES TO PRODUCE AN OUTCOME

SCIENCE:

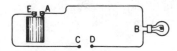

25 The set-up in the above diagram can be used to find out whether an electric current will flow through an object. To do this, you would place the object so that it would contact —

1 B and D   3 A and B
2 C and D   4 E and C

MATHEMATICS:

71. Mr. Nelson built a garage on the lot next to his home. He had to borrow $2000 from the bank. If the annual interest rate on the bank loan was 8%, how much was the interest for the first year?

1) **$20**   3) **$1600**
2) **$160**   4) (Not given)

72. The total area of the roof of the garage was 600 square feet. The shingles Mr. Nelson chose cost $9.00 for 100 square feet. How much did he pay for enough shingles to cover the entire roof?

1) **$54**   3) **$540**
2) **$150**   4) (Not given)

knowledge of court procedure to tell what will happen next in a given situation.

EVALUATING OTHER ABILITIES

It has been found that objective-type test items can be used quite successfully to measure the abilities of knowledge, translation, interpretation, and application discussed in preceding sections. Work carried out by the authors indicates that most items on published achievement tests can be categorized as measuring one of these abilities. This suggests that the beginning teacher who has learned to develop items covering these taxonomy categories will be in a position to produce tests that are about as comprehensive in types of abilities

Figure 3.6

TEST ITEMS MEASURING APPLICATION OF PRINCIPLES
TO EXPLAIN SOME REPORTED OR EXISTING OUTCOME

SCIENCE: 31

Two burning candles are placed under a pinwheel. The pinwheel spins because of the motion of the —

① pin   ③ wheel
② warm air   ④ flame

SOCIAL STUDIES: 10 For farming, plains usually produce more than hills because —

   5 topsoil erodes more easily from hills than from plains
   6 there is more rainfall on the plains
   7 the plains are warmer
   8 winds harm crops on the hills

Item 31 reproduced from the Stanford Achievement Test, Primary III, Form A, Test 10, Science, copyright © 1972, by Harcourt Brace Jovanovich, Inc. Reproduced by special permission of the publisher.
Item 10 reproduced from the Stanford Achievement Test, Advanced Battery, Form X, Test 7, Social Studies, Part A, copyright © 1964, by Harcourt Brace Jovanovich, Inc. Reproduced by special permission of the publisher.

sampled as objective-type tests can be. However, if this teacher relies solely on objective-type tests for assessing the achievement of pupils, certain important abilities will still not be evaluated. To assess abilities that are beyond the level of *application* in the hierarchical order of the taxonomy categories, procedures other than objective-type testing will have to be employed, despite the fact that the taxonomy gives examples of objective-type items that can be used to measure analysis, synthesis, and evaluation. Persons sophisticated in test-development procedures may be able to develop items for this purpose, but those who are less skilled will usually end up with items that in fact measure some simpler ability such as comprehension or application.

Synthesis is of course an essential ability that all teachers will want to evaluate. In most subject areas we are concerned with the pupil's ability to produce or create something in writing—a sentence, a paragraph, or a longer composition—and the most obvious means of such evaluation is an essay examination or an out-of-class assignment. In some subjects we may be concerned with the student's ability actually to synthesize or produce some physical object—a painting or other work of art, a poster, an industrial arts project, or something from the home economics kitchen. Here also the means

Figure 3.7

TEST ITEMS MEASURING APPLICATION OF PRINCIPLES
TO PREDICT A CONSEQUENCE

SCIENCE:

> Two fifty-pound steel balls, A and B, traveling in opposite directions on a level surface at a speed of 100 feet per second, crash head-on.

4 What happens after the crash?

5 B rolls away a greater distance.

6 They roll away equally in the same direction.

7 They bounce away equally in opposite directions.

8 A rolls away a greater distance

SOCIAL STUDIES: 34. The case of Sam Suspect has been tried, but the jury cannot come to an agreement. What will happen now?

34–1 Sam will be compensated for the time lost from work.

34–2 The case will be retried with a new jury.

34–3 The judge will send the case to a higher court.

34–4 The trial will begin all over, and the same jury will try again to reach a verdict.

34–5 The judge will determine the verdict.

of evaluation is rather obvious. We must first ask the pupil to create the product under certain conditions, and then we must assess the procedure used, the product itself, or both. In light of evidence of an increasing emphasis on creativity as a goal of education, it would seem that the evaluation of a pupil's ability with respect to synthesis should receive increased attention.

Although we have thus far been concerned largely with cognitive abilities, the teacher must always be concerned with the central importance of such affective variables as interest and attitude. In the first chapter we pointed out that because current devices for measuring variables in the affective domain are complex and relatively ineffective, little space would be devoted to them here. However, the teacher should be vitally concerned with the attitudes and interests of students, even though they will probably have to be assessed through informal, nonobjective procedures. But such procedures can be very useful. Certainly a teacher can investigate students' interests by talking with them, by listening to them, and by observing their actions. Such information can greatly help teachers to judge the effectiveness of their other teaching procedures and materials and, therefore, to plan pupil activities.

Summary

A common and frequently justified complaint about pencil-and-paper tests is that they measure only limited types of abilities—typically, the knowledge of facts. However, such tests can in fact be used to measure a variety of abilities. The starting point for ensuring this comprehensive type of evaluation is to specify instructional objectives that cover all the important types of abilities. Useful guidance in this task can be provided by an extensive and highly detailed taxonomy of cognitive abilities. This chapter has shown how objective-type test items can be used to measure such cognitive abilities as knowledge of specifics, knowledge of generalizations, translation, interpretation, and application. The teacher who plans evaluation instruments with the proper care and who employs some of the procedures described here should be able to develop tests that effectively measure such proficiencies. The assessment of higher-level cognitive abilities such as synthesis will probably require the use of nonobjective procedures—for example, essay examinations, out-of-class assignments, and the observation of pupil performance. The last of these procedures will also be used in appraising important affective variables such as attitude and interest. A wide variety of techniques is available for evaluating a great variety of instructional objectives.

SUGGESTIONS FOR CLASS DISCUSSION
AND FURTHER INVESTIGATION

1. Develop a matrix of objectives, such as the one presented in Table 3.1 of this chapter, for some course or unit of study that is of interest to you. Make certain that all objectives are stated in terms of pupil behaviors.

2. In the section on deriving specific objectives in Chapter 2, certain action verbs, such as *describe, explain, list,* and *compare,* were suggested as appropriate to the types of behavioral abilities that should be found in statements of specific objectives. For each of the six major taxonomy categories, develop a list of comparable action verbs that would be appropriate for objectives defined for that category.

3. Secure a copy of at least one standardized achievement test battery. Categorize every item in each test in the battery according to the taxonomy category that you feel it measures. Compare the various subject areas in terms

of percentages of items measuring the different taxonomy abilities. What do the different percentages reveal about what is stressed in teaching or testing in each subject?

SUGGESTIONS FOR FURTHER READING

For further orientation to the task of evaluating a variety of types of pupil abilities, the reader should study Benjamin S. Bloom, ed., *Taxonomy of Educational Objectives, Handbook I: Cognitive Domain* (New York: David McKay Co., 1956).

A rather comprehensive presentation with many examples on how to use test items to measure the various taxonomy categories in each of several subject-matter areas will be found in Benjamin S. Bloom, J. Thomas Hastings, and George F. Madaus, *Handbook on Formative and Summative Evaluation of Student Learning* (New York: McGraw-Hill, 1971).

4

Principles of Achievement
Test Construction:
Teacher-Made Tests

The first three chapters of this book have focused on the teacher's need for
the type of information provided by a good program of evaluation and testing.
It was emphasized that the value of such information is to be found in the
guidance that it can give the teacher in planning instruction and in making
decisions about pupils. Chapter 2 suggested specific procedures for outlining
the curriculum so that tests and other evaluation instruments can be made an
integral part of the teaching-learning process.

Since the particular curriculum organization used by any given teacher
will probably be unique, teachers will usually have to develop most of the
evaluation instruments they need. The evaluation device used most frequently
is undoubtedly the teacher-made test; therefore, it is essential that the beginning teacher be skilled in the development and use of such devices. The matter
of how to develop and use classroom tests has received considerable attention
in past years, and many useful criteria and suggestions have been prepared.
When carefully planned and developed, most types of classroom tests can
rate quite high on all the criteria discussed in Chapter 2—*validity, reliability, objectivity, comprehensiveness, economical use of class time* (because all
pupils are giving information about themselves simultaneously), and *simplic-*

ity in use. The *teacher-made* test can add to all this the advantage of highly specific appropriateness to a particular curriculum.

Types of Teacher-Made Tests

The types of test items most frequently written by teachers can be categorized as follows:

1. Essay items.
2. Completion or supply-type items.
3. Selection-type items.
   a. True-false.
   b. Multiple-choice.
   c. Matching.

Obviously the item types vary in the degree to which the examinee must supply the answer rather than making a selection from given alternatives and, therefore, in the degree to which the items can be scored objectively. In both the essay and completion types the students must provide the answer; however, in the completion items they supply only one or a few words, while in the essay they must provide everything. For this reason completion items are frequently classed with selection-type items and, with them, referred to as objective-type items. As we have seen, in the context of pupil evaluation the word "objective" means that the scoring can be done independently of the subjective judgment of the scorer. The selection-type items can, of course, be scored in a completely objective manner. Once a scoring key has been developed, the scorer does not need to make any subjective decisions, and scoring can be done just as effectively by a clerk or a machine as by the teacher. However, with completion or supply-type items this is not true. Here a scoring key will be developed and used, but it can be anticipated that students will supply some answers not listed on the scoring key that will have to be accepted as correct. Decisions in such situations will require the subjective judgment of the teacher. Hence, completion-type items are not altogether objective and probably should not be classed with selection-type items.

Essay Items

The type of test item whose scoring is the most subjective is the essay item. In answering essay items examinees must construct sentences, paragraphs, and written passages of varying length to demonstrate that they have the ability being tested. The length of the required responses may vary from a single sentence, which might be sufficient in a second-grade test, to a lengthy composition taking a day or more to complete, as in a comprehensive examination for some types of professional certification. The essential characteristic of the essay item is that it requires the examinee to write at least one sentence and that the answer must be assessed subjectively by the teacher or another authority on the content.

USING THE ESSAY ITEM

The essay item should be used only when it has been judged the most valid and efficient procedure for a given purpose. The teacher should not use it merely because he or she has developed the habit of relying exclusively on it or because it seems to be the simplest type of test to construct. The essay test can be extremely valid for evaluating certain kinds of objectives and may be helpful in promoting desirable study and planning by students. Also, it gives the examinee valuable practice in organizing ideas and trying to express them effectively. On the other hand, the typical unreliability of the scores obtained and the relative inefficiency in the use of testing time suggest that the essay test should not be chosen if some more objective procedure is equally valid.

If the purpose of the test is to determine the extent to which pupils have acquired certain knowledge, supply-type items or selection-type items will usually prove more effective than essay items. Essay examinations should be used to evaluate more complex abilities such as a student's competence to organize ideas, develop an argument, make comparisons, interpret information, and display other abilities involving original written verbal expression; and, when the intended objectives are stated in terms of such abilities, the essay test should be given first consideration.

CONSTRUCTING THE ESSAY ITEM

If an essay test is to be useful for measuring the desired abilities, considerable care must be taken in the development of the items. These items should not be dashed off hurriedly on the day of the test but should be planned well in advance so that they can be reexamined and edited before they are used.

An essay item must clearly specify the desired response. If examinees, in writing answers to an item, do not exhibit the desired ability because they do not understand the question, then low scores represent invalid information about their achievement. Each essay item should be worded so clearly and specifically that all pupils will interpret it correctly.

A mistake common in the writing of essay items is the use of questions that are too general. Consider, for example, a question that might be used with some of the content of this chapter: "Discuss the objective-type test." Answering an item worded in such broad terms, different examinees will probably concentrate on different aspects of the topic. One student might discuss the kinds of items that are usually considered objective and offer suggestions for the construction of each. Another might describe the problems of using this type of test to measure different abilities and compare it with the essay examination. Still another might explain how objective-type tests rate with respect to the various qualities that are generally sought in an evaluation device. If the teacher had one of these approaches in mind and penalized those students who did not use it, he or she would be making the judgment that failure to discuss this topic indicated lack of mastery of it; the judgment might not be valid.

To avoid ambiguity and to be certain of obtaining the same type of information about all examinees, one would have to rephrase the above question in more specific terms. An example might be: "Explain why certain kinds of test items are called 'objective.' Describe completion and multiple-choice items and compare their objectivity." Note that this essay item, although much more restricted in what it requests from the student, is necessarily much longer than the previous, more general, statement.

The revised form of our test question may be criticized because it does not require the student to display knowledge of other aspects of the topic; it is too restricted in its sampling of abilities. However, if greater sampling is desired, the student should be asked to respond to several relatively brief, specific items rather than to one broad, vague question.

SCORING ESSAY EXAMINATIONS

Because the major weakness of the essay examination lies in the subjectivity and possible unreliability of the scoring procedures, the scoring must be carefully planned. Two alternative procedures are quite widely used: (1) the *scoring key* procedure and (2) the *sorting* procedure.

1. *The scoring key procedure*—In using this method, one's first step is to develop a scoring key. Although this key will be somewhat different from that used with an objective-type test and cannot be applied with as much objectivity, it can contribute to more reliable scoring. The key typically consists of an outline of the ideal answer and indicates the number of points that are to be awarded to the student for including each element in the outline. For example, the key for scoring the essay question on objective-type test items might be outlined as follows:

1. Definition of objective-type item	2 points
2. Meaning of objectivity	2 points
3. The completion-type item	
a. Description	2 points
b. Degree of objectivity	2 points
4. The multiple-choice item	
a. Description	2 points
b. Degree of objectivity	2 points
5. Comparison of completion and multiple-choice	4 points

The arbitrary decision has been made that each of the first six elements in the outline is worth 2 points, while the final element is worth 4. The assignment of points to each element is made by the teacher on the basis of a judgment of the relative importance of each specific ability. Usually, however, the simpler the weighting system, the more reliable the results will be. In using the above key, the teacher will first look for the examinee's definition of an objective-type item. If it is stated in an essentially correct form, the answer will earn 2 points. If the definition is only partially correct, the answer may earn only 1 point. If the answer does not contain a definition, or if the given definition is totally incorrect, no points will be awarded. The teacher then goes on to score each element in the same manner. Note that the task of comparing completion and multiple-choice items has been judged to be of greater importance than any other single element in the answer and that here the scorer can award anything from 0 to 4 points. It should also be noted that if the teacher felt there were certain specific matters that should be included in the comparison, these could be listed as subcategories under Element 5, and each could be assigned some part of the total 4 points.

2. *The sorting procedure*—This procedure depends upon the scorer's making a judgment of the overall quality of an essay and does not involve the analysis of an answer in terms of its coverage of prespecified content. For this reason it may be more valid for assessing certain type of abilities such as those involving synthesis or some form of creative production. However, the sorting procedure is less objective than the scoring key method. In using the sorting procedure, the scorer decides ahead of time that each paper will be classified as falling into one of a limited number of categories, usually 3 to 5. For example, these categories may be the letter-grade categories of A, B, C, D, and E. In some cases a decision is also made as to the approximate percentage of papers that should be sorted into each category. The scorer, in reading each paper, makes a judgment as to its overall worth and assigns it to a category on the basis of this judgment. After this initial sorting is completed, the scorer should reexamine the papers in each category to determine if all are close enough in quality to be assigned the same score. This reexamination should also involve comparing the papers in one category with those in the adjacent categories to see if any shifts are suggested.

The reader will note that the *sorting procedure* results in a score that tells something about how a pupil's performance compares with that of other pupils. On the other hand, the *scoring key procedure* can provide rather exact information as to what the pupil has and has not mastered as well as permitting a comparison with other students. For this reason, in many situations the use of a scoring key in scoring essay examinations may be expected to provide more specific information for making decisions about instruction.

3. *Additional suggestions for scoring*—Whichever scoring procedure is used, certain other steps may be used to help increase the reliability and validity of results.

    1. If the essay examination consists of several items, score the answers

to the first item on all papers; then go on to score the second item, and so on. This procedure will increase the probability that for any given item the same standards will be used on all papers. It should also be helpful in reducing the "halo effect," or the probability that the scorer's judgment of the value of an answer to one item on a pupil's test paper will be influenced by an overall impression of the paper.

2. If possible, score each paper without looking to see the name of the examinee. This is another effort to reduce the "halo effect." If the scorer does not know whose paper is being graded, previous general impressions of the student cannot influence the score assigned. Scoring will then be on the basis of the present written answer alone.

3. During the process of scoring, periodically recheck some of the papers that were scored earlier. This review should improve the chances that a relatively uniform standard will be used for all papers.

Completion or Supply-Type Items

Completion items are statements with one or more missing words that must be provided by the examinee. The following items are simple examples of this form:

> During the Civil War, the commander of the Army of Northern Virginia was General _____.
> The chemical symbol for mercury is _____.

Another form of this item is a question that can be answered with one or a few words. The items given above can easily be reworded in question form:

> Who was the commander of the Army of Northern Virginia during the Civil War? _____
> What is the chemical symbol for mercury? _____

In either form, the essential features of this kind of item are that the answers consist of only one or two words and that these words must be supplied by the examinee rather than selected from a list of available alternatives.

USING THE COMPLETION ITEM

Completion items are useful in evaluating a variety of educational objectives. Here we will deal with their use in the *knowledge* category. They are appropriate whenever an objective specifies that the pupil should be able to name, list, or supply the answer. When the pupil is expected to have memorized certain terms, names of persons, dates, or symbols, the completion or supply-type item will probably be the most valid form of test question to use. It provides little likelihood of correct guessing, since the examinee can either supply the answer or not. Therefore, a correct response almost certainly represents actual knowledge—not just a lucky choice among alternatives—and can be considered highly reliable.

This kind of item has the advantage of being relatively easy to construct, particularly when compared with multiple-choice and matching items, since it does not require a list of plausible distracters.

As has already been mentioned, this form of item lacks complete objectivity. Because the person constructing the scoring key can seldom anticipate all the possible correct answers that students might insert, the scorer will frequently be required to make subjective decisions. In the classroom, the completion or supply-type item tends to be used primarily to evaluate memorization. Too much reliance on this type of item leads to overemphasis of this ability. Although rote learning is essential in most subject-matter areas, it is only one ability and must not be emphasized to the neglect of other, more complex abilities.

CONSTRUCTING THE COMPLETION ITEM

The following suggestions have been found helpful in the preparation of effective completion items.

1. Word each item so specifically that the desired answer is the only one possible. Consider the following:

World War II ended in _____.

A number of different expressions ("Japan," "victory," "1945") could be used to complete this statement correctly. If the item is intended to test whether the examinee knows the year in which the war ended, it should be worded:

World War II ended in the year _____.

This more specific statement rules out such answers as "Japan" and "victory."

2. Do not insert more than one or two blanks in any completion item. The addition of more typically results in a "butchered" sentence that could be answered correctly with a variety of combinations, for example:

The _____ type of test item is usually more _____ than the _____ type.

Of course, many different words could be used to complete this statement correctly, but each combination of words yields a sentence with a different meaning. A better item would be:

The supply type of test item is usually graded more objectively than the _____ type.

---

3. Word the statement so that the blank is near the end of the sentence. This practice ensures more efficient testing because the examinee will have the major idea of the statement in mind before having to think of the element that must be supplied; the informed examinee will then have to read the item only once. If the blank is near the beginning of the sentence, the student will have to read the item once to grasp the idea and then again to see if an answer is correct. One advantage of using the question form in supply-type items is that the blank necessarily appears at the end.

4. Do not use statements copied from textbooks or other lesson sources. A temptation in constructing completion items is to select key sentences from a textbook and to form test items merely by putting blanks in place of certain words. There are at least two important reasons for avoiding this practice. First, key sentences often are not specific enough to constitute good items. That is, the sentence may make sense only in context and by itself may not contain all the words necessary to make it clear and specific. Second, if students know that a teacher makes liberal use of sentences copied directly from the textbook, their study will tend to be essentially memorization of the phrasing of the text rather than its content. When material is taken from a printed source, it should be reworded so that verbatim memory alone will not be sufficient to enable the pupil to do well on the test.

5. In most cases the question form is more effective than the incomplete statement because (a) the question form tends to be more specific, (b) the blank is at the end of the item, (c) there is no chance of producing a "butchered" sentence, and (d) there is less likelihood that a question can be copied verbatim from a printed text.

True-False Items

In these items the examinee must decide whether a given statement is true or false. For example, the items used to illustrate the completion form could be reworded as follows:

The commander of the Army of Northern Virginia during the Civil War was General Robert E. Lee.	Ⓣ	F
The chemical symbol for mercury is Au.	T	Ⓕ

Variations in this two-alternative item include the use of such word pairs as "yes-no," "right-wrong," or "correct-incorrect" as the responses. Another variation is the "true-false with correction" item. In this latter type, the examinee is instructed to mark each item either true or false *and* to correct each false statement. In one procedure, the student is told to cross out the part of an item that makes it false and to write in the words necessary to make it true. In another procedure, each of the items has a key word underlined, and for each false statement the student is to substitute another word for the one underlined to make the statement true. The second procedure is preferable to the first because it makes scoring more manageable and reliable.

USING THE TRUE-FALSE ITEM

The true-false item should probably be used less frequently than it is. It is generally regarded as the weakest of the objective items. In most cases a teacher's evaluation of student achievement will be better if the multiple-choice rather than the true-false item is employed. However, use of the true-false or another type of two-response item may be justified where there are obviously only two alternatives and where the attempt to develop a multiple-choice item would result in highly implausible distracters.

A major weakness of the true-false item is of course the fact that if the pupil is totally uninformed about a given item and has to make a blind guess, there is still a 50 percent chance that the answer will be correct. Thus, scores from true-false tests are typically less reliable than are scores from multiple-choice tests. The high probability of guessing correctly often results in poor study habits. In addition, a pupil answering test items as true when actually they are false may retain this incorrect information.

One advantage of the true-false item is economy of pupil time; examinees typically can answer more items of this type than of other types in a given amount of time. When it is essential that the maximum amount of material be covered in a limited amount of time, the true-false test might be the most efficient procedure. Completely objective scoring is, of course, another advantage of this type of item.

Some teachers act on the assumption that an additional advantage of the true-false item is ease of construction. That is, they use this form because they find they can write a series of items rather quickly. This assumption is false, and the poor test items that usually result from it constitute a major reason why many teacher-made tests are of such poor quality. The construction of good true-false items actually requires careful planning and considerable time, and they are therefore not as easy to develop as might be expected.

CONSTRUCTING THE TRUE-FALSE ITEM

The teacher who uses true-false items should find the following suggestions helpful for improving test quality.

1. Construct statements that are definitely true or definitely false. This is important both for achieving valid and reliable test results and for avoiding the possibility that the examinee may acquire some incorrect ideas from taking the test. It is more likely that true-false questions will be unambiguous if the item writer takes the following advice.

a. Use relatively short statements.

b. Use language that is as exact as possible. For example, where feasible, one should use quantitative rather than qualitative terms.

c. Avoid the use of complex sentences containing more than one major idea; such sentences may yield incorrect information about a student's knowledge. Consider the following item, for example:

The Ohio and Mississippi rivers meet at Cairo, Illinois,
to form the Missouri River.   T (F)

A student may mark this item false because he or she (mistakenly) thinks that the Ohio River does not join the Mississippi at Cairo. This response, however, would be taken to mean that the student knows that when the Ohio joins the Mississippi at Cairo, the combined rivers continue as the Mississippi, and therefore it would be judged correct. The incorporation of two major facts has resulted in incorrect information concerning this pupil's knowledge.

d. Attribute opinions or attitudes used as item content to some particular source so that the examinee knows the teacher is not asking for personal opinion. Items of this type might start with such qualifying phrases as "From the point of view of the writer of our textbook" or "In the opinion of most authorities in this field."

2. Avoid giving the examinee verbal clues—clues that imply that a statement is true or false and result in the examinee's choosing the correct response regardless of his or her knowledge of the facts in question. Strongly worded items containing *all, always, definitely, never,* and *undoubtedly* are usually false. Statements with such indefinite qualifying words as *frequently, may, most, should,* and *some* are typically true. The teacher should be alert to this possibility of giving away answers and should edit all items to eliminate these clues.

3. True items and false items should be of about equal length. There is some tendency for item writers to include more qualifiers in a true item with the result that true items will be longer. This could provide an irrelevant clue to the test-wise student.

4. Do not copy sentences from textbooks or other printed lesson source materials. A sentence may be entirely true when it is read within context, but, because of a lack of explanation and clarification, it may not be true when it stands alone in a test item. Furthermore, the consistent practice of copying test items from printed lesson materials encourages undesirable rote learning of textbook sentences.

5. Do not be tempted to simplify scoring by arranging the items so that there is some easily memorized repetitive pattern to the correct responses (TFFTFF or TFFTTF, for example). Students soon discover such patterns and thus invalidate the test results. For a similar reason it is best to avoid the practice of consistently having many more true responses than false. Some

test experts recommend using more false items than true items, since there is a tendency for false items to better differentiate high achievers from lower achievers.[1]

Multiple-Choice Items

A multiple-choice item consists of a *stem* plus two or more *alternatives,* one of which meets the requirement demanded by the stem. The item stem may be an incomplete statement and the alternative responses possible endings for it:

---

1. Specific instructional objectives are most useful to the test developer if they are stated in terms of
   a. the specific content covered.
   b. the desired pupil behavior.
   c. the teaching activities to be carried out.
   d. what the pupil should know.

In another frequently used form, the item stem is worded as a question for which the examinee is to select the correct answer:

---

2. Which one of the following types of test item can be scored most objectively?
   a. True-false
   b. Essay
   c. Completion

Although these are the most commonly used, there are many other forms possible. For example, the stem may be a word followed by several pictures from which the examinee is to select the one best described by the word. The reverse is also frequently employed—the item stem is a picture, and the alternatives are words, only one of which fits the picture.

The number of possible forms that effective multiple-choice items may take is limited only by the test constructor's imagination. The beginning teacher can get many ideas by examining items on the better published tests.

USING THE MULTIPLE-CHOICE ITEM
The multiple-choice question is generally considered to be the most useful of the objective-type items. Tests using it are usually more reliable than those containing other types. Multiple-choice tests can be scored on a completely objective basis. The role that guessing plays in determining an examinee's score is reduced when each item is provided with several alternatives. Reduc-

---

[1] E.g., see Robert L. Ebel, *Essentials of Educational Measurement* (Englewood Cliffs, N.J.: Prentice-Hall, 1972), p. 180.

ing the possibility of guessing correctly increases the reliability of the test. Furthermore, multiple-choice items can be used to evaluate a greater variety of abilities than can the other items. Examples of this diversity were provided in Chapter 3. A multiple-choice item tests the ability to make fine discriminations by asking the pupil to select "the most important reason," "the principal cause," or "the best explanation."

The assertion that the multiple-choice item is generally superior to other forms is supported by the fact that almost all items on most published tests are of this form. Publishers have found that questions originally phrased as completion or true-false items can be made more effective through rewording as multiple-choice items. Most classroom teachers will find the same to be true concerning their own tests. They should find that their testing will improve if they make greater use of multiple-choice items and place less reliance on true-false and completion questions.

CONSTRUCTING THE MULTIPLE-CHOICE ITEM

The following suggestions may be useful for writing effective multiple-choice items.

1. Write as many items as possible in question form. In most cases a question makes the best item stem because it is worded specifically and deals with only one important idea. Phrasing a statement in question form also reduces the possibility that the item will be copied directly from a textbook. If the incomplete-statement form seems necessary, test the clarity and specificity of the stem by determining whether the statement contains all the information that would be included in the corresponding question.

2. Include at least three alternatives for every stem. A multiple-choice item with only two alternatives allows a 50 percent chance that a blind guess will be correct, thus giving no advantage over a true-false item. To minimize the probability that a pupil will merely guess the correct answer, provide four or five alternatives if possible.

3. Make certain that all the incorrect alternatives, the distracters, are plausible enough so that none can be dismissed as absurd by an examinee who does not really know the correct answer.

4. If the item stem is a statement, make certain that all distracters provide grammatically correct endings to the sentence. Sometimes, in the haste to add distracters, a teacher will word some of the listed alternatives so poorly that they can be dismissed simply because they do not form a sentence when read with the stem. A simple example is an item stem that obviously requires a singular response but is accompanied by plural distracters.

5. Avoid the use of negatively worded stems. Stems that contain phrases like, "which of the following is not," tend to be confusing to the examinee.

6. Make the responses as short as feasible by including in the item stem any words that would otherwise be unnecessarily repeated in each response. A poor item would be the following:

---

1. Columbus' ships
   a. were named the Godspeed, the Discovery, and the Susan Constant.
   b. were named the Nina, the Pinta, and the Santa Maria.
   c. were named the Maria, the Carla, and the Pinata.

The item could be improved simply by the inclusion of "were named the" in the stem. Note that this would result in an item stem implying the question, "What were the names of Columbus' ships?"

7. Do not consistently avoid any one of the response positions as the place for the correct answer. For example, do not get into the habit of never putting the correct response in the first position. The correct answers in a test should occur with equal frequency in each response position.

8. Try to make all the responses approximately the same length. Beginners in test construction frequently find that their correct answers are consistently longer than the distracters. This provides the examinee with an irrelevant clue to the correct answer.

9. The responses "none of the above" or "not given" may be useful in items with only one possible answer, as in problems involving numerical computation. They should not be used in a "best-answer" type of item. When this option is presented, care should be taken to make certain that it fits grammatically with the stem.

10. The response "all the above" should seldom be used by a beginning item-writer. If items requiring this response are not worded with great care, they can cause undesirable confusion for the examinee.

11. Use consistent and correct punctuation. Do not place any punctuation at the end of the incomplete-statement stem unless the sentence requires it. Each response should start with a lower-case letter (unless it is a proper name or other word requiring capitalization) and end with a period or other appropriate terminal punctuation. When the question form is used, the stem should end with a question mark, and each response should start with a capital letter. (See the examples on page 57.)

Matching Exercises

A matching exercise consists of two lists of words, phrases, pictures, or other symbols and a set of instructions explaining the basis on which the examinee is to match an item in the first list with an item in the second list. The elements of the list that is read first are called *premises,* and the elements in the other list are called *responses.* It is possible to have more premises than responses, more responses than premises, or to have the same number of each. In the example of a matching exercise that follows, the premises appear in the left-hand column, with the responses at the right, but in some cases the responses may be placed below the premises.

In the left-hand column below are titles given to some of the founders of our nation. For each title choose a name from the right-hand column and place the letter identifying it on the line preceding the number of the title. Each item in the right-hand column may be used once, more than once, or not at all.

_____ 1. Father of the Constitution	a. Alexander Hamilton
_____ 2. First Secretary of the Trea-sury	b. John Jay
	c. Thomas Jefferson
_____ 3. Proposer of the Virginia Plan	d. James Madison
_____ 4. First Secretary of State	e. Edmund Randolph
_____ 5. Leader of the Federalists	
_____ 6. First Chief Justice of the Su-preme Court	

A matching exercise may be thought of as a set of multiple-choice items in which all the stems have the same options. The example exercise above has six scoring units. That is, the examinee receives one point for each premise for which the correct response is selected.

USING THE MATCHING EXERCISE

As its name suggests, this type of test item evaluates a pupil's ability to match or associate related objects or ideas. Many school subjects require that a pupil be able to associate terms with definitions, names of places with locations, ideas or procedures with their uses, or names of persons with events. Where there are many such parallel relationships, the matching exercise is an efficient and effective testing procedure. A given number of premises, each of which constitutes a scoring unit, occupies much less space than would the comparable number of multiple-choice items. However, the matching exercise should be used only when every response is a plausible distracter for each of the premises. A useful rule is that the matching exercise should be used only when a number of possible multiple-choice stems require repetition of the same alternatives. Application of this rule helps to ensure that the matching form will be used only where it is naturally effective. In beginning to construct a matching exercise, the teacher frequently has two or three important relationships in mind and then seeks other relationships in order to complete the test. This artificial manufacture of matching items results in the testing of pupils' knowledge of some insignificant facts along with the original important ones, thus reducing the validity of the test.

The matching exercise can be scored on a completely objective basis. If each exercise is properly constructed with four or more responses, there is only a slight probability that the examinee can guess the correct answer. When used correctly, it has most of the advantages of the multiple-choice test and can be used to measure most of the same types of abilities.

CONSTRUCTING THE MATCHING EXERCISE

Many of the suggestions for the construction of other types of objective items apply to the writing of matching exercises. However, the following specific suggestions should also be helpful.

1. Make each matching exercise *homogeneous* in the sense that all premises and all responses refer to the same type of thing. The example on page 60 is homogeneous in that all the premises describe men active during the formation of the United States government, and all the responses are names of men prominent at that time. The following is a simple example of an exercise that is not homogeneous.

_____ 1. Largest city in Pennsylvania	a. William Penn
_____ 2. Flows through Harrisburg	b. Pittsburgh
_____ 3. Major steel-producing center	c. William Pitt
_____ 4. City located on one of the Great Lakes	d. Susquehanna River
	e. Philadelphia
_____ 5. Founder of Pennsylvania	f. Erie

Here we have three descriptions of cities, one of a river, and one of a man. The student who has no knowledge of Pennsylvania can easily get Item 2 correct because only one river is listed among the responses. For Item 5, the respondent needs only to guess between the two men's names. In other words, the test's validity is greatly reduced because not all the responses are plausible distracters for all the premises.

2. Give a full and careful explanation of the basis for matching. If this is not done, some students may find a logical basis for matching different from the one intended. Below is an example of a poor exercise that could cause confusion.

_____ 1. reclusive	a. ostracized
_____ 2. gregarious	b. hermitic
_____ 3. banished	c. social
	d. welcomed

A student without sufficient instructions might correctly match synonyms or antonyms. The necessary directions could say: "Choose from the right-hand column the word that most closely defines each word in the left-hand column."

3. Make certain that all responses are plausible distracters for each premise. An important step in achieving this is to have homogeneous premises and responses, as described in Suggestion 1 above. However, each exercise should also be checked to ensure that the examinee is not given unintended help by a mixture of plural and singular responses, by the fact that some premises begin with *an* and others with *a,* or by other similar grammatical clues.

4. Limit the number of responses in a given matching exercise to about ten. Longer lists cause the examinee to waste time searching through the responses. If the original version of an exercise is too long, it should be divided into two or more separate exercises. Of course, in certain situations it is possible to keep the response list short by permitting each response to be used more than once.

5. Avoid the "perfect matching" situation in which the number of responses equals the number of premises, and each response is used only once. If the examinee knows all the associations except one, the final one will necessarily be correct also, and thus the discriminating ability and the accuracy of the test as a measuring device will be diminished.

6. Make sure that the list of premises contains the longer phrases or statements while the responses consist of short phrases, words, or symbols. This arrangement provides for more efficient use of pupil time in that the good student working any matching exercise will need to read each premise only once but will scan the list of responses several times (at least once with each premise).

7. Try to arrange the responses in some meaningful order. Arranging them alphabetically, chronologically, or on some other logical basis should save the pupil time in finding the desired response.

8. The premises should be identified by number (since each one is a test item), and the responses should be identified by letter.

Assembling the Items into the Completed Test Form

The key step in the development of an achievement test is the actual writing of test items, but the writing of clear instructions and the planning of the format of the total test is also of major importance. If a test is to be effective, considerable attention must be given to its form. The examinees must understand what they are expected to do, and they should not be penalized because of vaguely worded instructions, an inadequate scoring procedure, or other deficiencies in the mechanics of the test. Some suggestions that should be helpful in the compiling of test items to create the completed test form are listed below.

1. Give the student clear and complete instructions on how to answer items and record answers. If students miss items because they misunderstand the instructions, the test will yield invalid results. It might be well to include in the instructions a sample item and, if necessary, some practice exercises. To obtain ideas as to the best way to word instructions, the teacher should study the directions found with good published tests.

2. Group items of the same type together. Putting multiple-choice, true-false, and completion items together in one section of a test causes unnecessary confusion for the examinee. A set of instructions applicable to

multiple-choice items should introduce a section of multiple-choice items. If another item type is to be used in the same test, these items also should be introduced with appropriate instructions.

3. Arrange the items in order of difficulty with the easier items near the beginning of the test. This arrangement will help prevent students from becoming stalled on a difficult item near the beginning of a test and therefore not having time to attempt later, easier items for which they know the answers.

4. Fit the procedure for recording answers to the age level of the examinees. With older students, it is possible to employ a separate answer sheet and thereby simplify scoring without confusing students as to the mechanics of marking their answers. It is usually better to have very young students record their answers directly on the test sheet by circling the correct answer or drawing a line between two elements that are to be matched.

Summary

Because teacher-made tests are undoubtedly the most widely used device for pupil evaluation, every teacher should be proficient in constructing them. The major types of item used are essay, completion, and selection (true-false, multiple-choice, and matching) items. Each type has certain strong and certain weak qualities and evaluates certain abilities more effectively than others. This chapter has enumerated the various types of item and has provided specific suggestions for writing them.

SUGGESTIONS FOR CLASS DISCUSSION
AND FURTHER INVESTIGATION

1. Consider the following essay item: "Discuss the problem of defining educational objectives." How could this item be improved? Write a better version and then outline the ideal answer to it. Does outlining the answer lead you to see the need for possible changes in the wording of your item?

2. Examine the "test" below, presented as a brief quiz covering the first four chapters of this text. Then list as many violations of the principles of test construction and item-writing as you can find.

TEST

1. _____ _____ should always be _____ in terms of _____ behavior.
2. The first major category in the *Taxonomy of Educational Objectives* by Blommers and others is *knowledge*.
3. The objective "The pupil will be able to use the rules for carrying to solve three-column addition problems" would be categorized under the taxonomy (a) category of knowledge, (b) category of

translation, (c) category of application, (d) category of understanding, (e) category of appreciation.

4. Matching:

a. true-false	1. An author of *Taxonomy*
b. multiple-choice	2. Requires homogeneity of premises
c. matching	3. Best item type for measuring discrim-
d. $S = R - W$	inating ability
e. Bloom	4. Correction for guessing formula
	5. Testee has 50 percent chance of guess-
	ing answer

3. Identify a unit of study in some course that is of interest to you. (This could be the unit used in Exercise 2 in Chapter 2.) Construct a unit pretest and unit posttest using the most appropriate item forms.

4. Identify four important principles that a pupil might be expected to learn in a social studies course or a science course. Construct multiple-choice questions to test a pupil's ability to apply these principles. Review Chapter 3 for suggestions as to how this can be done.

SUGGESTIONS FOR FURTHER READING

A rather comprehensive discussion of procedures for developing objective-type tests is presented in Robert L. Thorndike, ed., *Educational Measurement,* 2nd ed. (Washington, D.C.: American Council on Education, 1971). Chapter 4, "Writing the Test Item," by Alexander G. Wesman, and chapter 10, "Essay Examinations," by William E. Coffman, will be particularly useful for suggestions on item writing.

A variety of other sources discuss basic principles of item writing and deal with the problems of developing tests for various levels and subject areas. These include the following: Benjamin S. Bloom, J. Thomas Hastings, and George M. Madaus, *Handbook on Formative and Summative Evaluation of Student Learning* (New York: McGraw-Hill, 1971), (see particularly chapters 7, 8, and 9, although many other chapters will also be helpful); Robert L. Ebel, *Essentials of Educational Measurement* (Englewood Cliffs, N.J.: Prentice-Hall, 1972) chapters 6, 7, and 8; Julian C. Stanley and Kenneth D. Hopkins, *Educational and Psychological Measurement and Evaluation* (Englewood Cliffs, N.J.: Prentice-Hall, 1972) chapters 9 and 10.

5

Test Scores and Their Interpretation

As was indicated in Chapter 1, the concern of educators with evaluation and testing is basically a concern with the problem of how to acquire information necessary for making decisions about pupils and about the effects of instructional procedures. This information can be gathered through both formal and informal procedures. Informal procedures usually result in qualitative verbal statements about a pupil's ability, aptitude, personality, and interests. For a variety of reasons, it is generally desirable to supplement informal procedures with more formal techniques that yield some type of quantitative data—tests, inventories, and rating scales, for example. In this chapter we review a variety of types of quantitative data. In particular, we concentrate on test scores and their interpretation.

The Need for Quantitative Measurement

In many areas of human concern—especially in the various sciences and technologies—increased understanding and mastery have been accompanied by increased skill in quantifying important variables. Progress in science and technology has been accompanied by a change from rather gross, general descriptions to the relatively precise measurement of specific characteristics and qualities. Primitive peoples using a pole to pry or lift a rock probably knew that the difficulty of the task varied with the length of the pole and the location of the fulcrum. However, when the principle of the lever was applied to complex machinery, relationships of this type had to be expressed in quantitative terms. The reader can undoubtedly think of a great number of other examples where development and achievement in a given field have been related to success in obtaining precise measurement of variables and in expressing relationships in quantitative terms.

Although many of the human characteristics involved in learning and instruction may never be measured with absolute precision, very accurate tests and other procedures for measuring some of the important variables have been devised. Procedures for assessing achievement, aptitude, interests, and attitudes have made it possible for teachers and administrators to obtain quantitative information about their students and their instructional programs. Used properly, this quantitative information is useful in making qualitative decisions about individual students and about instructional procedures. Quantitative information has also enabled researchers to make studies of the relationships among a variety of variables involved in human learning.

Like persons working in the sciences, teachers and others dealing with the problems of education have benefited from advances in the development of tests and other devices for obtaining quantitative descriptions of pertinent variables.

1. *Quantification often provides a more exact description*—The teacher who knows that three pupils have spelling scores of 20, 50, and 90 on a representative sample of 100 words from a list of 2000 frequently misspelled words has more exact information about these pupils than if the pupils had simply been described as "not so good," "OK," and "pretty good" in their ability to spell.

2. *Quantification can lead to improved objectivity of a measuring procedure* —When rules are applied to a measuring procedure in a way that allows numerical scores to be obtained, the resulting scores can be used to study the objectivity of the measuring procedure. If two teachers score the same pupil's response to an essay question, we can study the extent to which the two teachers' scores agree. If two persons apply the same measuring procedure to the same examinee, then the procedure is said to be objective if the two persons assign the same score to that examinee's performance. The more the scores agree, the more objective (and less subjective) is the measuring procedure. This probability of essential agreement makes the resulting information more reliable than the information obtained from more subjective procedures. Reliable information often increases the validity of the decision being made.

3. *Quantitative procedures permit clearer and more efficient communication—* Whether the communication is a discussion between two teachers, a transmittal of a pupil's record from one school district to another, or a conference between a teacher and a parent, the usefulness of the communication is usually enhanced if it includes quantitative information. A rather extended written or oral communication would be required to convey anywhere near the same amount of information as that contained in a score on a test that is well known to both participants. Presentation of the quantitative information on which decisions are based often helps to clarify the basis for the decisions and thus can facilitate consideration of alternative decisions. Verbal descriptions, although frequently helpful, are neither as economical nor as precise in meaning as quantitative descriptions.

Cautions for the Use of Quantitative Measurement

From the above statements, the reader may be led to believe that the authors consider quantitative information a goal in itself. Overemphasizing the exactness and the importance of test scores to the detriment of human values and professional judgment is, in the authors' opinion, just as unjustifiable as complete rejection of quantification and sole reliance on subjective information and arbitrary judgments.

It is our hope that the reader will develop an attitude that test scores are simply helpful information and that they cannot make decisions for teachers. We feel that scores obtained from properly designed tests are useful information for decision-making. The responsibility for the decision itself rests with the user of the information—the decision-maker.

One would expect common sense to dictate the above cautions about overreliance on test scores; unfortunately that does not always happen. In one study of the ways in which tests are used in schools, Goslin[1] examined teachers' opinions about the accuracy of standardized tests in assessing a pupil's intellectual potential and the weight test scores should receive in various decisions about pupils. While there was a good bit of variation in the teachers' opinions, Goslin reported that, on the average, their opinions reflected general "good sense" with respect to the importance of test scores. Goslin pursued the question further by trying to estimate whether or not the teachers would display this good sense in practice. He gave them a "card sort" test,[2] in which they had to make decisions about students described on the

---

[1] David A. Goslin, "Social Impact of Testing," *Personnel and Guidance Journal 45* (1967), pp. 676–82.

[2] J. T. Hastings et al., *The Use of Test Results* (Urbana, Ill.: Bureau of Educational Research, University of Illinois, 1960).

cards. Each card contained information about a student's test scores and/or class grades and/or subjective evaluations by past teachers. The cards where the objective and subjective information were in disagreement or where one or the other of them was missing tested the degree to which the teachers relied on either objective or subjective information. When the teachers' *opinions* about the use of test scores were compared to the *decisions* they actually made on the basis of test scores in the card sort test, Goslin found no relationship between the opinions and the decisions. Thus, Goslin concluded that while

> teachers may have been exposed to enough literature concerning tests and their proper use to make it possible for them to give the 'right' answers on a questionnaire, when it comes to actually using test scores, all bets may be off. (p. 679)

Measurement Procedures: Raw Scores

When we want to measure the length of an object, say a table, we place a ruler along the table's edge and count the number of units (inches, centimeters, feet, etc.) between one end of the table and the other end. If we were concerned with comparing the lengths of two tables, we would repeat the procedure for each table. The number of units counted for Table A is then compared to the number of units counted for Table B. We can then make statements like: Table A is 36 inches (units) long, while Table B is 48 inches long. These numbers, 36 inches and 48 inches, are scores, although usually we don't think of them that way. Since these scores on the length characteristic of tables are obtained directly as a result of the counting-up process used in measuring, they are termed *raw scores*.

When we want to measure an educational or psychological trait or characteristic of a person, measurement procedures become more complex and less straightforward than the procedures for measuring length. To illustrate some of the difficulties involved in using raw scores to measure complex characteristics, we will examine two ways of measuring the simple characteristic, height (i.e., the length of a person). Through analogy we hope to illustrate why educational and psychological trait measurement becomes very difficult. Studying these two procedures should help you to interpret raw scores more meaningfully and to see their limitations.

EXAMPLE 1

Suppose that we wanted to measure the height of a person. To do this we might follow a procedure similar to the one stated in the first sentence of this section. However, instead of using a "ruler" we will follow a slightly different, but equivalent, procedure. The procedure we will follow is more closely analogous to the procedure a teacher would use when constructing a test for classroom use.

Recall that when we are measuring "how much" height or length a person possesses, we use a counting process—we count up the number of units there are from one end of the person to the other end of the person. At this point the important thing is the *unit*. In this example we will construct our units in the following way. Imagine that we have a long wooden rod (like a broom handle) and that we have cut up the rod into smaller pieces, each piece being 1 unit in length. This is shown in Figure 5.1(a). Further, suppose that we have a big barrel of these unit pieces.

Our procedure for measuring the height of a person is as follows. First, we ask the person to stand up straight against a wall. Then, we start taking the pieces out of the barrel in a random manner. We place the first piece on the floor beside the person's heels and start stacking the pieces on top of it one at a time until the stack of pieces reaches the top of the person's head. (We will assume that we are good stackers and that the stack of pieces will

Figure 5.1

ILLUSTRATION OF THE MEASUREMENT PROCESS
FOR EXAMPLE 1

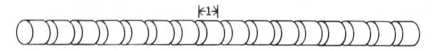

a. Constructing the units for Example 1

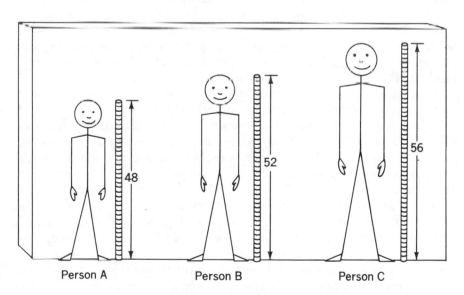

b. Measuring height by stacking units for Example 1

not collapse in the process!) We find the person's height by counting the number of pieces (or units) it took for the stack to reach the top of the person's head. Thus, Person A might be 48 units tall, Person B might be 52 units tall, and Person C might be 56 units tall. The procedure is illustrated in Figure 5.1(b).

We should note several things about this procedure before moving on to a new example. First, we note that each piece in the barrel is the same size. Thus, when we selected the pieces at random, it didn't matter which piece we happened to select—they were all the same. Second, the number we obtained for a person's height could be meaningfully referenced to zero. Another way to say this is that the number zero is legitimately interpreted as meaning "none of." In our case "none of" means that the thing being measured has no height. Third, differences between persons' height scores are unambiguous. Recall that Person A = 48 units, Person B = 52 units, and Person C = 56 units. The difference between a height of 48 units and a height of 52 units (52 − 48 = 4 units) has the same meaning as the difference between a height of 52 units and a height of 56 units (56 − 52 = 4 units). A difference of 4 units is interpreted to mean the same thing no matter how tall the two persons being compared may be.

EXAMPLE 2

In this example we will change some of the properties of the procedure used in Example 1. First, suppose that the pieces in our barrel are not all the same size. Some of the pieces are of length 1, others are of length 2, and still others are of length 3. These are illustrated in Figure 5.2(a). Second, let's assume that we have each person stand next to a table; we now measure the person's height by stacking a neat column of pieces on the table until the height of the stack reaches the top of the person's head. Assume that it is impossible for us to determine the height of the table. This is illustrated in Figure 5.2(b).

Again, the height score is obtained by counting the number of units from the top of the table to the top of the person's head.

Let's examine this example. First, we note that not all the pieces in the barrel were the same size. Thus, when we selected pieces at random, the pieces that happened to be selected changed the meaning of our height scores from person to person. For instance, if two people both were measured to be 48 pieces tall, we cannot be certain that they both have the same height. If by chance one person was measured by 48 pieces that all had length 1, and by chance the second person was measured by 48 pieces that all had length 2, then the second person would be taller than the first person even though our score (48 units) for each person was the same. The situation is even more complicated if we consider that the two persons having the same height score might be measured by different mixtures of large and small pieces, rather than all length 1 and all length 2 pieces as discussed above.

Figure 5.2

ILLUSTRATION OF THE MEASUREMENT PROCESS
FOR EXAMPLE 2

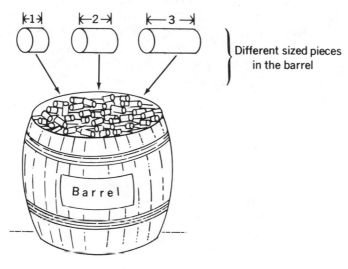

a. Illustration of the pieces in Example 2

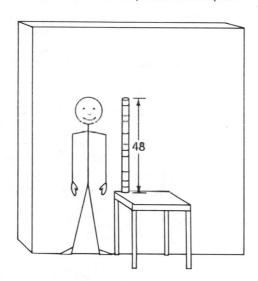

b. Illustration of the table and stacking procedure of Example 2

What about differences between persons' scores? Clearly, the difference
$52 - 48 = 4$ units would not necessarily mean the same thing as the difference $56 - 52 = 4$ units. If the 48 units going into Person A's measurement

are quite different from the 52 units going into Person B's measurement, and, similarly, the 56 units going into Person C's measurement, then we have no clear way to interpret what a difference of 4 units might mean.

On a third point Example 1 and Example 2 are quite different also. If we used the measurement procedure in Example 2, the scores could not be meaningfully referenced to zero. That is, we could not say that a person who had a score of zero has no height. If the top of a person's head came to just the top of the table, we would give this person a height score of zero. But clearly, the person's height is not zero. No meaningful zero exists in this height-measuring example.

ANALOGY TO EDUCATIONAL AND PSYCHOLOGICAL MEASUREMENT

Table 5.1 summarizes the examples above. Let us consider how these height-measuring procedures relate to educational and psychological test scores. First, we should note that in the height examples, we obtained the raw scores of the persons being measured by counting up the number of units. When we build an educational or psychological test, the units we count up are usually the number of test items the person answers correctly. Thus, the units of the height-measuring examples are analogous to the items on a test.

In Example 1, we saw that the units were constructed to be of equal size. Because they were of equal size, it didn't matter which units were selected to measure a given person and, further, scores obtained using this procedure were comparable from person to person. Seldom, if ever, do the items on a test possess this property. The size of the height unit is analogous to the difficulty *and* psychological meaning of a test item. That is, before one could claim that the items on a test are equivalent (or of equal size) one would have to establish that all the items are of equal difficulty to the persons being tested and that they all have the same psychological meaning for (or require the same psychological processes to be performed by) the persons being tested. For example, if our "barrel of units" was a pool of spelling words, we would have to establish that all words in the pool were equally difficult for all examinees and that the process each examinee used to spell each word was the same. Without establishing such facts about our pool of spelling words, we could not measure spelling ability in the same way that we measured height in Example 1.

Most general educational and psychological tests are analogous to the situations described by Example 2 in that the items are of unequal difficulty and require somewhat different psychological processes. That is, the units of measurement are unequal. Further, the way in which most tests are constructed makes them more like Example 2 in another way also. A meaningful zero score of "none of" the trait being measured is difficult (often impossible) to establish. If a person obtained a score of zero on a particular spelling test,

Table 5.1

SUMMARY OF THE MAJOR FEATURES OF THE
TWO HEIGHT-MEASURING PROCEDURES

Example number	Size of the units of measurement	Meaningful reference to zero	Meaning of equal scores	Meaning of equal differences
1	Equal units	Yes	Same meaning	Same meaning
2	Unequal units	No	Different meaning	Different meaning

does this mean that the person has "no spelling ability"? The raw score of zero here is ambiguous.

Another point to consider is this. In our examples we randomly selected units from the barrels to measure each person. When each person is measured by a different random sample of units and when the units are of unequal size (as in Example 2), then scores cannot be precisely compared from person to person. We saw that in this situation persons with equal height *scores* could in fact be of different actual heights. Further, even when the difference between one pair of scores was *numerically* the same as the difference between another pair of scores, such differences did not necessarily have the same meaning.

The analogy to educational tests is this. Suppose we give a different sample of test items—or a different test published by a different company—to each person. If the test items are of different difficulties and test somewhat different psychological processes (and for tests of different publishers this is bound to be true, even when test blueprints are similar), then the meaningfulness of person-to-person comparisons of scores is lost. Two people receiving the same score on different tests are not necessarily of equal ability. For this reason, when the purpose of educational and psychological measurement is to compare one individual with another, we take pains to administer the same test items to all persons.*

These illustrations can be helpful to us not only in thinking about the weaknesses in the measurements obtained from different tests, but also in recognizing the value of these less-than-perfect measurements.

It would probably be agreed that if the table-and-pieces method for measuring height as it appears in Example 2 were the only procedure available, it would yield more useful information than mere verbal descriptions such as

---

* We might note that even when the same items are administered to each person, differences in difficulty and in psychological processing will still not make differences between scores comparable in a precise way. You might think about this in relation to Examples 1 and 2.

"quite tall," "of average height," and "very short." The procedure in Example 2 could be improved if, instead of randomly selecting the pieces, the same pieces were used for each person and if they were stacked in the same order for each person. Measurements obtained in this latter way, despite their limitations, should at least be quite useful in describing the relative heights of the persons. In a similar manner, educational and psychological tests, despite limitations in the type of measurement they produce, can nevertheless be very useful in approximately describing the various mental qualities with which they are concerned. The informed educator, recognizing that test scores do not represent a perfect type of measurement, will not be tempted to give such scores an unwarranted exact meaning but at the same time will use these less-than-perfect measures to serve the essential purposes for which they are important and appropriate.

Measurement Procedures:
Criterion-Referenced Scores

Raw scores obtained by the simple counting-up processes are often hard to interpret. Some of the reasons for this have been discussed in the preceding section. To make an examinees' performance more interpretable for decision-making, this performance needs to be referenced to something outside of the test itself. The way this is done is through the development of a different type of score—a score that is *derived from* the raw score. These derived scores are developed so that they reflect the additional "outside" information in a more direct way than the raw score. If a derived score reflects the behavioral repertoire of an examinee, the kinds of things the examinee is able to do, this score is called a *criterion-referenced score*.[4] If a derived score reflects the examinee's location in a defined group of other examinees, then this score is called a *norm-referenced score*. In this section we will discuss criterion-referenced scores and in the next section we will discuss norm-referenced scores.

BACKGROUND OF CRITERION-REFERENCED TESTS
Although it may be true that criterion-referenced tests were used earlier, the term can probably be attributed to Robert Glaser. It was first mentioned in connection with proficiency measurement in military and industrial training[5] and later was applied to the measurement of educational achievement.[6] The

---

[4] Robert Glaser, "Instructional Technology and the Measurement of Learning Outcomes," *American Psychologist 18* (1963), pp. 519–21.

[5] Robert Glaser and David J. Klaus, "Proficiency Measurement: Assessing Human Performance," in R. Gagne, ed., *Psychological Principles in Systems Development*. (New York: Holt, Rinehart, and Winston, 1962), pp. 419–74.

[6] Robert Glaser, "Instructional Technology and the Measurement of Learning Outcomes," *American Psychologist 18* (1963), pp. 519–21.

motivation for this application to educational achievement measurement stemmed from a concern about the kind of achievement information required to make instructional decisions. Some instructional decisions concern individuals, for example, what competence an individual needs in order to be successful in the next course in a sequence. Other decisions center around the adequacy of the instructional procedure itself. Tests that provide achievement information about an individual only in terms of how the individual compares with other members of the group, or that provide only sketchy information about the degree of competence the person possesses with respect to some desired educational outcome, are not sufficient to make the kinds of decisions necessary for effective instructional design and guidance.

CRITERION-REFERENCED SCORES

Glaser called for the specification of the type of behavior the individual is required to demonstrate with respect to the content the test is designed to sample. "The standard [or criterion] against which a student's performance is compared . . . is the behavior which defines each point along the achievement continuum" (p. 519). A criterion-referenced test, then, is one that is deliberately constructed to give scores that tell what kinds of behavior individuals with those scores can demonstrate.[7]

As an illustration, consider the problem of assessing the competency of a student in elementary school geometry. Competence in elementary geometry can be analyzed into a number of behavior classes. A test can be constructed to measure these behaviors and to give scores that can be interpreted in terms of them. On such a test, a score of 30 might mean* that the student has demonstrated, along with a number of lower-level behaviors, the ability to

1. identify pictures of open continuous curves, lines, line segments, and rays.
2. state how these are related to each other; write symbolic names for specific illustrations of them.
3. identify pictures of intersecting and non-intersecting lines and name the point of intersection.

This score would also mean that the student could *not* demonstrate higher-level behaviors such as

1. identifying pictures that show angles.
2. naming angles with three points.

---

[7] Robert Glaser and Anthony J. Nitko, "Measurement in Learning and Instruction." In R. L. Thorndike, ed., *Educational Measurement* (Washington, D.C.: American Council on Education, 1971), pp. 625–70.

* The reader should keep in mind our previous comments that test scores should not be given an unwarranted importance as exact evaluations.

3. identifying the vertex of a triangle and an angle.
4. identifying perpendicular lines.
5. using a compass for bisection or drawing perpendiculars.

In like manner, a score of 20 might mean that the student could not demonstrate the more complex behaviors implied by the higher scores, but could demonstrate all lower-level behaviors up to and including behaviors such as:

1. naming the plane figures that comprise the faces of cubes, cones, pyramids, cylinders, and prisms.
2. naming these solids.
3. identifying pictures of these solids.

It is apparent, then, that there are four characteristics inherent in criterion-referenced tests:*

1. The classes of behaviors that define different achievement levels are specified as clearly as possible before the test is constructed.
2. Each behavior class is defined by a set of test situations (that is, test items or test tasks) in which the behaviors and all their important nuances can be displayed.
3. Given that the classes of behavior have been specified and that the test situations have been defined, a representative sampling plan is designed and used to select the test tasks that will appear on any form of the test.
4. The obtained score must be capable of being referenced objectively and meaningfully to the individual's performance characteristics in these classes of behavior.

EXAMPLE OF AN APPLICATION
OF CRITERION-REFERENCED TESTING

One practical example of the application of criterion-referenced testing to an instructional program is found in the testing program used with the mathematics curriculum of Individually Prescribed Instruction (IPI) that is described in Chapter 9 (pp. 193–201). IPI mathematics is a procedure for individualizing arithmetic instruction in the elementary school and involves the specification of sequences of units and of objectives, the development of tests to measure pupil performance on each objective and each unit, and the use of procedures that permit each pupil to start at an appropriate point in the curriculum and to proceed at his or her own individual pace. You should read

---

* It should be noted that many commercially available tests that claim to be "criterion-referenced" do not in fact possess these characteristics. Caution should be exercised when using such tests to make the criterion-referenced interpretations suggested in this chapter.

pages 193 through 201 before continuing with the paragraphs below if you are not already familiar with the IPI approach.

Some idea of how criterion-referenced tests may be employed in individualized instruction can be obtained by examining the procedure used in IPI for starting each student at an appropriate point in the curriculum. The way in which the IPI math curriculum is structured may be seen by examining Figure 9.1 (p. 197). It will be noted that curriculum is organized in terms of topics (Numeration/Place Value, etc.) and levels (Level A, Level B, etc.). A given topic at a given level, such as Level B Addition, constitutes a unit, and each unit involves a certain number of specific objectives. To get individual students started at the proper point in the math curriculum, one must determine the unit in which they should start and the objectives in that unit with which they should begin studying. The IPI testing program has been developed to accomplish this.

The first task of placement testing, then, is to determine to what level a student has progressed in each topic. Each topic has been developed in such a way as to constitute a hierarchy of prerequisites in which the abilities learned at each level build on those acquired at the preceding level and are prerequisite for those to be learned at the next level. In this sense, the sequence of levels within each topic (for example, A Numeration/Place Value, B Numeration/Place Value, C Numeration/Place Value, D Numeration/ Place Value, etc.) constitutes a hierarchy. Placement testing first involves finding where students' capabilities place them along this hierarchy. For example, placement testing within the Numeration/Place Value topic might indicate that a student has learned Levels A, B, C, and D but has not learned any levels above this (see Figure 9.2, p. 196). In essence, the report is that the student has a "score" of Level D in Numeration/Place Value. This is a criterion-referenced score. (It should be noted that the score need not be a letter.)

Because of the relatively gross nature of the information provided by these placement test scores, further criterion-referenced testing must be employed before a student actually starts instruction in any topic. The score of Level D in Numeration/Place Value obtained by the hypothetical student described above tells us that this student is ready to start work in Level E in the Numeration/Place Value continuum. However, it is also important to determine whether or not the student has mastered any of the specific behaviors identified by the six objectives in Level E. That is, the placement test score tells us that the student has not learned all of the Level E, but this does not preclude the possibility that he or she has learned some of the individual objectives in that unit. To determine whether or not this is the case, we need additional criterion-referenced information.

If the objectives in Level E Numeration/Place Value could be sequenced in order of prerequisites, it should be possible to develop a scaled test yielding a criterion-referenced score for that level. IPI unit tests are still only rough approximations of this ideal and do not themselves yield such precisely scaled scores. However, the IPI program does employ criterion-referenced tests known as unit pretests that help to provide criterion-referenced information at this point. These tests are structured so as to provide a sub-score for each objective within the unit and are scored so as to indicate whether or not the student has mastered each objective. This criterion-referenced information tells the teacher what the pupil can and cannot do with respect to the skills covered in a unit and enables the teacher to make instructional decisions about what the pupil should study. Thus, a combination of criterion-referenced scores from the *placement tests* and criterion-referenced information from the *unit pretest* serves to provide rather exact information concerning the specific competencies that the pupil does and does not possess.

While this example illustrates the use of criterion-referenced scores in a particular instructional context, the use of such scores need not be limited to this context. Criterion-referenced tests are not yet readily available for all applications. The emphasis on criterion-referenced testing is a relatively recent one and has not been fully accepted by all measurement specialists. It would appear, however, that there will be an increasing demand for and use of tests yielding criterion-referenced scores. A general review of criterion-referenced testing is provided by Klein and Kosecoff.[8]

Measurement Procedures: Norm-Referenced Scores

The need for norm-referenced information as well as criterion-referenced information should be apparent. It is useful under certain circumstances to know not only what level of competence an individual or group has attained, but also how that competence is related to other individuals or groups that are similar in composition, have similar educational experiences, or have similar aspirations. It is also important at times to know relative standing in groups that are basically different.

Pupils often seek answers to such questions as: "Where do I rank among all members of the class?" and "Where does my score stand with respect to the average of the class?" In much the same way, teachers and school administrators are frequently concerned with such questions as: "How do my pupils compare with pupils in other classes?" and "How does our school rank in comparison with other schools?" For the answer to these types of questions a raw score can take on additional meaning when it is compared

---

[8] S. P. Klein and J. Kosecoff, "Issues and Procedures in the Development of Criterion-Referenced Tests," ERIC/TM Report 26 (Princeton, N.J.: ERIC Clearinghouse on Tests, Measurement, and Evaluation, 1973).

with the scores of other persons or other groups who have taken the same test. For this reason a variety of procedures have been developed for transforming raw scores into types of scores that tell something about the relative meaning of a given performance.

Before we begin our discussion of these types of norm-referenced scores, it should be pointed out that the usefulness of either criterion-referenced scores or norm-referenced scores can only be interpreted in terms of purpose. In order to determine which kind of information to collect or emphasize, one must know what kinds of decisions need to be made. In some decision contexts norm-referenced information is inescapable. It has been pointed out, for example, that in some parts of the world it may be that it is financially impossible to offer advanced education to all individuals. Here relative competence, or relative standing, with respect to all such applicants for education becomes one of the most important types of information that is needed for decision-making. At the local classroom or school level, often parents want to have both criterion-referenced and norm-referenced information. They seek to evaluate the educational progress of their children both in terms of the competence the children have acquired and in terms of the relative standing of the children's competence in comparison to other children with whom they have been studying. The answer to the question of which type of score to obtain will be determined to a large extent by the type of information the decision-maker—pupil, parent, teacher, or administrator—will need.

THE PERCENTILE RANK

A rather obvious and direct way of interpreting a raw score so that it tells something about an individual's performance in comparison with other persons in a given group is to report on his or her relative rank within the group. This would mean saying such things as "This is the highest score in the class," "This score ranked third from the top," or "This score ranked twenty-seventh from the top." The only difficulty with this procedure is that it does not take into account the size of the group. To overcome this difficulty the *percentile rank* (also called the "centile rank") is used. The percentile rank is a number that tells what percentage of individuals within the specified norm group scored lower than the raw score in question. That is, if the percentile rank corresponding to a raw score of 37 is 68, 68 percent of the individuals in the norm group had raw scores lower than 37.

A simple procedure for computing percentile ranks will illustrate their meaning and can also be used for the transformation of raw scores to percentile ranks. The following formula (where N is the total number of pupils) is applied:

percentile rank = [Eq. 1]

$$\frac{\text{number of persons below score} + \frac{1}{2} \text{ of persons at score}}{N} \times 100$$

Assume that the numbers shown below represent scores on a certain test for 30 pupils in a given class.

71	65	61	60	57	52
69	64	61	60	57	50
67	63	61	59	56	47
66	63	60	59	55	46
65	62	60	58	54	43

To determine the percentile rank of a score of 57, we would note that eight pupils have scores lower than this and that two pupils have scores at 57. Substituting 30 for N in Equation 1, we would have

$$\text{percentile rank} = \frac{8 + 1}{30} \times 100 = 30$$

That is, 30 is the percentile rank of a raw score of 57.

To determine the percentile of a raw score of 62, we note that 20 pupils have scores lower than 62 and that only one pupil has a score at 62. The percentile rank of 62 would then be

$$\text{percentile rank} = \frac{20 + 0.5}{30} \times 100 = 68.3$$

Note that when only one person has received the raw score for which the percentile rank is being determined, we add one-half of one, or 0.5, to the number of persons below the score. This procedure emphasizes the fact that we are determining the percentile rank of a *point* on the score scale. Under the usual assumption concerning the value of a raw score on a test, the raw score of 62 occupies the interval of 61.5 to 62.5. The exact point 62 is then at the mid-point of this interval, and it is logical to assume that of all persons scoring 62 (that is, from 61.5 to 62.5), half score above and half score below the exact point of 62.

A further study of statistical methods will reveal a variety of formulas and procedures for determining percentile ranks, including graphic methods and methods for use with *grouped frequency distributions.** However, all these procedures are either equivalent to or approximations of the procedure presented here. Some of them may be simpler to use under certain circumstances, but the present method is always usable when raw scores are available.

In many circumstances, particularly in the use of standardized tests, the term *percentile* (or centile) is used in conjunction with tables of percentile ranks. It is important to grasp the distinction between these two terms. If the raw score of 57 has a percentile rank of 30, then the 30th percentile in this distribution is 57. That is, the *percentile rank* is a number that tells the *per-*

---

* Grouped frequency distributions are based on a coarser grouping of scores than one score unit. For example, instead of the interval 61.5 to 62.5, we might have an interval that is three units wide, say, 60.5 to 63.5. This procedure facilitates the handling of large amounts of data.

cent of persons scoring below a particular point on the score scale. On the other hand, the *percentile* is a *point on the score scale* such that an indicated percent of persons falls below it.

Sometimes the beginning student is confused by the terms percentile rank, percentile, and *percentage score*. A percentage score is used quite frequently in classroom testing and refers to the percent of items on the total test that a given individual has answered correctly. For example, if there were 80 items on a test and a pupil received a raw score of 57, then the percentage score would be $100 \times (57 \div 80) = 71.25$. In our example of the test scores of a given class of pupils, the percentile rank, percentile, and percentage score for the raw score of 57 on an 80-item test would be:

percentage score $= 71.25$
percentile rank $= 30$
thirtieth percentile $= 57$

Since this terminology tends to be confusing, the student should practice discriminating among these three terms.

STANDARD SCORES

Another way of giving relative meaning to a raw score is to speak of it in terms of whether it is above or below "average" and how far above or below it is. A fairly refined procedure for doing this is represented by the *standard score*. A standard score tells us how far any given performance is above or below the arithmetic *mean* in terms of the relative variability of the distribution (or collection of scores) as measured by the *standard deviation*. Understanding the standard score, then, requires some comprehension of the two statistics upon which it is based, the *mean* and the *standard deviation*.

THE ARITHMETIC MEAN

Most persons are well acquainted with the arithmetic mean, or "mean." It is what is commonly implied when we speak of the "average" of a set of numbers or measures.* It is determined by dividing the sum of all the measures by the number of measures involved. This method is commonly represented by the formula

$$M = \frac{\Sigma X}{N} \qquad \text{[Eq. 2]}$$

where M represents the mean, N represents the total number of scores involved, and Σ (Greek capital sigma) represents "sum of" or "summation of,"

---

* Another kind of "average" is the *median*. The median is the 50th percentile of a set of scores. One-half of the scores will be higher than the median and one-half will be lower. This is not necessarily a characteristic of the arithmetic mean.

signifying that whatever separate values are symbolized by what follows it are to be added to each other—in this case the various values of X, or in other words, all the particular measures involved.

To illustrate the application of this formula let us determine the mean of the following scores.

23	13	22	16
18	24	21	9
16	18	14	10
21	17	19	8
14	15	17	19

The sum of all 20 scores is 334. Applying the formula gives

$$M = \frac{334}{20} = 16.7$$

When a teacher is computing a mean for a small number of pupils, it is simplest to use the definition formula given above. Where greater numbers of students are involved, the increasing availability of pocket and desk-type calculators, digital computers, and test scoring and analyzing services makes it unlikely that paper-and-pencil procedures will need to be used. For these reasons, procedures for working with grouped frequency distributions are not presented in this text; they may be found in many conventional testing and statistics texts.

THE STANDARD DEVIATION

As mentioned above, the standard score describes an individual's distance from the mean in terms of the relative variability of the distribution involved. The measure of variability used for this purpose, as well as for a variety of other purposes, is the *standard deviation,* typically symbolized by *SD, s,* or σ (lower-case Greek sigma). First we will present the formula for determining a *SD*, and then we will comment on its meaning.

The basic formula that serves to define the standard deviation is

$$SD = \sqrt{\frac{\Sigma(X - M)^2}{N}} \qquad \textbf{[Eq. 3]}$$

The sum to be placed in the numerator is obtained by first subtracting the mean from each score (that is, finding $X - M$ for each score), squaring each $(X - M)$ value, and then obtaining the sum of all such squared values. This sum is divided by N, and the square root of this value is the standard deviation.

For example, let us assume that a small class of 6 students made the following scores on a quiz:

18, 15, 14, 20, 18, 11

To simplify our calculations we can arrange these scores in order of magnitude and then carry out the necessary steps for calculating the standard deviation:

X	X − M	(X − M)²
20	4	16
18	2	4
18	2	4
15	−1	1
14	−2	4
11	−5	25

$$\Sigma X = 96 \qquad \Sigma(X - M)^2 = 54$$

$$\frac{\Sigma X}{N} = M = 16$$

$$SD = \sqrt{\frac{\Sigma(X - M)^2}{N}}$$

$$SD = \sqrt{\frac{54}{6}} = \sqrt{9}$$

$$SD = 3$$

The X column shows the 6 raw scores arranged in descending numerical order, together with the sum and the mean (M). The second column shows the deviation of each score from the mean (X − M), and the third column contains the square of each such deviation. As the definition formula (Equation 3) indicates, the standard deviation is calculated by dividing the sum of the squared deviations from the mean, $\Sigma(X - M)^2$, by the number of scores, N, and then finding the square root of this result. In our example the sum of the squared deviations from the mean is 54, and when this is divided by N (here, 6), the quotient obtained is 9. The square root of 9 is 3, and thus 3 is our standard deviation for this set of 6 scores.

The standard deviation is the most generally used measure of variability, and the test user will encounter it several times in most test manuals. Our example shows that the SD measures how much the scores in a distribution "spread out," in that the basic measure is the distance of each score from the mean. Beyond this, the reader should not expect to be able to interpret the SD in any simple, absolute manner. A common error of beginning students in statistics is to try to give the SD more meaning than it actually has. When it is used to express the variability of a distribution, it can be meaningful to the extent that we can compare the SD of one distribution with that of another distribution when both groups have taken the same test. In this way we can compare the variability of the two distributions by using numerical indices. For example, if the SD of one group of scores is large relative to another group, it is more heterogeneous in the characteristic being measured by the test. This implies that the teacher's instruction will have to accommodate more individual differences in the group with the larger *SD*.

The following three points summarize what is important to remember about the standard deviation.

1. It is a measure of variability dependent on the deviation of each score from the mean.
2. It is useful as an index number for comparing the variability of two or more distributions, when the same test has been administered.
3. It serves as the basic unit of measure in standard scores.

As is true with the mean and with most other statistical measures, there are a variety of essentially equivalent formulas for computing the standard deviation. Since our goal in this presentation is some understanding of the meaning of this statistic, rather than skill in computation, only Equation 3 will be presented. Persons interested in a more complete presentation of this and other measures of variability should consult a statistics text.

THE STANDARD SCORE

The basic type of standard score is generally referred to as a "z-score" and is defined by the following formula:

$$z = \frac{X - M}{SD} \qquad \text{[Eq. 4]}$$

This formula tells us that the z-score corresponding to any given raw score is equal to the raw score's deviation from the mean divided by the standard deviation. Using the same distribution of scores with which we illustrated the computation of the standard deviation, we can determine the z-score corresponding to each raw score:

X	X − M	z-score
20	4	1.33
18	2	.67
18	2	.67
15	−1	− .33
14	−2	− .67
11	−5	−1.67

Note that raw scores below the mean have negative z-scores. What happens when we use z-scores can be illustrated by calculating such scores for another distribution of six test scores. In this case we have made each score three times the size of the scores in the preceding distribution. The mean and standard deviation are also three times those in the first distribution; that is, $M = 48$ and $SD = 9$.

X	X − M	z-score
60	12	1.33
54	6	.67
54	6	.67
45	− 3	− .33
42	− 6	− .67
33	−15	−1.67

The student can check the accuracy of these figures by calculating the mean and the standard deviation. It appears as if the new distribution has a much greater variability than the preceding one, as reflected both in the range between the low and high scores in each of the distributions and in the standard deviations. However, since the z-score represents the distance from the mean in terms of the relative variability of the distribution, the z-scores for the two distributions are equivalent. This is an illustration of how z-scores serve to make scores from the two distributions relatively equivalent even though the original distributions may differ greatly in their apparent variabilities.

The z-score is the basic type of standard score in that it tells how far a given raw score is above or below the mean in terms of standard deviation units. However, the fact that z-scores involve negative numbers as well as fractions or decimals makes them somewhat confusing. As a result, most published tests use a standard, minor modification of the z-score which we will call the "SS-score." The goal in this modification is to eliminate both negative and fractional scores. The SS-score is defined by the following formula:

$$SS = 10z + 50 \qquad \text{[Eq. 5]}$$

First the z-scores are calculated, and then each z is multiplied by 10 and the result (usually rounded to the nearest whole number) is added to 50 to obtain the SS-score. Multiplying by 10 and rounding off eliminates the fractional digits, while adding 50 serves to make all scores positive in value.

To understand the use of SS-scores, the reader can return to our preceding distributions and note that for a z-score of 1.33, SS would be obtained thus: $10 \times 1.33 = 13.3$, and $13.3 + 50 = 63.3$. This reported SS-score would then be 63. For a negative z-score such as −1.67, the corresponding SS would be determined in the same way: $10 \times (-1.67) = -16.7$, and $-16.7 + 50 = 33.3$, or 33.

Some test publishers employ the SS-score as a standard score. Others use some other modification of the z-score. Some multiply each z by 20 and then add 100, while others use still different constants. The test user should consult the test manual in each case to determine the constants used in calculating standard scores. One result of all such conversions is that the multiplier becomes the standard deviation of the *SS*-scores, while the constant added becomes the mean.

INTRODUCTION TO NORMAL DISTRIBUTIONS

When one administers a standardized achievement or psychological test to a large number of people and then tallies up the proportion of persons at each score point, one often finds that larger proportions of persons have scores near the middle of the score range and that there is a gradual reduction or "tailing-off" of scores toward the low end and high end of the score range. Often, too, these distributions are not perfectly symmetrical. Since different tests may yield differently shaped score distributions, test developers have found that it is sometimes convenient to transform the scores so that the distributions have a common form. The common distributional form toward which many test score distributions have been transformed is known as a *normal distribution.*

A normal distribution (or *normal curve,* as it is sometimes called) is really a mathematical model. It is defined by a particular equation that depends on the numerical value of the mean and the standard deviation. In other words, there are many normal distributions, each one having a different mean and/or standard deviation. Several normal distributions are illustrated in Figure 5.3. The normal curves shown in Figure 5.3 were obtained with the mathematical equation, which gave points to be plotted on a graph. In Figure 5.3(a) the mean is the same for all of the curves, but the standard deviation is different for each one. Notice that they are all centered at the same point on the *X*-axis but that the larger the standard deviation, the flatter and more spread out the curve looks to the eye.

Figure 5.3(b) shows normal distributions that have different means but the same value for the standard deviation. Thus, these distributions have the same degree of spread, though each of them is centered at a different point on the *X*-axis.

Notice that all of the curves are smooth and continuous. They are all symmetrical and can be described as bell-shaped in form.

The histogram in Figure 5.4 shows the actual distribution of the raw scores of 505 twelfth-grade students who took the creativity test of the Project TALENT test battery in 1960.[9] The solid continuous curve superimposed on this histogram is the normal curve that has the same mean and standard deviation as the distribution of raw scores of these twelfth-graders. You can see that the normal curve model approximates the actual distribution of creativity test scores but does not match it exactly.

---

[9] This data was obtained from P. R. Lohnes and W. W. Cooley, *Introduction to Statistical Procedures: With Computer Exercises* (New York: John Wiley and Sons, 1968), pp. 248–52.

Figure 5.3

ILLUSTRATIONS OF DIFFERENT
NORMAL DISTRIBUTIONS

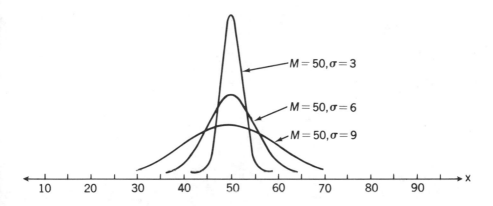

a. Normal distributions having the same mean but different standard deviations.

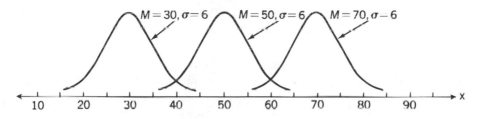

b. Normal distributions having different means but the same standard deviation.

Test publishers sometimes make the distribution of test scores approximate a normal distribution more closely by transforming the raw scores into *normalized standard scores*. Just how they do this is beyond the scope of this book.* The effect of the transformation is to squeeze and stretch the score scale so that the distribution of scores more nearly matches a normal distribution. In this way the mathematical theory of the normal curve model can be used more easily by test publishers.

Sometimes students believe that because test scores (raw scores or transformed scores) tend to be distributed like a normal distribution, then

---

* If you would like to know how to make this transformation you might check Howard C. Lyman, *Test Scores and What They Mean* (Englewood Cliffs, N.J.: Prentice-Hall, 1963), pp. 114–15.

Figure 5.4

ILLUSTRATION OF THE ACTUAL DISTRIBUTION (HISTOGRAM)
OF CREATIVITY TEST RAW SCORES FOR 505 TWELFTH-GRADE
STUDENTS AND A NORMAL CURVE (SMOOTH CURVE) THAT
HAS THE SAME MEAN AND STANDARD DEVIATION

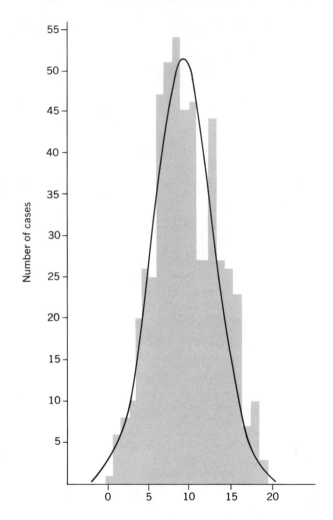

the actual ability underlying the scores must be normally distributed. At one time it was believed that many human characteristics and abilities followed a normal distribution. This is now known to be untrue. The distribution of scores depends on the particular population of people who are tested and on the properties of the particular test being administered. The developer of a test can put items in a test that will make the resulting distribution of scores take on almost any shape the developer wants the distribution to have. For example, if a test is composed mostly of items that are easy for a group of persons to answer correctly, then many people will have high scores. The distribution of test scores will be skewed negatively—that is, there will be a pile-up of high scores with fewer scores in the middle and low range.

By using a normal distribution as a model and referring to special statistical tables that mathematicians have developed for the normal distribution, one can determine the probability that certain scores will occur when a random sample of scores is drawn from the entire distribution. One can also find the percentile rank of any score in a normal distribution (without having to compute it by the procedure shown in Equation 1) by using these tables. Note, however, that the distribution of actual scores must approximate the normal curve model before the probabilities and percentile ranks taken from the special tables of the normal curve can be considered accurate.

For example, consider the various kinds of information in Table 5.2. As can be seen, the values of the percentile ranks and probabilities obtained for these raw scores from the normal curve model approximate the actual values obtained with the distribution data.

Table 5.2

DATA BASED ON THE DISTRIBUTION OF CREATIVITY
TEST SCORES IN FIGURE 5.4

Raw score*	Actual percentile rank	Actual probability of drawing this score	Percentile rank of this score in a normal distribution	Normal curve probability of drawing this score
2	1.8	.016	2.3	.012
5	11.5	.051	10.8	.048
10	53.5	.087	51.8	.102
15	88.9	.051	90.7	.043
18	98.4	.020	98.2	.102

* As on page 80, a score is assumed to occupy an interval.

If a normal distribution is cut up into sections so that each section is one standard deviation in width, then, regardless of which normal distribution we are referring to, each section will have a fixed percentage of cases. This is shown in Figure 5.5. The section from the mean to one standard deviation above the mean contains about 34% of the cases. The same is true of the section from the mean to one standard deviation below the mean. Thus, about 68% (34 + 34) of the cases fall between the score points located one standard deviation below the mean and one standard deviation above the mean.

Figure 5.5

ILLUSTRATION OF THE CORRESPONDENCE BETWEEN
PERCENTILE RANKS AND Z-SCORES FOR A NORMAL CURVE

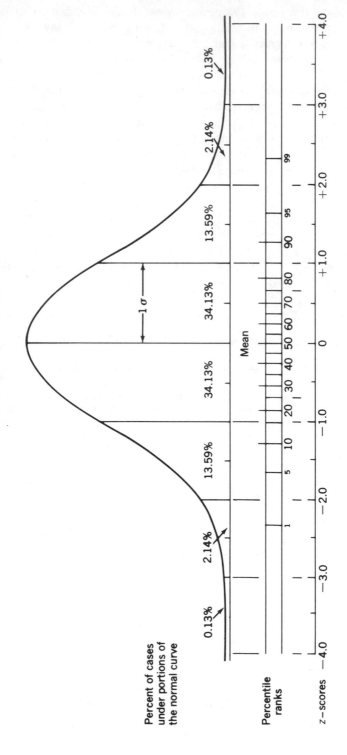

Modified from *Methods of Expressing Test Scores*, Test Service Bulletin No. 48 of the Psychological Corporation, 1955.

Figure 5.5 also shows the percentile ranks of various points on the score-scale and the z-scores for these points. You can see that the range of scores for the top 10 percent of the distribution is much greater than the range of scores for the middle 10 percent. That is, to include 10 percent of the cases (or area under the curve) near the center of the distribution we would need a shorter range along the score scale than we would if we wished to include 10 percent near one of the extremes of the distribution. (Compare, for example, the distance between the 50th and 60th percentiles and between the 90th and 99th percentiles.) As a result, differences between percentile ranks near the center of the distribution have a different meaning in terms of raw score differences than do equal distances between percentile ranks near the extremes of the distribution. Studying the table of percentile ranks on almost any standardized test will verify this. Such a study will reveal that the difference in raw score units between the 50th and 55th percentiles will be much smaller than the difference between the 90th and 95th percentiles. That differences between percentiles have varying meanings at different points along the score scale is often cited as a weakness of the percentile rank. It might better be considered an obvious quality of such scores and one that prevents the informed test user who is aware of it from drawing unwarranted conclusions concerning the meaning of score differences.

STANINE SCORES

The *stanine score,* another widely used derived score, is based on the assumption that educational achievement is normally distributed. The meaning of these scores can be understood through reference to Figure 5.6. In the original development of the stanine score, the distance from a z-score of −2.75 to a z-score of +2.75 was divided into 11 equal intervals, each of which was 0.5 of a standard deviation in width, as shown in Figure 5.6, where the limits of the intervals are represented by such z-scores as −2.75, −2.25,
1.75, etc. The limits of the total distribution are set at −2.75 and 2.75, since essentially all (actually 99.4 percent) of the area under a normal curve lies between these two points. When a normal distribution is partitioned in this way, the percentages of cases found in each interval are those shown in the first row of Figure 5.6. The scores falling into any given interval could then be given the number between 0 and 10 assigned to that interval, as shown in the middle row below the figure. Actually, since the percentage of cases having a score of 0 or a score of 10 on this scale is so small, and since there is some advantage (particularly for entering data on punch cards) in having only single-digit numbers as scores, the developers of the stanine scale elected to combine scores in the 0 and 1 intervals, assigning them all a stanine of 1, and to combine scores in the 9 and 10 intervals, giving them a stanine of 9. The result is that the actual scale of stanine scores and the percentage of cases included in each stanine are as shown in the last two lines of Figure 5.6.

Figure 5.6

GRAPH OF NORMAL DISTRIBUTION
INDICATING THE RELATIONSHIP
OF STANINE TO Z-SCORE INTERVALS
AND PERCENTAGE OF CASES IN EACH STANINE

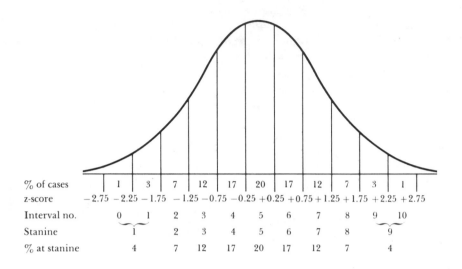

% of cases	1	3	7	12	17	20	17	12	7	3	1
z-score	−2.75	−2.25	−1.75	−1.25	−0.75	−0.25	+0.25	+0.75	+1.25	+1.75	+2.25	+2.75
Interval no.	0	1	2	3	4	5	6	7	8	9	10
Stanine	1		2	3	4	5	6	7	8	9	
% at stanine	4		7	12	17	20	17	12	7	4	

It can be seen then that the stanine score scale ranges from a low score of 1 to a high score of 9 and that the average score is 5. If further interpretation of a stanine score is necessary, use can be made of the percentage of cases at the given score and above or below it. For example, a stanine of 4 is a score slightly below the average: 17 percent of persons in the norm group make scores of this size; 23 percent make lower scores; and 60 percent make higher scores.

Since stanine scores are based on the division of the score scale into equal units (except in the cases of the first and ninth stanines), then for a distribution that is normal or assumed to be normal, equal differences between stanines represent equal differences on the raw score scale.

In the treatment of stanines up to this point, we have assumed a normal distribution of raw scores. What happens if a distribution is not normal? In practice, the computation of stanines is usually based on the percentage distribution of scores. That is, in the distribution being used as the reference group or norm group, the lowest 4 percent of the scores are given a stanine of 1, the next 7 percent a stanine of 2, the next 12 percent a stanine of 3, and so on. The result is that the transformation to stanines changes the distribution of measures so that it looks more like a normal distribution. The use of stanines, then, is based on the assumption that whatever the test is measuring actually is normally distributed and that the only reason the original raw scores are not normally distributed is that there are inadequacies in the score scale produced.

One caution should be voiced here in connection with the conversion of test scores to stanines via the percentile rank method described above. The test user should not assume that this conversion automatically results in a normal distribution of stanines. If the original distribution of test scores is not roughly bell-shaped but, rather, highly skewed, then it may be impossible to have stanine values of 9, 8, or 7 or stanine values of 1, 2, or 3. The former situation will arise when the test is very easy for most of the population of persons taking it; the latter, when the test is very hard for most persons. For example, some standardized tests are designed to be "diagnostic" and seek to identify only the poorest students in a given area of the curriculum. By design, these tests are not developed to identify the best students. It turns out that many students can obtain perfect or nearly perfect scores on some of these tests. Thus, there is a pile-up of high scores in the distribution with fewer scores in the lower parts of the score scale. While it is legitimate to build a test to identify the poorest students who may be in need of special instruction, converting the scores to stanines by the percentile method results in useless stanines for the better students. For example, a pupil could get a perfect score and receive a stanine of 5 or 6. Clearly, a perfect score cannot reasonably be interpreted as being "average" or "slightly above average." Yet, these kinds of mistakes are commonly made by persons who rely too heavily on superficial knowledge of the tests they are using. Again, this points up the relationship between tests and decision-making and the fact that a test score is only one piece of information that goes into the decision-making process.

GRADE-EQUIVALENT SCORES

Another type of norm-referenced score that is frequently used with achievement test batteries at the elementary school level is the grade-equivalent score. The grade-equivalent score is reported as a mixed decimal fraction, such as 3.1 or 4.3. The whole number part of this score refers to a grade level, for example, grade three or grade four. The fractional part of the score refers to a month of the school year within that grade level, for example, the first month (.1) or the third month (.3). The grade-equivalent score is designed to reference the raw score obtained on a test to a grade placement norm group. That is, a grade-equivalent is the grade placement for which the obtained raw score is the average. If a raw score of, say, 25 has a grade-equivalent score of 4.3, this is interpreted to mean that of all those pupils taking the test during the third month of fourth grade, their average test score was 25.

As we have noted, the months of a school year are assigned a decimal fraction. For convenience, the school year is usually considered to have nine months. The table below shows that September is assigned a decimal equivalent of .0, October .1, November .2, etc.

Month of school year	September	October	November	December	January	February	March	April	May	June
Decimal part of G.E.	.0	.1	.2	.3	.4	.5	.6	.7	.8	.9

Grade-equivalent scores are subject to much misinterpretation by teachers, administrators, and parents. To better understand this type of score, it would be useful to examine briefly how test publishers obtain these scores. (Teachers have no need to derive these scores themselves, since tests that employ grade-equivalents provide raw score to grade-equivalent conversion tables.) Most popular test batteries are designed to span several grade levels. A standardized achievement test battery usually contains several subtests, each testing a different subject area like vocabulary, reading, spelling, mathematics computation, and so on. To simplify the illustration we will limit the discussion to showing how grade-equivalent scores might be obtained for one such area, say, reading. Now, suppose we are interested in developing a reading test useful for grades one through eight. Clearly, a single test would be inappropriate. It would have to contain too many items to span from first-grade to eighth-grade reading ability. Many items would be too difficult for first-graders and many items would be too easy for eighth-graders. To avoid this difficulty, many test developers construct a series of reading tests that may overlap. For example, one test for grades one and two, one test for grades two and three, one test for grades four and five, one test for grades five and six, and one test for grades seven and eight. Each test would be appropriate for the grade levels it spans. The appropriate tests are then administered to a large national sample of pupils in each of the grades one through eight (usually just one time during the year). Since at any point in time there are large individual differences in pupils, there will be a distribution of scores for each test. These are shown in Figure 5.7. Notice that the tests in this hypothetical example were administered during February at each grade level.

The mean* score for all those first-graders who took the test during February is 10. Thus, the grade-equivalent of a score of 10 is 1.5. Similarly, the mean score for all those third-graders who took the test during February is 18. Thus, the grade-equivalent of a score of 18 is 3.5. Since the tests were not administered during every month of the school year, *actual grade-equivalents* can only be obtained at those points in time when the tests *were*

---

* Often the median (50th percentile) is used instead of the mean.

Figure 5.7

EXAMPLE OF DATA THAT CAN BE USED
TO OBTAIN GRADE-EQUIVALENT SCORES

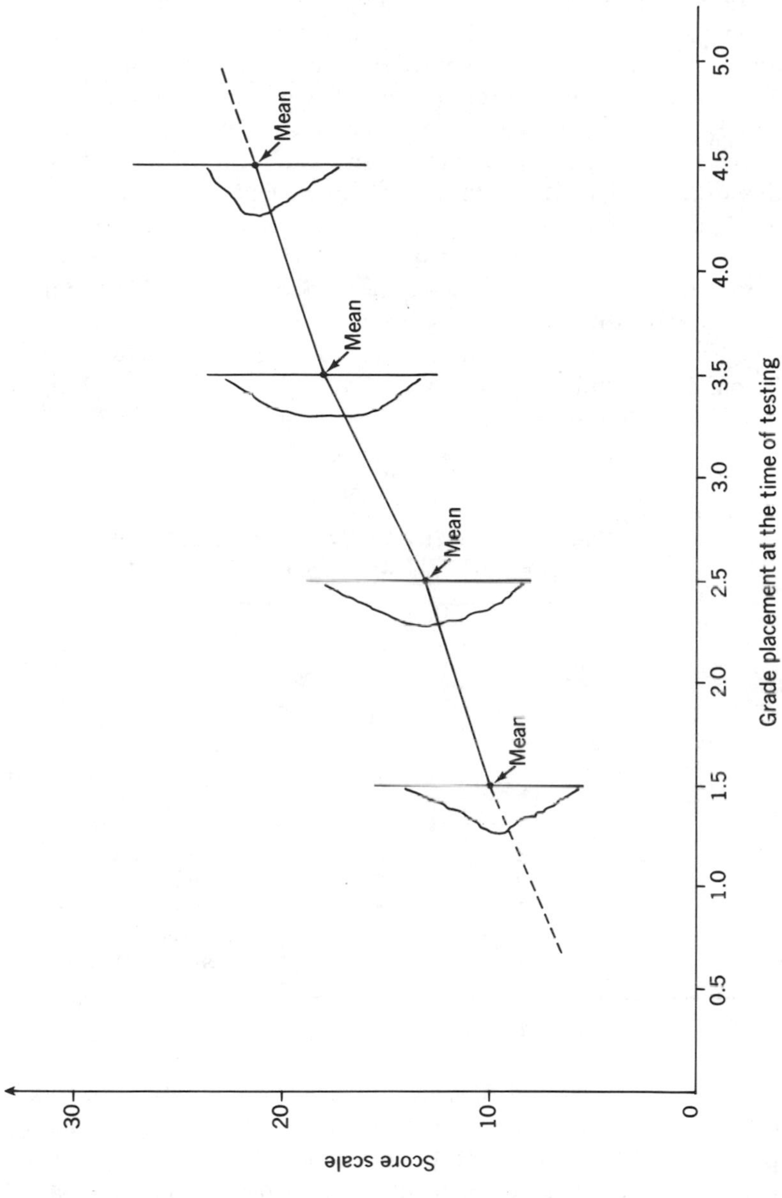

administered. But what about the other points on the grade-placement scale? Notice that a solid line connects the means of the actual distributions. This line can be used to interpolate and, thereby, estimate the in-between values. Thus, by interpolation, a score of 11 is assigned a grade-equivalent of 1.8, a score of 15 a grade equivalent of 3.9, and so on. Suppose a pupil obtained a score of 8 or a score of 22. In this example, no pupils were tested below a grade placement of 1.5 or above a grade placement of 4.5. However, grade-equivalent scores can be estimated for scores of 8 and 22 by extrapolation, that is, extending the line beyond the actual data according to our guess as to the trend of the distribution means. The dashed lines in Figure 5.8 show this extrapolation. Using these extrapolated parts of the line, a score of 8 would be assigned a grade-equivalent score of 1.0 and a score of 22 would be assigned a grade-equivalent of 4.8. Table 5.3 summarizes what we have said so far and is similar to a grade-equivalent conversion table one might find in a test publisher's manual. (The test publisher's table, however, will not indicate whether the grade-equivalent has been obtained from actual data, by interpolation, or by extrapolation.)

Table 5.3

GRADE-EQUIVALENT CONVERSION TABLE FOR THE
HYPOTHETICAL DATA IN FIGURE 5.7

Raw score	GE	How obtained
8	1.0	Extrapolation
9	1.3	Extrapolation
10	1.5	Actual Data
11	1.8	Interpolation
12	2.2	Interpolation
15	2.9	Interpolation
18	3.5	Actual Data
19	3.9	Interpolation
21	4.5	Actual Data
22	4.8	Extrapolation
23	5.1	Extrapolation

Extrapolation and interpolation are not the only problems with grade-equivalents. Other sources of misinterpretation contribute to the declining popularity of this type of score. One frequent misinterpretation is that of trying to compare the grade-equivalent scores on tests in different subject areas (*subtests*), for example, on a reading subtest and on a mathematics subtest. Grade-equivalents on two different subtests are not comparable, especially for high-scoring and low-scoring pupils. If a first-grade pupil had a reading grade-equivalent of 2.1 and a mathematics grade-equivalent of 1.9, the pupil may have in fact higher mathematics achievement than reading achievement. The pupil's percentile rank may be higher in mathematics than in reading. A second misinterpretation concerns the interpretation of growth at different parts of the grade-equivalent scale. A five-point difference on the raw score scale may mean a three-month difference at one part of the grade-equivalent scale but a one-year difference at another part of the scale. The grade-equivalent scale does not have equal units. (Recall the discussion of equal units on pages 68–74). A third misinterpretation is that a pupil ought to be in the same grade as his or her grade-equivalent score. For example, sometimes people will think a first-grader who receives a mathematics grade-equivalent of 3.0 ought to be placed in the third-grade arithmetic class the next year. What is closer to the truth is that the student has probably learned first-grade arithmetic very well; but promotion to third grade is not warranted by this score. A fourth misinterpretation of grade-equivalents is that grade-equivalent scores from similar tests developed by different publishers are comparable. You can see from Figure 5.7 and from our earlier discussion on pages 72 and 73 that the scores and grade-equivalents will depend on the types of test items each test contains and the particular group to which the tests were administered. Different test publishers will develop their grade-equivalents (and other types of norm-referenced scores) using different samples of pupils. This makes scores on different tests noncomparable.[10]

With all of these problems with grade-equivalents, the reader may wonder why they are used at all. Indeed, many testing experts feel that grade-equivalents should be abolished. The apparent simplicity of grade-equivalents has made them popular with school people, however, and they will probably continue to be used for some time. There is one advantage of the grade-equivalent score that often cannot be duplicated by the other types of norm-referenced scores we have discussed. This advantage centers around developing a measure of educational growth. A pupil who is learning well may be at the 75th percentile on the first-grade, the second-grade, and the third-grade tests. The fact that this percentile rank does not change (or changes very little) over time does not mean that the pupil has not learned over three years. Similarly, a person's location in a distribution of scores as reflected by a standard score may change very little over time.* Again, similar or identical standard scores would not indicate lack of educational growth. The grade-equivalent scores of such pupils will reflect this change, however. A student

---

[10] R. M. Jaeger, "The National Test-Equating Study in Reading: The Anchor Test Study," *NCME Measurement in Education 4* (1973).

* We are speaking here of standard scores that are computed separately for each grade level. This is not true when several grades are pooled and standard scores computed for this pooled group. See Chapter 7 for further information on this point.

who is at the 75th percentile each year from second through fourth grade would have a stanine score of 6 each year. Yet this student's grade-equivalent scores might be 3.4, 4.4, and 5.8, respectively.

To summarize some of the cautions we have given about grade-equivalent scores, we offer the following. Assume that we have administered a standardized achievement test battery to a third-grade class during May of the school year. Assume that the battery is determined to be valid and appropriate and that the test publishers' norms are useful. Then of all the statements below about students in that class, only the first is true—all the rest are false.

1. Pat's Reading Subtest grade-equivalent score is 3.8. This suggests that she is an average third-grade reader.
2. Ramon's Arithmetic Subtest grade-equivalent is 4.6. This means that he knows arithmetic as well as the typical fourth-grader who is at the end of the sixth month of school.
3. Melba's Arithmetic Subtest grade-equivalent is 6.7. This suggests that next year she ought to take arithmetic with the sixth-graders.
4. Debbie's Reading Subtest grade-equivalent is 2.3. This means she has mastered three-tenth's of the second-grade reading skills.
5. Sam's Arithmetic Subtest grade-equivalent is 4.2. This means that he has mastered two-tenth's of the fourth-grade arithmetic curriculum.
6. John's grade-equivalent profile is: Vocabulary = 6.2, Reading = 7.1, Language = 7.1, Work-Study Skills = 7.2, Arithmetic = 6.7. This means that his weak areas are vocabulary and arithmetic.
7. Two of Sally's grade-equivalents are: Language = 4.5 and Arithmetic = 4.5. Since her language and arithmetic grade-equivalents are the same, we conclude that her language and arithmetic ability are about equal.

COMPARISON OF VARIOUS NORM-REFERENCED TEST SCORES

It would be useful at this point to summarize and compare the various types of norm-referenced scores discussed above. This summary is shown in Table 5.4. It can be seen that each type of score provides a somewhat different kind of information about the location of a score in a distribution of scores. Perhaps the most useful score and the one easiest to explain to parents and pupils is the percentile rank. The z-score and the other standard scores become more useful if one understands the concept of the standard deviation and the ways in which these scores are developed using this concept. Most often, normalized standard scores and stanines are interpreted through the vehicle of percentile ranks. Since these normalized scores reflect the same percentage of cases from test to test, their meaning remains relatively stable

Table 5.4

COMPARISON OF VARIOUS NORM-REFERENCED SCORES

Type of score	Interpretation	Score	Examples of Interpretations
Percentile rank	Percentage of scores below this point in a given distribution	$PR = 60$	"60% of the pupils' raw scores are lower than this score."
Standard score (z-score)	Number of standard deviation units a score is above (or below) the mean of a given distribution	$z = +1.5$	"This raw score is located 1.5 standard deviations *above* the mean."
		$z = -1.2$	"This raw score is located 1.2 standard deviations *below* the mean."
Standard score (SS score or 50 ± 10 system)	Location of score in distribution that has a mean of 50 and a standard deviation of 10	$SS = 65$	"This raw score is located 1.5 standard deviations *above* the mean in a distribution whose mean is 50 and whose standard deviation is 10."
		$SS = 35$	"This raw score is located 1.5 standard deviations *below* the mean in a distribution whose mean is 50 and whose standard deviation is 10."
Stanine	Location of a score in a specific segment of a normal distribution of scores	Stanine $= 5$	"This raw score is located in the middle 20% of a normal distribution of scores."
		Stanine $= 9$	"This raw score is located in the highest 4% of a normal distribution of scores."
Grade-equivalent	The grade-placement at which the raw score is average	$GE = 4.5$	"This raw score is the obtained or estimated average for all those pupils whose grade placement is at the 5th month of the 4th grade."

in various situations in which the normal curve model is appropriate or can be assumed. Grade-equivalents provide some information that is not found in the other types of scores and can be used to obtain gross estimates of pupil growth from year to year. However, the grade-equivalent is easily subject to misinterpretation and, hence, should be used carefully and only when accompanied by percentile ranks.

If you are interested in pursuing the study of norm-referenced scores in greater detail, you should consult a very readable book by Howard B. Lyman titled *Test Scores and What They Mean.*[11]

Summary

Tests and certain other techniques enable the teacher to obtain measures of pupil achievement and other variables that are important in guiding instruction. Although the numerical results obtained in this way are only very rarely absolute or precise measures of the type obtained when a tape measure is used to determine length or distance, they do have certain qualities that make them very useful for describing student characteristics. Since a "raw score" obtained from a test has little meaning in and of itself, it needs to be referenced to something before it can be interpreted. Criterion-referenced tests yield scores that are referenced to the kinds of behaviors persons with a given raw score are likely to exhibit. The IPI placement testing procedure is one example of the use of criterion-referenced tests that yield scores that can be interpreted in terms of the kinds of curriculum behaviors a pupil is likely to be able to perform or not be able to perform. Norm-referenced tests yield scores that are referenced to other scores made by other persons taking the same test. A number of "derived scores" have been developed to provide this norm-referenced meaning. Examples of these types of scores include percentile ranks, standard scores, stanines, and grade-equivalent scores. Tests could yield both criterion-referenced and norm-referenced scores, but they are usually designed to provide scores for only one type of referencing system. The use of one or more of these scores in reporting and recording test results makes the results more meaningful and simplifies the process of comparing a student's performance on one test or occasion with his or her performance on another test or on another occasion.

SUGGESTIONS FOR CLASS DISCUSSION AND FURTHER INVESTIGATION

1. The distribution of test scores for a large number of students is often organized in the form of a simple frequency distribution as shown here:

---

[11] Howard B. Lyman, *Test Scores and What They Mean,* 2nd ed. (Englewood Cliffs, N.J.: Prentice-Hall, 1971).

Score	f	Percentile rank
40	4	
39	8	
38	11	
37	14	
36	6	
35	4	
34	2	4
33	0	2
32	1	1
	50	

The f (or frequency) column shows how many persons made each raw score. Determine the percentile rank of each raw score using the procedure described in this chapter. (Three have already been computed.) Note that the numerical differences between the percentile ranks for successive raw scores are not equal. Why is this so? What does it show about percentile ranks?

2. Compute the median (50th percentile) of the distribution of test scores shown above. Also compute the mean of this distribution. (Hint: to find the sum of the score, first multiply each raw score by the number of persons who obtained the scores, then add up these products.) Compare these two averages and interpret your findings.

3. Shown below are two hypothetical sets of test scores, A and B, each consisting of five scores. Compute the mean and standard deviation for each of the two sets. Then determine the z-score and SS-score corresponding to each score in each distribution.

A	B
9	28
7	24
6	22
5	20
3	16

In this case each original score in set B was obtained by doubling each score in set A and adding 10. Note how conversion to standard scores serves to eliminate the differences between the means and standard deviations in the two sets.

4. Explain the difference between "percentile rank," "percentile," and "percentage score." Use the collection of scores on page 80 to give several examples that illustrate the difference between these scores.

5. Discuss the advantages and disadvantages of criterion-referenced test scores and norm-referenced test scores in specific situations or for specific purposes. For example, which would be preferred by a teacher explaining test performance to a parent? Which would a school superintendent prefer when comparing the test performance of the several schools in the district?

6. Explain why each of the seven grade-equivalent statements on page 98 are true or false.

7. To test pupils' knowledge of single-digit addition facts, an elementary school teacher randomly selected ten different facts for each pupil and put them on a test. Thus each pupil had a different ten-item test. Discuss the advantages and disadvantages of doing this in terms of the height-measuring examples given on pages 68 through 74.

SUGGESTIONS FOR FURTHER READING

Rather detailed discussions of the meaning of measurement and of the problems involved in developing measuring devices in psychology and education can be found in E. F. Lindquist, ed., *Educational Measurement* (Washington, D.C.: American Council on Education, 1951) and in R. L. Thorndike, ed., *Educational Measurement,* 2nd ed. (Washington, D.C.: American Council on Education, 1971).

Descriptions of procedures to be used in determining the various statistical measures and scores discussed briefly in this chapter are found in a great number of available textbooks on statistics and measurement. The following represent a few of these: G. V. Glass and J. C. Stanley, *Statistical Methods in Education and Psychology* (Englewood Cliffs, N.J.: Prentice-Hall, 1970), chapters 1–6; G. H. Weinberg and J. A. Schumaker, *Statistics: An Intuitive Approach,* 2nd ed. (Belmont, Calif.: Brooks/Cole Publishing Co., 1969), chapters 1–8; H. B. Lyman, *Test Scores and What They Mean,* 2nd ed. (Englewood Cliffs, N.J.: Prentice-Hall, 1971).

Further readings on criterion-referenced testings include: W. J. Popham, ed., *Criterion-Referenced Measurement: An Introduction* (Englewood Cliffs, N.J.: Educational Technology Publications, 1971); R. Glaser and A. J. Nitko, "Measurement in Learning and Instruction," in R. L. Thorndike, ed., *Educational Measurement,* 2nd ed. (Washington, D.C.: American Council on Education, 1971) pp. 625–70; R. Glaser and R. C. Cox, "Criterion-Referenced Testing for the Measurement of Educational Outcomes," in R. Weisgerber, ed., *Instructional Process and Media Innovation* (Chicago: Rand McNally, 1968) pp. 545–50; S. P. Klein and J. Kosecoff, *Issues and Procedures in the Development of Criterion-Referenced Tests.* ERIC/TM Report 26, 1973 (Princeton, N.J.: ERIC Clearinghouse on Tests, Measurement, and Evaluation, 1973).

6

Technical Concepts
Used to Appraise a Test

The preceding chapter dealt with procedures used in summarizing and analyzing test scores in order to obtain information about students. The usefulness of test scores as information, however, depends on the quality of the test from which they are obtained. No matter how elegant or refined derived test scores may be, they must originate from tests of good quality, or they have little value. It is the purpose of this chapter to examine technical concepts and procedures that are used to judge the quality of tests. The teacher should note that the quality of a test is judged primarily in terms of the decisions that will be made on the basis of test results. In the last chapter we pointed out that the desirability of using criterion-referenced information, norm-referenced information, or both depended primarily on the type of decision being made. We stress the point again in this chapter, where we view the quality of the test as a whole. In general, the quality of a given test will be high for some purposes and low for others. The question "Is this a good test?" can be answered only after we have answered the question "Good for what?" Answers are of the form "This test is good for this purpose, but not good for that purpose."

The major sources of information that are generally available to teachers for use in judging the quality of a published test are (a) a copy of the test itself and (b) the test manual that accompanies the test. Test manuals, in addition to giving directions for the administration of a test, provide certain types of data that describe in a general way the final form of the test and its development. (More detailed information is often found in the test's technical reports, which will contain more complete statistical analyses of test results and more information on how the test was developed.) Although publishers of tests of good quality make some effort to interpret the data in the test manuals for the test user, it is ultimately the professional responsibility of the test user to make these interpretations and judgments for the particular situation in which the test results will be used. In the final analysis, the user is responsible for good or bad use of a test. Thus, professional teachers should have command of the technical concepts and procedures used to judge the quality of tests. They can apply them to tests they have developed themselves and will find it essential to use such concepts in evaluating published tests.

Another Statistic:
The Correlation Coefficient

In Chapter 5 we discussed two useful statistical indices: the mean and the standard deviation. In this section, we will introduce another statistical index, the *correlation coefficient*. This statistic is used a greal deal in test manuals —particularly with norm-referenced tests but sometimes with criterion-referenced tests as well. Test manuals often present a test's correlation coefficient as indicating certain aspects of its quality. Some understanding of this index and its characteristics are, therefore, prerequisites to the discussions later in this chapter that deal more directly with judging the quality of a test.

In the analysis of test results, a variety of questions can be answered on the basis of how one set of scores is *related to* another. How are pupils' scores on a scholastic aptitude test related to their later scores on an achievement test? Are the measures obtained from Form A of a given test closely related to the measures that would be obtained if Form B of the test were administered to the same students? The use of the correlation coefficient helps to answer such questions. Notice that we use the term *related to* in a particular way. We don't say "caused by" or in any other way imply causality. When we ask how closely one set of scores is "related to" another, we mean: "How well can we predict or estimate the scores on one test from knowledge of the scores on the other?" When the two sets of test scores are highly related, we can quite accurately predict one set of test scores on the basis of the other. When two sets of test scores are unrelated, we cannot do this.

To further refine this concept of relationship, let us consider something we have already discussed. In Chapter 5, we discussed the z-score:

$$z = \frac{X - M}{SD}$$

This score represents the number of standard deviation units a given raw score is above (or below) the mean. When we speak of a relationship between two sets of scores, we have two scores for each person. We consider a person's z-score on each test. For convenience, let's call one test X and another test Y. The question we are asking is: "How does a person's z-score on test X relate to the same person's z-score on test Y?"

The correlation coefficient gives us the answer to this question. Looking at the formula for it will help explain why. The symbol for the correlation coefficient is r_{XY} (or sometimes ρ_{XY}). The formula that defines it is

$$r_{XY} = \frac{\Sigma z_X z_Y}{N} \qquad \text{[Eq. 1]}$$

We obtain the sum that is placed in the numerator by first finding each person's z-score on test X (i.e., z_X) and on test Y (i.e., z_Y), multiplying, for each person, z_X by z_Y, and then obtaining the sum of all such z-score products. This sum is divided by N to give the value of the correlation coefficient. (N is the number of persons who have both X and Y scores.)

Although our objective in presenting Equation 1 is not to have you learn how to compute the correlation coefficient, it will help you understand this statistic if you see the application of the equation in a couple of examples. These examples are presented in Table 6.1.

Table 6.1

HYPOTHETICAL SCORES FOR 10 PUPILS
ON A VERBAL APTITUDE TEST, A READING TEST,
AND AN ARITHMETIC TEST

Pupil	Verbal Score (V)	Reading Score (R)	Arithmetic Score (A)	z-scores z_V	z-scores z_R	z-scores z_A	Product of z-scores $z_V \cdot z_R$	Product of z-scores $z_V \cdot z_A$
A	83	82	60	1.42	1.38	0.17	1.96	0.25
B	80	77	68	1.22	1.01	0.91	1.23	1.10
C	75	75	75	0.87	0.86	1.55	0.75	1.35
D	71	70	51	0.59	0.49	−0.65	0.29	−0.39
E	65	71	45	0.18	0.56	−1.20	0.10	−0.21
F	62	64	74	−0.03	0.04	1.45	−0.001	−0.04
G	56	58	60	−0.44	−0.40	0.17	0.18	−0.08
H	49	52	50	−0.93	−0.85	−0.74	0.78	0.69
I	45	45	56	−1.20	−1.37	−0.19	1.64	0.23
J	38	40	42	−1.69	−1.74	−1.47	2.93	2.48

$$\Sigma z_V z_R = 9.86 \qquad\qquad \Sigma z_V z_A = 5.38$$

$$r_{VR} = \frac{9.86}{10} = 0.986 \qquad\qquad r_{VA} = \frac{5.38}{10} = 0.538$$

This table shows the scores of ten pupils on each of three tests. The pupils have been arranged in descending order according to their verbal (V) aptitude scores. Looking first at the columns of test scores, we see that the V test scores and the reading (R) test scores order the pupils in about the same way. However, we do not see the same strong relationship between the V scores and the arithmetic (A) scores.

This is more apparent when we look at the columns of z-scores that correspond to the test scores. We can see that the correspondence between the verbal z-scores and the reading z-scores is quite close. This indicates a high relationship (or *correlation*) between verbal aptitude scores and reading scores. On the other hand, the correspondence between the verbal z-scores and the arithmetic z-scores is not very close. This indicates a somewhat lower correlation between verbal aptitude scores and arithmetic scores for this group of pupils.

For each pupil we computed the products of the z-scores for the verbal and the reading tests and for the verbal and the arithmetic tests. These values appear in the last two columns of Table 6.1. Then we added up the products in each column. The two sums are shown at the bottom of the table. When we divide each of the two sums by the number of pupils, we obtain the *correlation coefficients*. The correlation between verbal scores and reading scores is .986, while the correlation between verbal scores and arithmetic scores is .536. You can see that these numerical values for the correlations reflect the degree of relationship that you observed when you compared the scores in Table 6.1 visually. The value .986 indicates a high relationship, while the value .536 indicates a more moderate relationship.

The relationship between the *paired scores* developed from two sets of scores can also be seen if the data are presented in graphic form as in Figure 6.1. In these graphs verbal aptitude scores are measured along the horizontal axis, achievement scores along the vertical axis. The way in which entries are made is illustrated by the mark in Figure 6.1(a) made for Pupil A, whose verbal aptitude and reading scores were 83 and 82, respectively. This mark, in the extreme upper righthand corner of the graph, is located at the intersection of the dashed lines, one running vertically from the verbal aptitude score of 83, the other running horizontally from the reading score of 82. This intersection locates the point marking the paired scores for this student. The paired scores of all other pupils have been located in the same way.

The overall picture of the relationship in Figure 6.1(a) shows that the marks lie almost in a straight line running from the lower lefthand corner to the upper righthand corner of the graph. In contrast, the marks in Figure 6.1(b), although showing a general trend from lower left to upper right, do not come at all close to lying on one straight line. The tendency of such plotted points to lie in a straight line is a key to the concept of correlation. The closer the points come to lying in a straight line, the higher is the correlation between the two sets of measures being studied. The extent of this correlation is described by the numerical value of the correlation coefficient. A

Figure 6.1

SCATTERGRAM SHOWING THE RELATIONSHIP BETWEEN
(A) VERBAL APTITUDE AND READING SCORES AND
(B) VERBAL APTITUDE AND ARITHMETIC SCORES
FOR THE 10 PUPILS IN TABLE 6.1

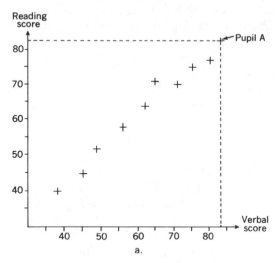

a.

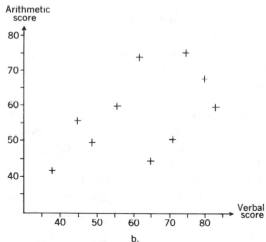

b.

perfect *positive* correlation, one in which the plotted points in a graph would all fall exactly on a straight line extending upward from left to right, would yield a correlation coefficient of +1.00 ($r = +1.00$). An absolute lack of relationship would result in an r of 0.00. A perfect *negative* correlation, in which the plotted points in a graph would all fall exactly on a straight line extending downward from left to right, would yield a correlation coefficient of -1.00 ($r = -1.00$).

Although the computation for a correlation coefficient is relatively simple and straightforward, it can be rather time-consuming if there are many scores. For this reason, and since the ability to compute a correlation coefficient is not necessary for an understanding of it, computational procedures will not be presented here. The beginning student in testing and measurement will gain sufficient understanding of the concept of correlation by studying graphs or correlation charts such as those in Figures 6.1 and 6.2.

In Figure 6.2, seven different correlation charts show the correlation coefficients resulting from different degrees of relationship as represented by plotted points for paired scores. The scatter diagram (a) in the upper left-hand corner shows that when the points lie exactly on a straight line, r will equal 1.00. Another way of illustrating perfect correlation is to note that if we knew a person's score on one test, we could predict exactly what that person's score would be on the other test. Perfect correlation permits perfect prediction. Figure 6.2(d) also shows a perfect correlation. However, this is a perfect negative correlation ($r = -1.00$). The *strength* of the relationship illustrated by Figure 6.2(d) is the same as that illustrated by Figure 6.2(a). The difference is that in Figure 6.2(d) high scores on one test go along with *low* scores on the other, whereas, if the relationship is positive, as in Figure 6.2(a), high scores on one test go along with *high* scores on the other.

Of course, it should be added that perfect correlation (either $r = +1.00$ or $r = -1.00$) is really never obtained in the study of relationships among test scores. The complexity of the factors affecting such relationships as well as weaknesses in the tests themselves essentially eliminates this possibility.

Figure 6.2(b) depicts a correlation of $+0.90$, while Figure 6.2(e) depicts a correlation of -0.90. Where test data are involved, this would be considered a very high correlation. Notice that the degree of relationship is the same for a correlation of -0.90 as for $+0.90$, even though the direction of the relationship is different. Here there is a tendency for the plotted points to approach a straight line pattern although they do not all lie in one line. Note, too, that such an arrangement would not permit us to tell exactly what score a pupil made on one test by knowing the pupil's score on the other. However, since the relationship is quite strong, a prediction could be made with considerable accuracy, though we would always have to recognize that the predictions will contain some error.

When we turn to the correlation of 0.70, pictured in Figure 6.2(c), and the correlation of -0.70, pictured in 6.2(f), we see that the plotted points depart much further from the straight line arrangement. In Figure 6.2(c) there is still a general tendency for high scores on one test to be associated with high scores on the other, and for low scores on one to be associated with low scores on the other. Also, in Figure 6.2(f) there is a tendency for high scores on one test to be associated with low scores on the other. If these plotted points represented the relationship between verbal aptitude and reading

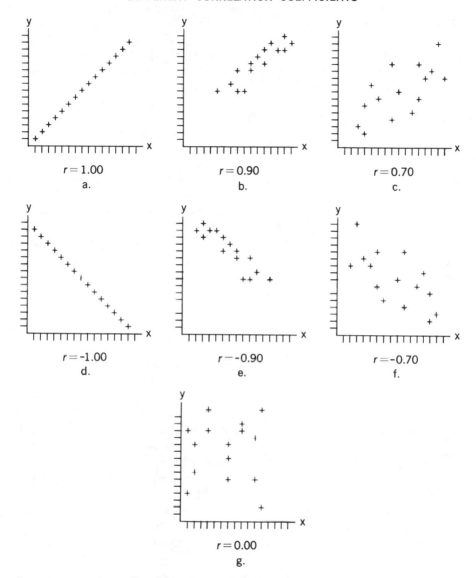

Figure 6.2

PLOTTED POINTS FOR PAIRED SCORES YIELDING
DIFFERENT CORRELATION COEFFICIENTS

$r = 1.00$
a.

$r = 0.90$
b.

$r = 0.70$
c.

$r = -1.00$
d.

$r - -0.90$
e.

$r = -0.70$
f.

$r = 0.00$
g.

achievement, it would be of some value to know a pupil's verbal score if we wished to predict a reading score, but the prediction would have to be made within a broader margin of error than if the correlation was -0.90 or $+0.90$.

Finally, Figure 6.2(g) depicts the situation in which there is no relationship whatsoever ($r = 0.00$). Here there is no tendency for high scores on one variable to be associated with high scores on the other or vice versa. A pupil with a high score on one test might have a high score, an average score, or a low score on the other. Knowledge of a pupil's score on one test would not help us predict what the pupil would do on the second test. In studying relationships among actual data, an r of exactly 0.00 will seldom be attained, but anything very close to this can be thought of as representing no relationship. The correlation coefficients $r = -1.00$, $r = +1.00$, and $r = 0.00$ are seldom actually obtained, but they serve to define the limits in degree of relationship, and coefficients computed from actual data take on meaning in terms of the extent to which they approach these limits.

In studying correlation we are concerned with a procedure for examining the relationship between different sets of measures made on the same individuals. A correlation coefficient can be thought of as an index number telling us something about the strength of the relationship between two such sets of variables or about the accuracy with which we can predict one from the other. A correlation coefficient obtained in any given situation takes on meaning as we are able to compare it with others obtained in comparable circumstances. Various purposes for which correlation coefficients are used and the size of the coefficients typically obtained in applying correlation to these purposes will be discussed in the remaining sections of this chapter.

Test Validation: Introduction

Chapter 2 provided a brief introduction to the concept of validity and explained how this quality must be considered in decisions about how pupil achievement can best be evaluated. The discussion of validity in the present chapter will extend this concept. This more complete understanding of validity is essential if the classroom teacher is to make use of the information provided in the typical test manual and is to be able to make informed choices among tests being considered for a given purpose.

To ask whether a test is a good test is to ask whether the test gives you information about pupils that helps you make better decisions about these pupils. In the end, decision-making is a judgmental process directed toward some goal. Professional judgment is improved when it is based on relevant information of known quality. The relevance of the information provided by educational and psychological tests can only be expressed in terms of the kinds of decisions one wishes to make with that information. A test that provides relevant information in one decision context may have little or no relevance in another context.

Psychologists, educators, and psychometricians have done much in recent years to help clarify the relationships between the concepts of test validation and decision-making. Much of this clarification and synthesis can be attributed to the work of Professor Lee J. Cronbach of Stanford University. We will draw heavily on Professor Cronbach's work in this chapter.[1]

Test validity is not a simple unitary concept. What is ultimately involved in deciding whether a test is valid for a given set of decisions is the integration of a wide variety of kinds of information. Seldom do practical requirements in schools allow one test to be used for only one decision. More often than not one test will be used to make several decisions. This means that in the long run the test that is selected for use will serve some decisions well and serve other decisions less well.

Decisions about pupils and interpretations of test scores go hand in hand. Often a decision about a pupil is based not just on the score the pupil obtained but also on an interpretation about what cognitive functioning that test score "really" represents. For example, some schools give readiness tests to pupils before formal reading instruction begins. On the basis of these test scores and various sorts of informally acquired information, a teacher might subdivide a class into small groups for reading instruction. In doing this, the teacher is making certain judgments about the cognitive skills possessed by pupils with different test scores. On the basis of an interpretation of what "really" lies behind test performance, the teacher will design and carry out different kinds of instructional procedures for pupils with different scores.

To ask about the validity of a test, then, is to ask about the soundness of the interpretations that can be made of the test scores and about the soundness of the decisions that can be made using the test scores.

Assessing the Adequacy of the Sample of Items in a Particular Test

When a test is used to measure the outcomes of instruction, a central question concerns the importance of exercises (items) that appear on a test. When examining an educational achievement test, we ask ourselves whether this test is measuring the important objectives of instruction that are the focus of our teaching. If a test contains a large percentage of items that do not measure our objectives or are measuring nonimportant behaviors, then we cannot justify using the test to describe the educational attainment of students. We should seek tests that measure important educational outcomes.

Even if our judgment leads us to conclude that it is important for our pupils to be able to answer correctly the items appearing on a particular test, the test still may not be an adequate one for our purposes. Any test (whether it is built by the teacher or by an outside agency) can only contain a sample of test items. The pupil's performance on this sample of test items is used to

[1] Lee J. Cronbach, "Test Validation," chapter 14 in R. L. Thorndike, ed., *Educational Measurement,* 2nd ed. (Washington, D.C.: American Council on Education, 1971), pp. 443–507.

make an inference about what the pupil's performance would have been if the pupil had been asked to respond to the entire domain of test items from which the sample has come. To take a simple example in elementary school arithmetic, suppose that we are interested in the very narrow domain of column addition. Our objective may be concerned with whether or not the pupil can correctly perform problems containing three, four, and five addends, with the limitation that each addend be a single digit from 0 through 9. The domain of items here consists of 111,000 addition problems. Any one test would have only a few of these problems on it. The question we ask about the test is: "How representative of the domain is this sample of items?" If the sample of items on the test is not adequately representative of the domain of items to which one wishes to make an inference, then the test scores will be a poor basis for judgments and decisions about a pupil.

To ask whether the test adequately represents the domain of objectives that the test developer claims to be sampling is to ask about the *content validity* of the test. For educational achievement tests, content validity is one of the most important—if not *the* most important—of all validity considerations.*

Another set of questions relates to the test developer's definition of the domain from which the test's items are sampled. While the test developer may have sampled adequately the domain that is defined, that domain may not be the domain which the test user wants to evaluate. For example, a reading test may sample the students' ability to read paragraphs and sentences, but may not sample the students' word attack skills directly. The user's concern for a direct measure of word attack skills must be satisfied by the way the test developer has specified the domain. If the test developer does not include the specific area of word attack skills in a definition of reading achievement, then content validation is only concerned with whether the actual test items sample the areas the developer has stated. Therefore, if the user's definition of the reading domain is different from that of the test developer's, then the user needs to seek another test developer whose definition corresponds more nearly to the user's.

Another point that should be made here concerns whether a test should measure only those behaviors specifically taught by the curriculum at a given school. Sometimes when examining a test, the teacher may discover that the test measures certain behaviors that are not taught by the lessons the teacher develops or the materials the pupils have used. Centering the concern about a test only on whether specific test content has been used in the curriculum may often lead to improper decisions. The reasoning behind the selection of an

---

* Questions about content validity apply to teacher-made tests as well as published tests. A verbal statement of an objective usually implies quite a large collection or domain of test items. The teacher should prepare a detailed description of the domain of test items implied by an objective that can be used to decide whether the actual items appearing on a test are an adequate sample from that domain.

achievement test rests on determining the educational importance of what the test is designed to measure and whether or not the sampling of test items from those important areas is adequate. When a school has judged that certain categories of pupil outcomes are important and when the test samples these outcomes adequately, then testing these outcomes becomes important. It may turn out, for example, that pupils perform adequately in certain areas even though systematic formal instruction has not been provided. This is useful information to the curriculum maker and those who are evaluating the school. It is useful to know a pupil's status with respect to certain areas, even though the pupil hasn't been given specific instruction in those areas. However, it would be unfair to judge a pupil as a poor student if the pupil has not had the opportunity to learn in these areas. Similarly, it would be unfair to judge the teacher because pupils did not learn material for which the teacher was not held responsible. (It may also be unfair to judge the teacher on the basis of the test scores of the teacher's pupils, even in those areas for which instruction was provided. Many other factors, beside the adequacy of the teacher, enter into pupil performance on a test.)

Determining What the Test Really Measures

As teachers and as students we have all taken a test of one sort or another and then raised the question to ourselves concerning what that test "really measured." Even though the content and purpose of the test were clearly spelled out to us, somewhere in the recesses of our mind we might have said, "Yes, that is true but . . ." The "but's" might, for example, express our concern that the test in question really measured our speed of responding rather than our knowledge of the subject-matter or, perhaps, our memory of specific idiosyncratic vocabulary rather than our grasp of certain principles and their application.

Whenever we raise questions about how a test result is to be interpreted, or what the test really measures, we are asking about the validity of the test in terms of the *constructs* used to interpret the results of the test.[2] Thus, this type of validity has been called *construct validity*. Constructs, for our purposes, are terms and phrases invented for ideas, experiences, or observations as considered within a given logical framework. In educational and psychological measurement these constructs abound: verbal ability, quantitative ability, spelling ability, reading comprehension, scientific thinking, self-concept, etc. In the discussion of instruction and evaluation, such constructs are often used to describe internal mental processes that persons are presumed to go through in the performance of certain tasks. Of the many constructs in this book, a number have been used in the clarification of certain instructional

---

[2] Ibid.

objectives. The words *knowledge, comprehension, application, analysis, synthesis,* and *evaluation* are such constructs.

PROCEDURES USED TO EXAMINE CONSTRUCT VALIDITY

The procedures that are used to examine the validity of construct interpretations of a test are considerably diverse. Many of these procedures require a sophisticated use of statistical techniques that are beyond the scope of this introductory book. In simplest terms, the process of construct validation consists of constantly seeking evidence that the performance on a test that claims to measure a given construct cannot be explained by other factors unrelated to the construct in question. These procedures often rely heavily on both psychological theories and on empirical evidence. As Professor Cronbach says, three broad methods of inquiry need to be integrated when the validity of a construct interpretation of a test is questioned.[3]

1. *Logical Analysis*—By examining the nature of the test and the performance it requires and integrating this with one's experience and knowledge of theory, one can question the plausibility of the given construct interpretation. Often alternative explanations or interpretations of good or poor test performance can be hypothesized.

2. *Correlational Studies*—Often the theoretical framework that forms the basis for defining a construct postulates that persons high or low on the qualities of the construct behave in certain ways. The construct is said to be related to certain other constructs and unrelated to still others. Correlational studies are conducted to see if various tests measuring the same, as well as different, constructs show the postulated relationships. If the postulated relationships are not confirmed by these correlational studies, the interpretation of performance on a test that says it measures a certain construct is open to question.

3. *Experimental Studies*—Here the investigator deliberately attempts to modify the scores persons attain on a test by introducing certain experimental treatments. If scores on the test can be changed by experimental conditions that are theoretically unrelated to the construct the test is designed to measure, then there is evidence that the interpretation of test performance in terms of the proposed construct is open to question.

READING COMPREHENSION AS AN EXAMPLE

The discussion above is somewhat abstract and complex. It might be useful to try to illustrate some of these ideas by taking a specific example. One of the

---

[3] Ibid.

examples that Professor Cronbach uses in his discussion of construct validation concerns the construct of reading comprehension. Since reading comprehension is a construct frequently used in education, it would seem useful to present this example here.

Reading comprehension tests typically contain the following types of exercises. A passage of one or two paragraphs is presented, followed by several multiple-choice questions. The directions to the examinees are to read each passage and then answer the questions that follow the passage. At first glance, it appears that the passages require reading and that to answer the questions the examinee needs to read and understand the passages.

A thorough logical analysis of reading comprehension tests was done by Vernon.[4] As a result of that analysis, he postulated several other factors that might account for an examinee's test performance beside "reading comprehension" per se. Here are some of them:

1. Technical bias—A passage may cover a specific theme such as a certain literary work, a specific scientific topic, or a particular historical period. An examinee who has a lot of prior knowledge about the particular passage content may not need to read it in order to answer the questions.

2. Speed conditions—Most tests are timed. Perhaps test performance is largely determined on the basis of speed of reading rather than comprehension.

3. Attitudes and motivations—Performance on a test can be influenced by the way in which the test administrator presents the test to the examinees. An examiner who attempts to motivate high performance in the examinees may increase their scores substantially.

4. Sophistication of the examinee—Some examinees are "test-wise." They know how to pick up clues that aid in answering questions. They use their testing time efficiently, or they may have an ability to answer certain types of questions better than their peers. Test-wiseness would not be considered to be reading comprehension.

5. Understanding the test directions—Some students may misunderstand the directions for taking the test. This may result in poor test performance and, thus, the test may not measure these examinees' reading comprehension very well.

6. Answer marking ability—Many multiple-choice tests require that the answer be marked on a separate answer sheet. Examinees appear to differ in the speed and accuracy with which they can accomplish this task. If this is a major influence on whether or not an examinee scores well, then the test will not measure reading comprehension very well.

---

4 Philip E. Vernon, "The Determinants of Reading Comprehension," *Educational and Psychological Measurement 22* (1962), 269–86.

These are a few examples of how a logical analysis of the test and the construct it is supposed to measure can raise questions about the interpretation of test performance in terms of the postulated construct. But these are only questions or counterhypotheses about the reading comprehension interpretation of test performance, and as such they need to be empirically investigated and then either confirmed or rejected.

For example, take the hypothesis that student motivation can influence reading comprehension test scores. An experiment designed to test this hypothesis should reveal this influence. Students whom the experimenter has motivated by giving them a "pep talk" or offering them prizes or money for good test performance should perform substantially better than students for whom no such motivators were provided. If this is borne out by an experimental study, then the interpretation of test performance as measuring only reading comprehension should be questioned. A different, and perhaps more complex, interpretation is required.

Similarly, correlational studies could be conducted. The scores of students taking a multiple-choice reading comprehension test can be correlated with the scores of the same students when they are individually given oral tests after reading similar passages. If the correlation is low, then the two measures would be unrelated. They would be measuring different abilities. One would have to decide which testing procedure, the paper and pencil test or the oral test, is the "real" reading comprehension measure.

Construct validation, then, is a continuous process of checking the adequacy of test performance interpretations. The teacher, of course, cannot become a researcher and conduct these studies. The test developer and test publisher can conduct such studies, but we cannot expect that they will provide exhaustive evidence on all aspects of the construct validity of a test. Because of this, the professional teacher will need to exercise considerable judgment when interpreting test results in terms of the constructs the test is supposed to measure. The validity of a construct interpretation such as reading comprehension or intelligence is always open to question when a particular test is used with a particular group of students. Being aware of this, the teacher will examine the test carefully, trying to identify reasonable counterexplanations of test performance. Reading professional journals that deal specifically with measurement topics should keep the teacher informed about current developments and recent research relevant to the interpretation of test results.

Relating Test Scores
to Criterion Performance

An important use of test scores is to help the decision-maker predict the future performance of pupils. Thus, for example, a scholastic aptitude test might be given to college applicants and used as one piece of information to help the college admissions committee estimate how well each applicant might perform during the first year of college. This estimate of future performance usually takes the form of a prediction of the scores persons would obtain on a second measure from knowledge of persons' scores on a first measure. The second measure most often used for the college admissions situation is the grade-point average (GPA) at the end of the first year (sometimes at the end of the first term) of college. Thus, the scholastic aptitude test scores are used to predict or estimate each applicant's GPA. The GPA is called the *criterion-variable* in this case. Evidence about the validity of a test for predicting a criterion-variable score is called *criterion-oriented* validation evidence.

While criterion-oriented validation evidence is used in many situations, both in education and outside of education, there are two types of educational situations in which it is most frequently emphasized. The first of these situations is the *selection* of students with the purpose of keeping some while rejecting others. The second is *placement* of students. Here decisions must be made assigning each student to one of several instructional treatments. For example, if two methods of beginning reading instruction are available to pupils, placement is concerned with deciding which students will learn best with which reading method. The latter is not a selection decision; we do not "select" some students to read and ignore the rest of the students—all students must be taught to read. When all students have to be accounted for in the decision context, then we have a placement situation.

VALIDITY FOR SELECTION

When a test is to be used in selection decisions, we need evidence that the test is indeed useful for that purpose. This evidence is usually reported in the test manual in terms of correlation coefficients. If test scores are highly related to or correlated with the criterion scores, then there is evidence that the test is useful in predicting the criterion performance. When we are actually using the test as a selection device for a group of examinees, we do not have criterion scores for that group available to us (if we did we would have no need to predict; we would just use the criterion scores). Thus, before a test can be used in selection situations, certain studies need to be conducted. There are two kinds of studies that test developers report.

One type of study that is conducted is called a *predictive validity* study. To illustrate this kind of study, let us return to the college admissions example. In the ideal case, we would proceed as follows. First, we would administer the admissions test to all those who apply to the particular college. We would then put aside these scores and admit all of the applicants. This is done so that we would not bias the results of this study by using the test actually to select people. Then we would wait until all of the admitted students had completed, say, one semester of course work. We would obtain the GPA of each student. Finally, we could correlate their admissions test scores with their GPA's. If this correlation is high, then we have evidence that the admissions test is a useful predictor of "success" during the first semester of college. The criterion of success is limited to GPA's in this example. If other criteria of success are desired, then they would be measured and correlated with admissions test scores.

We noted that the above example represented the ideal case. In practice, colleges do not admit all applicants in order to study the predictive validity of an admissions test. One common procedure that is used to approximate the ideal procedure is known as a *concurrent validity* study. Here the admissions test would be administered to those students who are already admitted on the basis of other measures (e.g., another test or, perhaps, a high school grade-point average). The college GPA of these students may be obtained at essentially the same time as the scores of the test being studied, hence the term *concurrent validity study*. The correlation between the scores on the admissions test under study and the college GPA's would provide some suggestive evidence of the validity of the test in predicting a new student's GPA.

Note that in this latter case, concurrent validity correlation coefficients should not be uncritically accepted as providing data on predictive validity. If there is no time lapse between the administration of the predictor test and the obtaining of criterion data, the relationship between the two sets of measures is not indicative of predictive value of the test involved. A coefficient of concurrent validity obtained in this way would probably be an overestimate of the predictive validity of the test, because in actual prediction situations rather natural and expected changes in the mental and physical conditions of students from the first testing to the second testing will contribute to the lowering of the correlation and the predictive value of the test. When the predictor and the later criterion measuring device are administered concurrently, such changes are not involved, and the obtained correlation tends to be spuriously high. A further problem is that often concurrent validity coefficients are based on groups of persons who have been preselected in some way, such as those already meeting college admissions criteria. When the range of the scores one is likely to obtain is restricted in this way, the correlation is likely to be lower than that which would have been obtained had the range not been restricted. Concurrent validity coefficients showing the relationship between an aptitude test and some measure of achievement should be interpreted merely as indicating the extent to which the two measures are assessing the same abilities, and not necessarily as an indication of high predictive validity.

Information on predictive validity from a test manual is quite helpful in determining the value of a test for a particular purpose. However, when starting to use a test, teachers are advised to study its predictive validity in their own situations and for their own purposes. This can be done by studying the relationship between the scores pupils make on the given predictor test and their scores on a later measure of achievement. One can examine the relationship by graphing the results as illustrated in Figure 6.1. Studying a graph or correlation chart of this type may well be all that a teacher needs to do by way of examining the actual predictive validity of an instrument being used. However, teachers who wish to go further and compare the validity of the test as shown by their own data with that reported by the test publisher can consult a statistics textbook and actually compute a validity coefficient based on the data.

VALIDITY FOR PLACEMENT*

One important category of educational decisions is concerned with how to assign pupils to the different instructional methods that are best suited to each pupil, so that learning is optimized. For example, suppose we have two methods of teaching beginning reading. Some pupils will learn to read better when one of the methods is used with them, while other pupils will learn better when the second method is used. If we could find a way to measure a pupil's aptitude for a particular kind of instruction, then we could use this measure to help make this placement decision.

Notice that placement decisions are different from selection decisions. We do not select some students to read and ignore the rest of the students. Schools are required to teach all pupils to read. Further, the concept of placement requires that we have at least two instructional procedures available for students and that both procedures, when used, will lead to the same outcome.

The state of the art of testing is currently such that there are few tests designed explicitly to help make placement decisions in the instructional context. In the past, a prevailing philosophy of education has been to direct attention toward the selection process in education. Tests, by and large, have followed suit and have been directed toward this end. More recently, it has come to be realized that the schools' obligation is to teach basic skills to all pupils and that this often will require different instructional procedures for different pupils. Building tests to help in these decisions is not an easy job. Some specialists in measurement doubt that it can even be done.

What kind of evidence should test developers provide if they claim that a test is useful for placement decisions? They should report the results of experiments that demonstrate that, when test scores are used to place students in different instructional procedures, better achievement results. A full treatment of the topic of technical evidence of placement test validity is beyond the scope of our purpose for this book. Basically, the teacher should know that if a test is to be useful for deciding which instructional method is best for each student (in order to accomplish the same goals for each), then evidence that shows that performance is improved when students with different

---

* One type of placement testing is quite commonly used in programs for individualized instruction. This involves placing a student at the point in a sequential curriculum which is appropriate in terms of what units and objectives he or she has mastered. This type of placement testing is described in Chapter 9.

test scores are placed into different instructional procedures should be provided.

SUMMARY OF TEST VALIDATION

We have discussed three broad classes of questions asked in connection with the validation of tests. One class of questions concerned the adequacy with which the items on a test represented the domain or universe the test was supposed to represent. Another class of questions centered on whether the test really measured the trait or construct it claimed to measure. Finally, there was a class of questions that asked how well test scores relate to criterion performance. This latter class of questions was further subdivided into (a) questions about whether the relation between test scores and criterion performance could be used to select persons for a job or for advance training and (b) questions about whether the relation between test scores and criterion performance could be used to assign persons to different treatments or instructional methods in order for these persons to achieve the same or similar goals. Our answer to the question "Is this a valid test?" will depend on what classes of questions about validity are being asked. Different kinds of decisions will require different classes of questions to be answered. This means that we will need to specify the kind of decision to be made before we can ask the proper test validation question. Having asked the right question will allow us to search for the proper information about the validity of a test. These classes of test validation questions and the procedures for answering them are summarized in Table 6.2.

Test Reliability: Introduction

Another concept related to the technical quality of a test is the concept of reliability. We have spoken previously about the fact that any given test is but a sample of performance. We might extend this notion somewhat and say that a test contains one sample of observations of human performance. When we make observations of human performance, we are concerned with how accurate our observations might be. For example, if a student teacher is observed by a supervisor on Tuesday, will the rating the student teacher receives be an accurate reflection of teaching ability? Many factors enter into the notion of accuracy here. If the same lesson were being taught to the same pupils at the same time of day, but on Thursday instead of Tuesday, would the rating by this supervisor be the same? Or, suppose that on Tuesday a different supervisor observed and rated the student teacher. Would the ratings of the two supervisors agree? Would one supervisor rate higher than another? Again, suppose that the supervisor rated the student teacher's teaching ability on Tuesday, but that the type of lesson being taught differed. Would the

Table 6.2

QUESTIONS ASKED IN VALIDATION RESEARCH

Question asked	Procedure	Principally applied to	Example
	CRITERION-ORIENTED		
How do measures of some valued performance (criterion) relate to the test scores?	Give test. Collect data on the criterion, ordinarily after the person has spent some time in training, on a job, or in therapy. There may be different treatments for different groups. Examine the correspondence of criterion scores to test scores.	(a) Tests used in selecting employees and students.	(a) Admission test for law students is checked against later marks.
		(b) Tests used in deciding what treatment should be given a patient or student.	(b) To find out what sort of persons respond well to an antidepressant drug, the drug is given to people with different personality test scores.
		(c) A test intended to substitute for a more cumbersome assessment procedure.	(c) Diagnosis of brain damage from Block Design performance is compared with a neurological examination.
	CONTENT		
Do the observations truly sample the universe of tasks or the situations they are claimed to represent?	Examine the test items and the responses called for. Compare with a full description of the universe the test is supposed to represent.	(d) Tests used to evaluate educational programs.	(d) Content of a test of shorthand ability is compared with content of office correspondence.
		(e) Observation procedures in research on typical behavior.	(e) A schedule for observing what questions children put to their teachers is checked for representation of types of lesson, time of day, etc.

Question asked	Procedure	Principally applied to	Example
	CONSTRUCT		
How can scores on the test be explained psychologically? Does the test measure the attribute it is said to measure?	Set up hypotheses regarding the meaning of test scores, stating how high scorers and low scorers are expected to differ, or what influences are expected to alter scores. Test the hypotheses one by one.	(f) Tests interpreted as measuring mental processes or personality traits. Includes tests used to describe the individual in diagnosis or guidance. Includes outcome measures in scientific research and educational evaluation.	(f) A test of art aptitude is studied to determine how largely scores depend on art training, on experience in Western culture, on mental set to be unconventional, etc. A measure of "suggestibility" is studied experimentally to see if scores are influenced by (e.g.) previous relations with the tester.

"Questions asked in validation research" from *Essentials of Psychological Testing,* 3rd Edition, by Lee J. Cronbach (Harper & Row, 1970), Table 5.1, pp. 124–125.

rating of teaching ability be different if the lesson was a reading lesson instead of an arithmetic lesson?

In each of these situations, we might be concerned with measuring (observing and rating) the "teaching ability" of a student teacher. If our purpose were to estimate the teaching ability of a student in general, then the accuracy of measurement would be influenced by the conditions that were included in our sample of observations. Accuracy of measurement or reliability of measurement is a matter of how well we can generalize one set of observations over the conditions or circumstances that are of interest to us. If we were concerned with whether teaching ability is stable over time, we would be interested in whether the rating given on Tuesday was an accurate indication of the rating that would be given on Thursday. If it turned out that ratings were not stable over time, we would have little confidence that our measurement procedure or observation procedure gave us an accurate or reliable estimate of teaching ability from one day to the next.

On the other hand, if our concern were whether ratings given by one supervisor would agree with ratings given by another supervisor, then our definition of reliability would be different. We would not necessarily be concerned with the stability of ratings over time. Rather, we would be concerned with the consistency among raters at a given time. If it turned out that the rating a student teacher received was not consistent from rater to rater, we would have little confidence that any one of the raters' estimates of teaching ability was accurate.

These two major categories of reliability estimates—reliability over time and reliability over conditions—are discussed below. These categories of reliability estimates can be applied to any measurement procedure—be it ratings and observations or paper and pencil tests. The two categories help us focus our attention on the type of reliability question we are asking. Sometimes we want to know if a test score would be the same if a different sample of the test content were administered to examinees. Here our focus is not on changes due to time, but change due to the conditions (test items) sampled at a given time. The other broad category of reliability questions focuses on how stable a test score is from one time to the next. Would the examinee score the same if the test were administered next week instead of today?

Procedures for Estimating Reliability on a Single Occasion

Suppose a teacher administers a test to a class of students and after scoring the test notices that some of the pupils scored higher (or lower) than expected. The teacher may wonder whether these pupils' scores might have been different if a set of test items different from but similar to those on the test had been used. The teacher in this situation is asking about the consistency of two sets of scores (one from each of two comparable tests) obtained on the same occasion.

ALTERNATE FORMS RELIABILITY

One way a test developer can provide information relevant to the type of reliability question the teacher posed in the situation above is to administer two forms of a test to a group of examinees and report the correlation between the scores. This correlation is known as an *alternate forms reliability coefficient*. The tests are administered on the same (or nearly the same) occasion.

Table 6.3 shows the alternate forms reliability coefficients for Form J and Form K of the *Otis-Lennon Mental Ability Test*. The table shows two levels of the test (Primary II and Elementary I) and three grades of children. For each level of the test there are two forms. The alternate forms reliability coefficients are above 0.80. Attention should also be given to the means and

Table 6.3

ALTERNATE FORMS RELIABILITY COEFFICIENTS WITH MEANS
AND STANDARD DEVIATIONS FOR RAW SCORES ON
FORMS J AND K, GRADES 1–3, FOR THE OTIS-LENNON
MENTAL ABILITY TEST

Test level	Grade	Number of pupils	Number of items	Raw scores Form J Mean	Raw scores Form J S.D.	Raw scores Form K Mean	Raw scores Form K S.D.	r
Primary II	1	1,047	55	40.66	8.66	41.67	8.30	.87
Elementary I	1	376	80	36.36	9.99	35.91	10.37	.84
Elementary I	2	920	80	44.50	12.28	44.94	11.90	.85
Elementary I	3	968	80	53.27	12.48	53.02	12.44	.89

standard deviations of the two forms of the test at each level. In this example, Form J and Form K are quite similar with respect to mean and standard deviation. This will not be true for all standardized tests that have two or more forms, however. If the means and standard deviations of two forms are different, then, even if the correlation between them is relatively high, the forms are not interchangeable. That is, the numerical value of pupils' scores are likely to be systematically different on the two forms of the test, even if the relative ordering of the scores on the two forms is quite similar.

INTERNAL CONSISTENCY RELIABILITY

Another way a test developer might provide information about how scores of pupils might differ when a different sample of content is included on a test is to split a test into two or more equivalent parts and then compare the scores of the parts. This type of procedure is called an *internal consistency reliability procedure.*

One type of internal consistency reliability estimate is called the *split-halves procedure.* When we spoke of the alternate forms procedure, we thought of the forms of a test as being made up of samples of items drawn from a common pool of items that could be used in testing in the given area. The split-halves procedure can be thought of as a modification of this procedure in which one test is thought of as being split in two, each half being a sample of possible test items. The correlation between scores from the two halves then yields something like an alternate forms coefficient. However, the coefficient obtained in this way estimates the reliability of a test that is only half as long as the actual test, and the coefficient must be modified if it is to be taken as an estimate of reliability.

The usual procedure in applying the split-halves method is to give the test in question only once. After the responses have been marked correct or incorrect, two separate scores are recorded for each paper. There are several ways to split a test into halves, and several corresponding methods are available to estimate reliability. One commonly used method is to consider the odd-numbered items as one of the halves of the test and the even-numbered items as the other. Two scores are thus obtained. One score represents the total of odd-numbered items answered correctly; the other represents the total of correct even-numbered answers. This specific method is described as the *odd-even split-halves procedure.*

As indicated previously, the correlation between scores on odd-numbered items and scores on even-numbered items, or between any two halves of a test, is a measure of the correspondence between the scores on two tests each of which is only half as long as the actual test. Since a shorter test, giving a less adequate sample of an examinee's ability, can be expected to be less reliable than a longer one, a standard formula is applied to the correlation between the two halves in order to raise it so that it represents an adequate estimate of the reliability of the full-length test. This is the Spearman-Brown prophecy or correction formula and can be represented as follows:

$$\text{split-halves reliability coefficient} = \frac{2r_{hh}}{1 + r_{hh}} \qquad \textbf{[Eq. 2]}$$

Here r_{hh} represents the original correlation between the two halves. To illustrate the application of the formula, let us assume that the correlation between two halves of a test is found to be .70. The Spearman-Brown formula would then be applied as follows:

$$\text{split-halves reliability coefficient} = \frac{2 \times .70}{1 + .70} = \frac{1.4}{1.7} = .82$$

The split-halves reliability coefficient would be reported as .82.

Table 6.4 provides an example of actual split-half reliability data. This data is for the subtests of the Primary I Battery of the *Metropolitan Achievement Tests.* The test developers tell us that the data are based on all second-grade pupils tested in the fall of 1969 with Form G of the Battery. The split-half procedure used was the odd-even method.

Another type of internal consistency reliability estimate is known as the *Kuder-Richardson Formula 20.* We will not illustrate the computation of this type of estimate here. This procedure is used quite frequently by test developers, however. The beginning student can perhaps best understand the meaning of the coefficient if it is interpreted as representing the average of all possible split-half coefficients that could be determined for a given test. By all possible split-half coefficients, we mean not just the odd-even split, but all possible different splits that could divide a test into halves. This coefficient reflects not only the content sampling differences but also how heterogeneous or "lumpy" the test is in terms of the trait being measured by the items comprising the

Table 6.4

ODD-EVEN RELIABILITY ESTIMATES FOR SECOND-GRADE
PUPILS TESTED DURING THE FALL OF 1969 WITH THE
PRIMARY I BATTERY OF THE METROPOLITAN ACHIEVEMENT
TESTS FORM G

Subtest	Split-halves coefficient
Word Knowledge	.94
Word Analysis	.94
Reading	.96
Total Reading	.97
Total Mathematics	.96

Reproduced from *Metropolitan Achievement Test, Manual for Interpreting,* copyright © 1973, by Harcourt Brace Jovanovich, Inc. Reproduced by special permission of the publisher.

test. Since split-half coefficients tend to be based on a planned splitting of a test into two equivalent halves (rather than a random splitting), split-half coefficients often are a little larger than Kuder-Richardson coefficients unless the items of a test are very homogeneous.

Procedures for Estimating Reliability over a Time Period

Suppose that the teacher referred to in the preceding section asked a different question. Instead of asking whether the unusual scores of the pupils tested were due to the particular sample of items administered to them, suppose the teacher wondered whether the scores were a result of the pupils' psychological state at the time the test was administered. If the same test were administered on another occasion, perhaps the scores would be different. Here the concern is not with the particular sample of items, but whether the scores on a given sample of items would stay the same from one time to another.

TEST-RETEST RELIABILITY

One way a test developer can provide information to the user to answer the question about the stability of test scores over time is to administer the test to a group of persons on two occasions. If the same test (rather than alternate forms of the test) is administered at two different times, then the correlation between the scores on the two occasions is known as the *test-retest reliability estimate.*

What is important to the user of tests when interpreting test-retest coefficients are the time interval between test occasions and how stable the trait being measured is expected to be. For example, we might expect attitude toward school to change over time if a special motivational program is introduced. Stability over a long time period is not expected. On the other hand, sometimes we wish to make long-range predictions, say from the beginning of the year to the end of the year. If our concern is how stable the measures are over a long period of time, then we should look for test-retest coefficients based on data obtained over a long time period.

The teacher concerned with whether test scores can be affected by pupils' having a "bad day" would probably be interested in the stability of scores over a relatively short time period, say, a week or a month. The test-retest correlation over this short time period should be looked up in the test manual.

One important point to keep in mind when examining test-retest coefficients is that the time period between the two testings should be long enough to ensure that there will be little likelihood that examinees will remember specific items or answers but should not be so long as to allow changes in the actual ability of the examinees. This is to ensure that the inconsistencies observed in the scores on the two testings can be interpreted as inconsistencies due to the occasions sampled. Otherwise, it would be difficult to say to what the inconsistencies observed can be attributed.

DELAYED ALTERNATE FORMS RELIABILITY

Another commonly used procedure for estimating reliability over a time period is to administer one form of a test on one occasion and an alternate form on another occasion. Here we have a new sample of test items and a new sample of occasions. The correlation between the scores on the two occasions will be influenced by both the content and the occasion factors.

The question that this procedure addresses is "How will the scores on the test be affected if a different sample of items is given on a different day?" This is an important question when we are using a test to infer a person's status on the quality being measured and when we wish to generalize over samples of items and samples of time. Many educational decisions require this kind of generalization. To return to our example of rating the "teaching ability" of a student teacher—our interest is focused on how accurate the rating of teaching ability is on different occasions and with different raters. We probably are not interested only in confining our inference of teaching ability to one occasion or to one supervisor's rating. How well we can infer beyond a single occasion and a single rater is indicated by a delayed alternate forms type of coefficient. In this example, the delay is reflected by the later occasion on which the student teacher was observed, and the "alternate form" would be the different rater.

SUMMARY OF RELIABILITY COEFFICIENTS

We have discussed two broad categories of reliability questions. One class of questions concerned the effect on test scores when time is held constant and content (or test items) is allowed to vary. The other broad category of questions concerned the effect on test scores when time is allowed to vary and when content is either held constant or varied. Our answer about the reliability of a given measurement procedure will be different depending on which of these classes of questions we are most interested in. Different procedures will examine different sources of inaccuracy. These are summarized in Table 6.5.

Table 6.5

TYPES OF RELIABILITY COEFFICIENTS AND THE SOURCES OF INACCURACY OF MEASUREMENT THEY ARE ADDRESSING

Type of Reliability	Sources of Inaccuracy Addressed
Alternate Forms (immediate)	Content Sampling
Split-Halves	Content Sampling
Kuder-Richardson	Content Sampling and Homogeneity
Test-Retest	Time Sampling
Alternate Forms (delayed)	Time Sampling and Content Sampling

Modified from Anne Anastasi, *Psychological Testing*, 3rd edition. © Copyright Anne Anastasi, 1968, published by the Macmillan Company.

Standard Error of Measurement

Another statistical index used in describing the adequacy of the reliability of a test is the *standard error of measurement*. One way to describe the concept of reliability would be to measure the same thing many times and note how much all the measurements vary. The standard error of measurement provides evidence of this type. If a test could be given over and over again to a student (without changing his or her ability with respect to the quality being measured), the standard deviation of this distribution of actual scores for that one person would be the standard error of measurement of that test for that person. The mean of this distribution of actual scores is considered to be the person's theoretical true score. Of course, because it is not possible to continue retesting persons in this way without changing them, the standard error of measurement is not determined by actual trial but is estimated by using the formula

$$SE_{meas} = SD\sqrt{1 - r_{tt}} \qquad \textbf{[Eq. 3]}$$

where *SD* represents the standard deviation of scores from the test in question and r_{tt} represents its reliability. The standard error of measurement computed by this formula is an estimate of the standard deviation of the errors of measurement that would result from repeated testing as described above.

The standard error of measurement may be thought of as telling something about how closely an actual score approximates a person's theoretical true score. The usual way of explaining it is to assume that any person's hypothetical distribution of actual scores is normally distributed and to state that 68 percent of the time a person's actual score is within a distance of one standard error of measurement of his or her true score.* Hence, the standard error of measurement provides information as to the accuracy of the scores yielded by a test. The smaller the standard error of measurement of a test, the greater the likelihood that the person's actual score on the test will be close to his or her true score on the test. If the reliability of a test was $r_{tt} = .84$, and the standard deviation of the test was $SD = 10$, then the standard error of measurement would be

$$SE_{meas} = 10\sqrt{1 - .84} = 4.0$$

Using the normal curve interpretation described above, we would say that 68 percent of the time we administer this test, the score a person gets would be within 4 points of the person's true score on the test. Conversely, 32 percent of the time a person's test score will be more than 4 points away from the person's true score. If instead of 10, $SD = 5$, then the $SE_{meas} = 2.0$. Thus, we can see that if the reliability remains at .84, the standard error of measurement is smaller when *SD* is smaller. This illustrates an important point: the interpretation of the reliability of a test as a measuring device should take the standard error of measurement into account. One cannot tell from the reliability coefficient alone how reliable the tests are.

Other Uses of Correlation

The two most important purposes for which correlation coefficients are used in describing a test are as ways of expressing validity and reliability. However, test manuals sometimes use correlation coefficients to present other types of information.

CORRELATION OF ITEMS WITH TOTAL SCORE

It is possible to compute a correlation coefficient that expresses the relationship between a person's performance on any individual test item and the person's overall score on the test. This coefficient provides some information

---

* Refer to Figure 5.5 (p. 90) to verify the validity of this interpretation when the normal curve model is adopted.

concerning the extent to which an item measures the same type of thing as the total test. If all such item-test correlations are quite high for a given test, the test is said to be quite homogeneous in that all items appear to be related to the same ability. Information of this type is sometimes obtained for a preliminary form of a test and is used to eliminate those items that are not to be used in the finished version. Data on the average correlation between individual test items and total test score are sometimes presented as information about the content validity of a test. This is essentially a misrepresentation of these data and can be misleading to the uninformed or partially informed person. An instrument may have a high average item-test correlation and be quite poor in its content, concurrent, predictive, or construct validity.

CORRELATIONS AMONG SUBTESTS

Many tests actually composed of a number of discrete subjects, each yielding a separate score, include data in the manual showing the intercorrelations among these subtests. Such correlations are particularly meaningful where the various subtests are supposed to measure different abilities and are supposed to be useful for diagnostic purposes. An example of information of this type is presented in Table 6.6. The first correlation in the table (.83) shows the correlation between vocabulary scores and reading comprehension scores

Table 6.6

INTERCORRELATIONS AMONG STANFORD ACHIEVEMENT TEST
ADVANCED BATTERY SUBTESTS, GRADE 8,
FORM A, FALL TESTING

Test Name	Vari-able	2	3	4	5	6	7	8	9	10	11	12	13
Vocabulary	1	.83	.71	.66	.73	.72	.75	.83	.79	.93	.75	.88	.89
Reading Comp.	2		.74	.70	.75	.73	.80	.85	.82	.98	.78	.92	.92
Math. Concepts	3			.82	.83	.65	.75	.78	.77	.76	.93	.87	.87
Math. Comput.	4				.81	.67	.75	.73	.73	.72	.94	.86	.85
Math. Appl.	5					.64	.74	.80	.78	.77	.94	.87	.87
Spelling	6						.80	.70	.68	.76	.70	.86	.84
Language	7							.79	.79	.82	.79	.92	.91
Soc. Sci.	8								.86	.87	.82	.88	.92
Science	9									.84	.81	.87	.91
Total Reading	10										.80	.94	.94
Total Math.	11											.92	.92
Tot. Basic Batt.	12												.99
Tot. Compl. Batt.	13												

for the *Stanford Achievement Tests Advanced Battery*. This relatively high correlation shows that there is a tendency for students who score high on reading comprehension to score high also on the vocabulary subtest. Notice also that the vocabulary subtest correlates 0.73 with the mathematics applications subtest. In this test battery, the mathematics applications subtest consists of a number of items of the word problem type. This correlation may mean that the better students have larger vocabularies and also are able to solve mathematics word problems better. We cannot say that a large vocabulary causes better performance on this mathematics test. The general pattern of positive intercorrelations in this table is rather common with achievement test batteries of this type. One explanation is that each of the subtests measures, in part, a common trait that might be called "general intellectual ability." Another explanation is that since all subject areas are taught to pupils, the pupils grow in all areas in similar ways. Growth in one area goes hand-in-hand with growth in other areas.

Summary

This chapter has reviewed some of the technical measurement concepts that are used to judge the quality of a test. A test is said to yield valid information for certain interpretations and decisions when it can be demonstrated that using test scores will improve those decisions and interpretations. One class of validity questions concerns the adequacy with which a given test samples important objectives of instruction. Another class of validity questions asks whether the test really measures the quality it says it is supposed to measure, or whether other, supposedly irrelevant, factors influence scores. Still another type asks how well scores on a criterion can be predicted by the scores on a test. Finally, we can ask if test scores can be validly used to place students in different kinds of instructional treatments.

Another technical characteristic of a test is reliability. Here we ask whether test scores will change much if a new, but equivalent, sample of test items is administered to the same persons. Or, we can ask if the test scores will remain stable from one occasion to another.

The type of reliability and validity evidence we should look for will depend on which types of questions we are asking. The questions we ask should be determined by the types of decisions we want to make with the test scores of the pupils.

SUGGESTIONS FOR CLASS DISCUSSION
AND FURTHER INVESTIGATION

1. For each of the following questions decide which type of validity or reliability is of concern to the questioner. Explain what type of evidence could best be used to answer the question.

a. Will my students show about the same reading score on this test if I gave it today as they will if I give it next week?
b. Would my students score differently if a different sample of test items were used?
c. Will this test, if given at the start of the term, give me some idea as to how well the students will do on the final examination for this course?
d. Would this test be useful for dividing my class into groups so that I can teach by one method for one group and by another method for another group?
e. Does this test really measure arithmetic concepts? What factors might account for test performance other than the students' knowledge of arithmetic concepts?

2. Write an instructional objective for a subject area of your choice. What are all of the possible test items you could write that would measure this objective? How could you sample from this domain of test items to make up a test? Can questions or concerns about sampling adequacy (content validity) be raised about your procedure?

3. What kind of evidence would you look for to support the claim that the rating given to your teaching is a *reliable* indication of your teaching ability? Do the same for the claim that your rating is a *valid* measure of your teaching ability.

4. Use this data to compute the standard error of measurement: $r_{tt} = .75$, $SD = 10$ and $r_{tt} = .84$, $SD = 12.5$. Compare these values and offer an interpretation of the accuracy of measurement.

5. List all of the things you can think of that might make an alternate forms reliability coefficient (both delayed and not delayed) lower than a split-halves reliability coefficient for the same test.

6. Should validity for selection or validity for placement be the focus of elementary school tests? High school tests? College tests? Explain your answers and compare them with the answers of other persons in your class. What educational philosophies and value systems underlie your answers and those of others?

7. Distinguish between criterion-oriented validity and criterion-referenced testing. Is the term "criterion" used to mean the same thing in both cases?

SUGGESTIONS FOR FURTHER READING

Presentations on the computation and use of the correlation coefficient can be found in most elementary statistics textbooks. The following are a couple of examples of such sources: G. V. Glass and J. C. Stanley, *Statistical Methods in Education and Psychology* (Englewood Cliffs, N.J.: Prentice-Hall, 1970), chapters 7–9; G. H. Weinberg and J. A. Schumaker, *Statistics: An Intuitive*

Approach, 2nd ed. (Belmont, Calif.: Brooks/Cole Publishing Co., 1969), chapters 16–18.

Rather extensive discussions of the topics of validity and reliability will be found in: L. J. Cronbach, "Test Validation," chapter 14 in R. L. Thorndike, ed., *Educational Measurement,* 2nd ed. (Washington, D.C.: American Council on Education, 1971); J. C. Stanley, "Reliability," chapter 13 in R. L. Thorndike, ed., *Educational Measurement,* 2nd ed.

Good discussions of the issues involved in prediction and in selection and placement are found in: P. A. Schwarz, "Prediction Instruments for Educational Outcomes," chapter 11 in R. L. Thorndike, ed., *Educational Measurement,* 2nd ed.; J. R. Hills, "Use of Measurement in Selection and Placement," chapter 19 in R. L. Thorndike, ed., *Educational Measurement,* 2nd ed.

7

Standardized
Norm-Referenced Tests

Jan Miller (the beginning third-grade teacher to whom we were first introduced in Chapter 1) had just been told that standardized achievement tests would be administered at her school during the first week in May. Jan's only previous experience with such tests had been when she had taken them herself as a student, and at the time, she had viewed them only as a necessary evil to be faced at the end of every school year. To help her understand the use of these tests and to provide her with the guidance necessary for administering them, the principal of her school had given her copies of two test manuals, "Directions for Administering" and "Manual for Interpretation." These booklets provided rather clear directions for giving the tests but contained a lot of other information that she found difficult to comprehend—information on reliability, the test standardization program, norms, and a variety of types of scores. Jan realized that if she were to understand this information, she would have to do a lot of additional studying and perhaps get some assistance from the school's guidance counselor, who seemed well-informed about tests.

Jan had another concern. During this first year of teaching she had learned quite a bit about how to develop and use her own tests and other simple evaluation procedures. But she always developed them for some specific purpose, knowing beforehand how she would use the results. Now she would be taking almost three full school days to test her students with instruments for which she could not see any specific use. Why was the school forcing her to take so much time to give these tests? What use would the results be to her? Could she use these scores in making decisions about pupils or in planning her classroom instruction?

The concerns raised here by Jan Miller are probably representative of the concerns felt by many classroom teachers when they are asked to take time from their busy classroom schedules and devote it to the administration of standardized achievement tests. How do such tests fit into a total program of evaluation? For the important task of evaluating the extent to which pupils have achieved the specific objectives of instruction, the most useful and valid devices are those produced by a teacher to meet the needs of his or her particular situation. Teacher-made tests can assess the abilities outlined in the specific objectives for a course, thus providing the teacher with essential information about pupil mastery of those abilities. In this sense they provide *criterion-referenced* measures.

At times, however, it is useful for a teacher, a pupil, or a parent to know how the achievement of pupils in a given school compares with the achievement of their peers in other schools. Are the pupils in this fourth-grade class doing as well in arithmetic computation as pupils in typical fourth-grade classes? Is their reading comprehension as good? Answers to such questions will be important in evaluating the effectiveness of an instructional program or in comparing the relative proficiencies of students. Standardized norm-referenced achievement tests help provide these answers.

The meaning of the term "standardized test" is fully understood only by someone who has become familiar with such tests and has used them for a variety of purposes. However, it will be useful to start our study of these instruments with a definition. *A standardized norm-referenced test is a published test, accompanied by specific directions for administration and scoring, that has been given to a group of subjects representative of the group of students for whom the test was designed. The performance of any subsequent examinee can be compared with the performance of typical examinees through the use of derived scores and norms.* This chapter will enlarge on this definition by explaining how these tests are developed, providing descriptions of a few representative tests, and offering suggestions for their selection and use.

The Development of a Standardized Norm-Referenced Achievement Test

The task of developing a standardized achievement test for general use is a lengthy process involving many steps and the work of many persons. In the paragraphs below we will describe these development phases briefly.

PLANNING AND WRITING THE INITIAL VERSION

As in the development of teacher-made tests, the first step in the construction of a standardized test is the determination of what the instrument shall measure. Obviously, the general area with which the test is concerned is determined by the interests of the author or the desires of the publisher. Some tests are limited to one subject area, such as reading, arithmetic, chemistry, or world history. Others are test batteries made up of subtests in many subject areas. Decisions must be made concerning the exact content and abilities to be covered within the subject area and grade level for which the test is intended.

Test authors and publishers vary greatly in the care with which they describe in their test manuals what their instruments are designed to measure. Some present a detailed outline showing the plan on which the selection of content was based. Others provide only a few descriptive statements. Some test authors determine the basic content of their tests by surveying the textbooks most widely used for that particular subject and by analyzing course outlines followed by some of the larger school systems. In general, test producers try to develop tests that cover the material studied in typical school systems at the time the test is being developed. They do not attempt to set the pace by suggesting what content the pupils should master; instead they endeavor to construct tests that are useful to, and hence salable to, a large portion of the country's schools.

A statement by a test producer or author of what a test is intended to measure, although a valuable aid, should not be accepted as the final word on what it actually does measure. The user can determine this only after a careful examination of the test items themselves.

Planning for the test requires a number of decisions besides those involving content. Decisions must be made about the number and types of items to be used and the relative emphasis to be placed on the different abilities listed in the test's outline of content. When all such issues have been settled, the actual writing of items begins. This may be done by one person who is competent both in the content being covered and in techniques of item-writing. More frequently, however, it is a team effort involving both specialists in the subject area and specialists in test construction. In any case, the effort typically involves considerable consultative and editorial assistance, which is provided by experienced members of the test publisher's staff. Many more items are prepared than will be used in the final version of the test. The poorer items are discarded or revised after the item analysis phase.

TRYOUT AND ITEM ANALYSIS PHASES

When preliminary versions of the standardized test have been prepared, they are administered to a relatively large group of students who are judged to be representative of persons for whom the test is intended. This group is often not as large nor as truly representative as that used in the standardization of the final form of the test, since it is used only to determine the relative effectiveness of the various original items. However, if the item analysis program is to be meaningful, the group must consist of pupils who are in fact typical of those who will be using the completed test. Particularly important considerations are socio-economic level, size of city, and geographic region. Detailed information about performance on each item is summarized to indicate the item's *difficulty* and *discriminating capacity*.

1. *Item Difficulty*—Information about item difficulty is important for (a) making certain that a final version of a test consists of items with a suitable range of difficulty, (b) balancing alternate forms with respect to this quality, and (c) arranging items within a test in an approximate order of increasing difficulty. It is usually expressed merely in terms of percentage of persons answering the item correctly. On the basis of results obtained from the tryout stages of test development, items that are too difficult or too easy are discarded or rewritten. The goal is usually to choose items that will be answered correctly by somewhere between 50 and 65 percent of persons in the middle of the group for which the test is intended.* For example, if a test is intended for use with third, fourth and fifth graders, it would be expected that 50 to 65 percent of the fourth-grade group would answer each item correctly. Some test publishers check the difficulty of test items for various subgroups of pupils—e.g., boys vs. girls, black students vs. white students—in an effort to determine if a test item might be biased toward one of the groups.

Some actual data on item difficulty for one of the subtests on the Iowa Tests of Basic Skills are presented in Table 7.1. Not all items have been taken by pupils at all grade levels, but there is some overlapping from grade to grade. A close study of the table tells us, for example, that Item 23 was passed by 34 percent of third graders, 46 percent of fourth graders, and 56 percent of fifth graders. Note that the items included at each grade level have an average difficulty level of about 50 percent and that the range in difficulty of items is approximately the same within all grades.

The reader should find it interesting to examine Table 7.1 in terms of this grade progression in item difficulty by looking at the percentage answering an item correctly at each grade level. This has already been seen in the case of Item 23. As another example, the table tells us that Item 25 was answered correctly by 30 percent of third graders, 40 percent of fourth graders, and 48 percent of fifth graders. Both Items 23 and 25, then, seem to possess satisfactory properties in terms of the criterion of increasing per-

---

* Note that it is primarily in norm-referenced tests that items are of carefully distributed levels of difficulty, the goal being to distinguish different levels of ability with a single test. This is not necessarily a goal for teacher-made tests or criterion-referenced tests, where items are usually designed to measure specific behaviors and not relative ability.

Table 7.1

DISTRIBUTIONS OF ITEM DIFFICULTY INDEXES FOR TEST L-4: LANGUAGE USAGE (FORM 5) NATIONAL ITEM NORMS FOR MIDYEAR

Item Difficulty Index (% of pupils getting item right)

ITEM DIFF.	Grade 3 Level 9	Grade 4 Level 10	Grade 5 Level 11	Grade 6 Level 12	Grade 7 Level 13	Grade 8 Level 14	ITEM DIFF.
98							98
96							96
94							94
92							92
90							90
88							88
86							86
84							84
82							82
80							80
78					45		78
76				45			76
74		20			52	57 71	74
72							72
70	3		30 45	52			70
68		14			57		68
66		13	24	34	48		66
64	20	17 19 30	52	33 36 42 57	47 71		64
62		12 15 24			50	63	62
60	9				44 63	55	60
58	10 13		29 42	47 48		56	58
56			23 33 36	39 63			56
54	1 2 8 24			35 41 50	49	70 74	54
52	14 15		34	40 44	46 55 74		52
50	4 6 17 30	16 22 29	27 35 47 48	38	56	58 75	50
48	5 7 11 12 19	35 42	25 31	46 49 55		61	48
46		18 21 23	40 41 44		51 75	59	46
44		33 36	26 28 32 39 50	43	61 70	64 67	44
42	22	34	38 49	37	53 58	76	42
40	29	25 31	37 46	51 56 61	54 67	60 65 66 78	40
38	16	40			59	62 82 84	38
36	18 21	26 27 28 37	43 51		64 66	86	36
34	23	32 39 41		54 58	60 65	81	34
32		38		53 59	62	69 72 77	32
30	25 31					68 73	30
28		43				83	28
26	26 27		53 54	60 64	72	79 85	26
24	28 32				68 69		24
22				62	73		22
20							20
18							18
16						80	16
14							14
12							12
10							10
8							8
6							6
4							4
2							2

E. F. Lindquist and A. N. Hieronymus, *Manual for Administrators, Supervisors, and Counselors,* Levels Edition, Forms 5 and 6 of the *Iowa Tests of Basic Skills,* published by the Houghton Mifflin Company, 1974, p. 74.

centage of correct responses with increase in grade since they measure something in which students gain proficiency as they progress through these grades. If an item does not show a pattern of increase in correct responses with an increase in grade level, it may be a poor item in which some extraneous factor, such as guessing, is playing a major part, it may be measuring something pupils do not become more proficient at as they progress, or it may be measuring some specific knowledge that is taught at one grade level but not retained. In any case, the item probably would be discarded or rewritten.

2. *Item Discriminating Capacity*—If a test item is to provide reliable information and contribute to the overall reliability of a test, it must discriminate between persons who have the ability that the item is intended to measure and persons who do not. Test producers use several procedures to estimate the extent to which an item has this capacity for discrimination. One procedure commonly used to determine discriminating capacity is the computation of the correlation between examinees' getting the item right or wrong and their total score on the test. The assumption here is that pupils with high total test scores are advanced students with respect to the overall content of the test whereas those with low scores are less advanced students in that respect. An item is judged to be discriminating, then, if it correlates well with the total test score.

Another procedure employed is selection of the top and bottom 27 percent of test papers (in terms of total score) and use of these as representing advanced students and less advanced students, respectively. For each item the percentage of upper students and the percentage of lower students choosing each option are determined. Data of this type for one item across three grade levels is shown in Figure 7.1. In grade three, for example, 90.1 percent of the upper group, 25.6 percent of the lower group, and 63.1 percent of the total group answered the item correctly. Notice also that 5 percent of the third-grade group, 1.3 percent of the fourth-grade group, and 2.5 percent of the fifth-grade group omitted the item. The percentage of pupils at each grade level who answered the item correctly increases from grade three through grade five (63.1, 83.2, and 90.5 percent, respectively). The discrimination index, which is the correlation between correct answers on the item and the total test score, is given in the right-hand column of the figure. This index in this case indicates that the item works better for third and fourth grades (the grades for which it was intended) than for the fifth grade.

There is no simple, set standard for deciding whether a test item displays an adequate discriminating capacity. The problem of developing discriminating items is simpler in some subject areas than in others. Usually a test producer will weigh information about discriminating capacity along with data on item difficulty and information about the importance of the content covered and will then select or reject items on the basis of all these criteria. An item will be retained, usually, if it is needed to fulfill the test content specifications, regardless of its statistical properties. Other things being equal,

Figure 7.1

ITEM ANALYSIS DATA FOR A MATHEMATICS COMPUTATION ITEM
FROM THE ELEMENTARY BATTERY OF THE
METROPOLITAN ACHIEVEMENT TESTS SHOWING THE PERCENT
OF PUPILS AT THREE GRADE LEVELS CHOOSING EACH OPTION

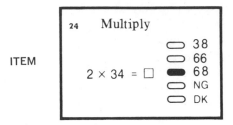

Number of Pupils	Grade Level		Option Number						Discrimination Index
			1	2	3*	4	5	Omits	
301	3	Upper 27%	2.5	0.0	90.1	4.9	2.5	2.5	
		Lower 27%	12.2	11.0	25.6	11.0	25.6	14.6	.66
		Total Grp.	8.3	4.7	63.1	9.6	9.3	5.0	
297	4	Upper 27%	0.0	0.0	98.8	1.3	0.0	0.0	
		Lower 27%	14.8	4.9	48.1	14.8	12.3	5.1	.68
		Total Grp.	4.0	1.7	83.2	6.1	3.7	1.3	
325	5	Upper 27%	0.0	0.0	97.7	1.1	0.0	1.2	
		Lower 27%	3.4	4.5	76.1	8.0	2.3	5.7	.44
		Total Grp.	0.9	1.2	90.5	4.3	0.6	2.5	

* Correct option.

the test developer will select the items that show the greatest discriminating power.

Teachers will probably find it useful to gather information, such as the type suggested above, about the discriminating capacities and difficulty levels of their own test items. For objective-type items, it would also be useful to tabulate the percent of pupils choosing each option. This frequently provides some insight into teachers' capabilities with regard to item-writing as well as the effectiveness of their instruction. However, such data should not be taken as absolute authority as to the worth of an item but should be considered along with other information.[1]

This description of item analysis procedures has touched briefly on the principal techniques employed for this purpose. The student who wishes to become more fully informed on this topic should study the descriptions of specific procedures in the manuals of published achievement tests.

After the item analysis has been made the test producers, using this information together with the original plans and specifications for the test, assemble the items into the final form, or multiple equivalent forms, of the test. Then revisions of directions for administering and scoring are prepared, and the test is ready for standardization.

THE STANDARDIZATION PHASE

An essential quality of a standardized norm-referenced test is that it provides a means of comparing the performance of pupils in any one school or classroom with that of a much larger reference group of pupils. The procedure that yields results making this type of comparison possible is referred to as *standardization*.

To standardize a test, publishers administer it to a large group of students intended to be representative of the population at the grade level for which it is intended. This group is typically denoted as the standardization sample or norm sample. The extent to which it is truly representative of any particular population varies greatly from test to test. In some cases a major effort is made to see that the sample is representative of all pupils in the country. In other cases a much less representatively selected sample is taken. It is not the size of the sample that is of primary importance. Rather, it is the sample's representativeness of the group the test is intended for that should be the main focus.

Most often the test is administered once during the year to a large sample for standardization. (The test may be administered to smaller samples at other times during the year for special purposes such as reliability and validity studies or for the equating of scores on one form of a test to scores on another form.) An example of how a standardization phase is carried out is the procedure used in the development of the Metropolitan Achievement Tests. The Metropolitan Achievement Tests were standardized both in October and in April of the 1969–1970 school year. This is the way these standardization samples were selected:

> The first step in the actual mechanics of selecting the standardization sample involved dividing the national population into 16 cells (4 geographic regions × 4 classifications of community size) and deriving from

---

[1] A useful discussion about item analysis procedures for certain types of classroom tests can be found in Robert L. Ebel, *Essentials of Educational Measurement* (Englewood Cliffs, N.J.: Prentice-Hall, 1972), pp. 383–406.

Table 7.2

PERCENT OF PUPILS BY CITY SIZE AND GEOGRAPHIC
REGION IN NATIONAL POPULATION AND IN
METROPOLITAN STANDARDIZATION SAMPLES

City Size	250,000+	25,000–249,000	2,500–24,000	Rural
National Population[a]	22	20	28	30
MAT Sample[b]	21	21	29	28

Geo. Region	Northeast	Midwest	Southeast	West
National Population[a]	27	29	22	22
MAT Sample[b]	23	28	27	22

[a] National population statistics are from the 1960 U.S. Census.
[b] Metropolitan data are averages for fall and spring standardization groups combined.

Reproduced from the *Metropolitan Achievement Test: Manual for Interpreting*, p. 23, copyright © 1973, by Harcourt Brace Jovanovich, Inc. Reproduced by special permission of the publisher.

census data the percentage falling within each cell. Then, the average socioeconomic index [based on median family income and median years of schooling of persons over age 24] was determined for each cell. Next, a large pool of potential participants was developed: school systems classified with respect to region, size of city, and socioeconomic status. A subsample of approximately 70 systems which matched the desired percentage of cases in each of the cells, was drawn from this pool; these schools were invited to participate in the standardization program. Two alternate school systems were selected for each invited system in the event that the invited system declined to participate. After the school systems were selected, their characteristics were compared with those of the national population on an extensive list of descriptive variables. Minor adjustments were made in a few instances to improve the match between population and sample values on sampling variables within a cell.[2]

Tables 7.2 and 7.3 show the percentage of students in the standardization sample from various demographic categories, which include geographic region and size of city. These tables also report the national population statistics (based on the 1960 U.S. census) for each of the categories.

For every standardized test, the manual or some other publication made available by the test producer provides a description of the composition of

[2] G. A. Prescott, *Metropolitan Achievement Tests: Manual for Interpreting* (New York: Harcourt Brace Jovanovich, 1973), p. 22.

Table 7.3

CHARACTERISTICS OF THE METROPOLITAN STANDARDIZATION
SAMPLES AND NATIONAL POPULATION

Characteristic	Fall Sample	Spring Sample	National Population[a]
Median Family Income	$5,500	$5,600	$5,600
Median Years of School	10.7	10.7	10.6
Percent Black	10.2	9.4	10.5
Percent Other Non-White	.3	.3	.9
Percent of Pupils in Non-Public Schools	12.0	7.0	12.5
Median Class Size	28	28	28

[a] National data from the 1960 U.S. Census.

Reproduced from the *Metropolitan Achievement Test: Manual for Interpreting,* p. 23, copyright © 1973, by Harcourt Brace Jovanovich, Inc. Reproduced by special permission of the publisher.

the standardization sample for that test. The prospective user of a test should always examine these descriptions to determine whether these standardization samples seem to represent the country adequately. Seldom will a national standardization sample be similar in composition to a particular local school system. This means that for most meaningful local norm-referenced comparisons, the local school system should also collect and analyze its own data on a given test.

THE SCALING PHASE

When a test has been administered to the standardization sample, the test developer has information from which various types of norm-referenced scores can be computed. The development of various norm-referenced scores is sometimes called the *scaling phase* of test development. These various derived norm-referenced scores (see Chapter 5 for a complete description), once developed, permit an easy comparison of the relative performances of any pupil who will later take the test to the performance of other pupils who are represented by the standardization sample. Since a school system interested in norm-referenced information is also concerned with how pupils perform at the local and state levels, it will need to develop this information on its own. (Often test publishers provide this service to local school systems, and they usually state in the descriptive materials accompanying a test whether this service is available for that test and how much it will cost.)

The resulting tables, reproduced in the manuals accompanying published tests, are called *norms.* Typical norms produced in this way are *stanine* and *standard score* norms, *percentile rank* norms, *grade-equivalent* norms, and sometimes *age-equivalent* norms. The procedures for deriving and some explanation of the meaning of each of these norm-referenced scores was presented in Chapter 5. The reader may wish to review these before proceeding with the material below. In the following sections we will briefly review the meaning of these norms, indicate how they might be used, and show some examples of the norm tables test producers provide. We will also cross-reference each type of norm-referenced score to the appropriate pages in Chapter 5.

TYPES OF NORMS

Almost all standardized tests provide for the reporting of scores in a number of different forms, thus permitting test users to select the score or scores that will be most useful for their particular purpose. Since not all tests provide exactly the same types of scores or norms, one of the things that should be determined before a test is adopted is whether or not it provides the scores or norms that will be most useful for a particular testing purpose. The norms described below include those that are most commonly found on standardized achievement tests.

1. *Standard scores* (pp. 81–86)—Standard scores tell how far a raw score is from the mean in terms of standard deviation units. Standard scores are seldom used in explaining pupil performance either to pupils or to parents because other types of norms are more easily understood. The test user will find, however, that with many tests a first step in converting from raw scores to other types of scores is the translation of raw scores to standard scores, usually through a simple conversion table. These standard scores are then used in reading various tables to determine other norms. Standard scores are also regularly used in analyzing test results for research purposes.

When a test battery is designed to be used at several grade levels and when the test developers take special pains to administer more than one level of the battery to each grade level, then statistical procedures can be used to relate the overlapping score distributions to each other. In this way, the scores of pupils over several grades can be placed on a single standard score scale. In the overlapping testing program for the *Metropolitan Achievement Tests,* for instance, two or more levels of the battery were administered to each grade. Grade 3, for example, was administered the Primary I, the Primary II, and the Elementary levels of these tests. Grade 4 was administered the Primary II, Elementary, and Intermediate levels. The publisher's manual tells us that this overlapping testing was conducted in five school systems with a total sample of 8,252 pupils and spanned grades two through eight. When standard score norms are developed in this way, it is possible to use standard scores as indices of pupil growth.

An example of the type of raw score to standard score conversion tables that are available to teachers is shown in Table 7.4. A pupil with a raw score

Table 7.4

RAW SCORE TO STANDARD SCORE CONVERSION TABLE FOR THE METROPOLITAN ACHIEVEMENT TESTS, INTERMEDIATE LEVEL

STANDARD SCORES

Raw Score	Word Knowledge F,G,H	Reading F,G,H	Total Reading F,G,H	Language F,G,H	Spelling F	Spelling G	Spelling H	Math Comput. F,G,H	Math Concepts F	Math Concepts G	Math Concepts H	Math Pr. Solv. F,G,H	Total Math F,G,H	Science F,G,H	Social Studies F	Social Studies G	Social Studies H	Raw Score
60			82	87									88	93	88	88	88	60
59			81	87									87	92	88	88	88	59
58			81	86									87	91	87	87	87	58
57			80	86									86	90	86	86	86	57
56			80	86									86	89	86	86	86	56
55			79	85									86	88	85	85	85	55
24	72	79	57	64	75	78	77	87	88	85	88	92	67	70	67	67	67	24
23	71	78	56	63	74	77	77	86	86	84	87	91	66	69	66	66	66	23
22	70	76	54	61	73	75	76	85	84	83	85	89	65	68	65	65	65	22
21	69	75	53	60	71	74	75	84	83	82	84	87	63	67	64	64	64	21
20	68	74	52	59	70	73	73	83	82	80	83	86	62	66	63	63	63	20
19	67	73	51	57	69	71	72	81	80	79	82	84	61	65	62	62	62	19
18	66	71	49	56	68	71	71	80	78	76	80	83	60	64	61	61	61	18
17	65	70	48	55	67	69	70	79	76	75	78	82	59	63	59	59	59	17
16	64	69	47	54	66	67	69	78	75	75	76	80	58	61	58	58	58	16
15	62	67	45	52	65	66	66	77	73	73	75	79	56	60	57	57	57	15
14	60	65	44	51	64	65	65	75	72	72	73	78	55	58	55	55	55	14
13	59	63	42	50	63	64	64	74	72	71	72	76	52	57	54	54	54	13
12	57	61	39	48	62	53	63	72	69	69	71	74	50	56	53	53	53	12
11	55	58	37	47	60	61	61	70	67	67	69	72	48	55	52	52	52	11
10	53	55	34	46	59	60	59	68	65	66	67	70	46	53	50	50	50	10
9	51	52	32	45	58	58	58	67	64	64	65	68	44	52	49	49	49	9
8	49	50	29	44	56	56	56	65	62	62	63	65	42	51	48	48	48	8
7	48	48	27	42	53	53	53	63	60	60	61	62	40	49	47	47	47	7
6	46	45	22	41	51	51	51	61	57	57	58	59	38	48	45	45	45	6
5	43	42	18	40	48	48	48	58	54	54	54	56	37	46	44	44	44	5
4	40	38	15	38	45	45	45	55	51	51	51	52	34	45	42	42	42	4
3	36	35	12	37	42	42	42	50	46	46	46	47	29	43	40	40	40	3
2	31	29	8	35	39	39	39	45	40	40	40	38	24	40	38	38	38	2
1	24	23	5	34	35	35	35	37	33	33	33	29	16	37	36	36	36	1

Reproduced from the Metropolitan Achievement Test, Teacher's Handbook, Intermediate Level, copyright © 1973, by Harcourt Brace Jovanovich, Inc. Reproduced by special permission of the publisher.

of 20 on the Math Computation subtest would be given a standard score of 83. If this same pupil had a raw score of 20 on the Math Concepts subtest, the corresponding standard score would depend on which of the alternate forms of the subtest the pupil had taken. The pupil's standard score would be 82 if Form F had been used, 80 if Form G had been used, and 83 if Form H had been used.

2. *Percentile (or centile) ranks* (pp. 79–81)—A percentile rank tells the percentage of pupils in the norm group who scored at or below a particular point on the score scale. Norms in terms of percentile ranks are provided with most standardized tests and are meaningful if used appropriately. Table 7.5 provides an example of a norm table showing percentile ranks. The person scoring the tests would obtain the raw score for a student from the test itself, locate that score, or the one closest to it, in the proper column in the body of the table, and then look at the marginal columns to determine the percentile rank for the particular person. For example, a first grader who took this test at mid-year (February) and whose raw score for Total Reading was 92 would be given a percentile rank of 74. This means that 74% of the first graders in the standardization group who took these tests at mid-year had Total Reading scores less than 92. Notice that Table 7.5 shows two sets of percentile rank norms—one for the middle of grade one and one for the end of grade one. It is a common practice for achievement tests to report norms for two or more times of the year.* The teacher using these raw score to norm-referenced score conversion tables should be careful to use the tables that correspond to the time of the year that the pupils under consideration took the test. In our example, a raw score of 92 for Total Reading taken at the end of grade one has a percentile rank of 40. Thus, a pupil with a raw score of 92 has a much lower standing at the end of first grade. Differences such as this reflect the rapid rate of learning of pupils in the early grades.

In using tables of percentile ranks, the teacher should keep in mind certain characteristics of these scores.

1. A student's percentile rank tells what percentage of persons in a particular norm sample had lower raw scores. With most tests used in the elementary and secondary schools, the percentile norms are based on pupils at specific grade levels.

2. As with any type of test score, these scores have a certain degree of unreliability and must not be given too exact an interpretation. For example, if one pupil earns a percentile rank of 56 and another a percentile rank of 54 on the same test, this should not be taken as conclusive evidence that the first pupil is superior to the second. Scores are to be taken only as estimates of a pupil's standing and must not be viewed as exact measures that permit such

---

* Note that this reporting may be done even if the test was only administered once during the year for standardization. Norms for other times of the year would then be based on interpolation rather than actual data. (See Chapter 5, p. 96.)

Table 7.5

RAW SCORE TO PERCENTILE RANK CONVERSION TABLES FOR VARIOUS TOTALS OF THE STANFORD ACHIEVEMENT TESTS, PRIMARY LEVEL I BATTERY, FORM A

Middle of Grade 1

TOTAL NUMBER RIGHT

%ile Rank	Complete Battery*	Total Auditory	Total Reading	Total Mathematics	%ile Rank
99	243-274	59-63	141-147	56-64	99
98	233-242	55-58	134-140	54-55	98
96	221-232	53-54	127-133	52-53	96
94	211-220	52	118-126	50-51	94
92	205-210	51	113-117	49	92
90	201-204	50	111-112	48	90
89	198-200	49	109-110	47	89
88	195-197	48	107-108	46	88
86	192-194	47	103-106	45	86
84	187-191	46	101-102	44	84
82	184-186		98-100	43	82
80	181-183	45	97	42	80
78	179-180	44	96	41	78
77	177-178		95		77
76	175-176		93-94	40	76
74	171-174	43	92		74
72	169-170		91	39	72
70	167-168	42	89-90		70
68	164-166	41	88	38	68
66	162-163		86-87	37	66
64	160-161	40	84-85	36	64
62	158-159	39	83		62
60	155-157		81-82	35	60
58	153-154	38	80	34	58
56	150-152		78-79		56
54	148-149	37	77	33	54
52	145-147		76	32	52
50	143-144	36	75		50
48	141-142	35	74	31	48
46	138-140		73		46
44	136-137	34	72	30	44
42	134-135		70-71	29	42
40	132-133	33	69		40
38	129-131	32	68	28	38
36	128		67	27	36
34	126-127	31	66		34
32	123-125		65	26	32
30	121-122	30	63-64	25	30
28	118-120	29	62		28
26	116-117	28	61	24	26
24	114-115		60		24
23	113	27	59	23	23
22	112		58		22
20	110-111	26	57	22	20
18	108-109		56	21	18
16	104-107	25	55		16
14	101-103	24	53-54	20	14
12	99-100		51-52	19	12
11	96-98	23	50		11
10	93-95		48-49	18	10
8	89-92	22	46-47	17	8
6	84-88	21	42-45	16	6
4	79-83	19-20	38-41	15	4
2	72-78	17-18	32-37	13-14	2
1	63-71	16	29-31	12	1

*Does not include Spelling.

End of Grade 1

TOTAL NUMBER RIGHT

%ile Rank	Complete Battery	Total Auditory	Total Reading	Total Mathematics	%ile Rank
99	257-274	60-63	145-147	59-64	99
98	252-256	58-59	144	58	98
96	248-251	56-57	142-143	56-57	96
94	245-247	55	141	55	94
92	243-244	54	140	54	92
90	240-242		138-139		90
89	238-239	53	137	53	89
88	236-237		136		88
86	233-235	52	135	52	86
84	230-232		134	51	84
82	229	51	132-133		82
80	225-228	50	130-131	50	80
78	224		129	49	78
77	222-223		128		77
76	220-221	49	127		76
74	219		125-126	48	74
72	215-218	48	123-124	47	72
70	213-214		121-122		70
68	211-212	47	119-120	46	68
66	208-210		117-118	45	66
64	206-207	46	115-116		64
62	203-205	45	113-114	44	62
60	201-202		111-112		60
58	198-200	44	109-110	43	58
56	196-197		107-108	42	56
54	194-195	43	105-106		54
52	192-193	42	103-104	41	52
50	190-191		101-102		50
48	187-189	41	99-100	40	48
46	185-186		98	39	46
44	181-184	40	96-97		44
42	179-180	39	94-95	38	42
40	176-178		92-93	37	40
38	172-175	38	90-91		38
36	169-171	37	88-89	36	36
34	166-168		86-87	35	34
32	164-165	36	84-85	34	32
30	161-163	35	82-83		30
28	157-160	34	80-81	33	28
26	154-156	33	77-79	32	26
24	152-153		75-76	31	24
23	149-151	32	74		23
22	146-148	31	73	30	22
20	143-145	30	71-72	29	20
18	138-142	29	68-70	28	18
16	134-137	28	65-67	26-27	16
14	130-133	27	63-64	25	14
12	124-129	26	61-62	24	12
11	122-123	25	60	23	11
10	117-121	24	58-59	22	10
8	111-116	23	54-57	21	8
6	106-110	21-22	50-53	20	6
4	94-105	19-20	45-49	18-19	4
2	80-93	16-18	35-44	15-17	2
1	53-79	14-15	30-34	13-14	1

*Does not include Spelling.

Note: Total Auditory = Vocabulary Subtest + Listening Comprehension Subtest
Total Reading = Reading Subtest + Word Study Skills
Total Mathematics = Math. Concepts Subtest + Math. Computation and Applications Subtest

fine discriminations. To emphasize this point, some test publishers report "percentile bands" rather than exact percentile rank for raw scores. For example, instead of reporting a percentile rank of 55 for a given student, what might be reported is an interval from 48 to 62. This percentile band emphasizes the inexactness or unreliability of the scores and cautions the test user against overinterpreting small differences in pupil scores. On the negative side, the use of bands may cause errors of underinterpretation. That is, some real differences in pupil achievement may be masked when bands are used for score interpretation. If the band technique is to be used, then narrower bands are to be preferred over wider bands.[3] It should be emphasized that percentile ranks are no more unreliable than are any other type of score and that it would be quite reasonable to provide "bands" rather than exact scores for all types of norms.

3. Equal differences between percentile ranks do not necessarily represent equal differences in raw scores. This characteristic, discussed in some detail in the presentation on the percentile rank in Chapter 5, is illustrated by the data in Table 7.5. Note, for example, that for the Total Auditory scores, for the middle of grade one the 94th percentile is 52 and the 88th percentile is 48. A difference of 6 points in percentile ranks $(94 - 88 = 6)$ is associated with a difference of 4 points in raw scores $(52 - 48 = 4)$. Now, move down the scale and note that the difference between the 50th and 44th percentiles equals only 2 points, the difference between raw scores of 36 and 34. A further study of such differences will reveal a characteristic of any table of percentile ranks based on a standardization sample that is anywhere near a bell-shaped distribution: between successive percentiles the raw score differences will be quite small near the center of the distribution and will increase in size as they move toward either extreme.

If the cautions suggested above are kept in mind, the percentile rank can be a very useful type of norm-referenced score for the classroom teacher. It is quite simple to explain to pupils and to parents. Also, since it reports the student's standing in relationship to other pupils at the same level in school, it makes clear that, even though the pupil's score may be quite high or low, there are other pupils at that grade level who are scoring higher and lower. It does not suggest, as grade-equivalents might, that the pupil is entirely out of step with other pupils at the same grade level.

3. *Stanine scores* (pp. 91–93)—Stanines are a type of standard score involving single-digit numbers from a low of 1 to a high of 9. With the exception of stanines of 1 and 9 each stanine represents a distance of one-half a standard deviation along the score scale of a normal distribution. The relationship between percentile ranks and stanines is shown in Figure 7.2. This figure shows the percentage of persons at each stanine and the range of percentile

---

[3] Leonard S. Feldt, "A Note on the Use of Confidence Bands to Evaluate the Reliability of a Difference between Two Scores," *American Educational Research Journal, 4* (1967), 139–45.

Figure 7.2

STANINE SCALE FOR A NORMAL DISTRIBUTION

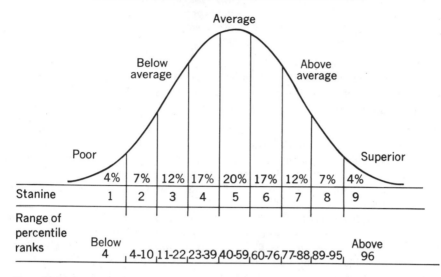

Reproduced from the *Stanford Achievement Test, Manual Part II*, Primary I, Norms Booklet, Form A, p 12, copyright © 1973, by Harcourt Brace Jovanovich, Inc. Reproduced by special permission of the publisher.

ranks associated with each stanine. For example all persons with scores having percentile ranks between 23 and 39 are assigned a stanine score of 4. Seventeen percent of the persons in the distribution are assigned a stanine score of 4.

Stanines are a widely used type of norm-referenced score. Among the advantages claimed for such scores are that they (a) involve single-digit numbers only, (b) have approximately equal units at all points along the scale, and (c) do not imply a greater exactness in measurement than warranted. Some test developers offer the following qualitative interpretations of each stanine score:

9 — highest level
8 — high level
7 — considerably above average
6 — slightly above average
5 — just average
4 — slightly below average
3 — considerably below average
2 — low level
1 — lowest level[4]

---

[4] G. A. Prescott, *Metropolitan Achievement Tests: Manual for Interpreting* (New York: Harcourt Brace Jovanovich, 1973), p. 53.

More general groupings can be made:

1 — poor
2, 3 — below average
4, 5, 6 — average
7, 8 — above average
9 — superior

These are shown above the curve in Figure 7.2.

Not all test experts agree that stanines and other standard scores are useful for interpreting achievement test scores. Some hold that stanines are in fact more difficult to interpret than percentile rank norms.

> The stanine scale is . . . regarded as unnecessarily coarse, particularly for relatively *reliable* tests. For example, all pupils scoring between the 40th and 60th percentiles are assigned a stanine of 5; however, a pupil scoring at the 59th percentile (Stanine 5) is probably much more similar in achievement to a pupil scoring at the 61st percentile (Stanine 6) than to one at the 41st (Stanine 5).
>
> Another important reservation about the use of stanines is that by *definition* they are equally variable from test to test and from grade to grade. There is evidence that skill development in the elementary schools is more variable in subjects such as reading, in which the pupils have many opportunities for advancing "on their own," than in subjects such as arithmetic, in which pupil progress is controlled through placement of concepts and processes in the curriculum. Also, it is to be expected that because some children progress at a faster *rate* than others, they grow farther apart as they progress through the grades. This increased variability is reflected in grade-equivalent scores but not in stanines. This reservation also implies to other standard score scales with a predetermined mean and standard deviation.[5]

4. *Grade-equivalent scores* (pp. 93–98)—A widely used norm-referenced score for standardized achievement tests is the grade-equivalent, which attempts to reference a person's test score to the grade level of the students for whom the score would be average. The procedure for developing grade-equivalent scores was described in Chapter 5 and involves giving the test to groups of students at various specified grade levels and then finding the average score for each group. This score is then assigned a grade-equivalent equal to the grade placement of the group.

The use of grade-equivalent norms assumes some uniformity in the subject-matter taught at a particular grade level. This assumption is more plausible at the elementary school and middle school levels where students are exposed to a common curriculum within a given school system. At the high school level students are usually not exposed to the same curriculum. For example, some students may be in a "college prep" curriculum while

---

[5] E. F. Lindquist and A. N. Hieronymus, *Iowa Tests of Basic Skills: Manual for Administrators, Supervisors, and Counselors* (Boston: Houghton Mifflin, 1964), p. 13.

others may be in a "general" curriculum. In some schools biology may be given in ninth grade, while in others it may not be given until eleventh grade. For these reasons grade-equivalent norms are seldom useful at the high school level and are typically not provided by test publishers.

Table 7.6

RAW SCORE TO GRADE-EQUIVALENT CONVERSION TABLE
FOR LEVEL 1, FORM A, OF THE CALIFORNIA ACHIEVEMENT TESTS

GRADE EQUIV-ALENT	READING			MATHEMATICS			LANGUAGE					TOTAL BATTERY	GRADE EQUIV-ALENT
	VOCAB	COMPR	TOTAL	COMPU	CONCPT & PROB	TOTAL	AUDG	MECH	USG & ST	TOTAL	SPELL		
0.6	0-51	0-4	0-58	0-10	0-19	0-31	0-7	0-6	0-6	0-21	0-3	0-119	0.6
0.7	52-53		59	11		32-33			7	22		120-123	0.7
0.8	54		60-61	12	20	34		7		23		124-128	0.8
0.9	55-56	5	62	13-14	21	35-36			8	24		129-132	0.9
1.0	57		63	15	22	37-38	8	8		25	4	133-137	1.0
1.1	58		64-65	16	23	39-40			9	26		138-143	1.1
1.2	59-60		66-67	17	24	41-43		9		27		144-147	1.2
1.3	61	6	68	18-19	25	44-45		10	10	28		148-152	1.3
1.4	62		69	20	26	46				29-30	5	153-156	1.4
1.5	63-64		70	21	27	47-48		11	11	31		157-161	1.5
1.6	65		71-72	22-23	28	49-51		12		32-33		162-167	1.6
1.7	66-67	7	73-74	24-25	29	52-54	9	13		34	6	168-174	1.7
1.8	68-69	8	75-77	26	30	55-56		14	12	35-36		175-181	1.8
1.9	70		78-79	27-28	31	57-59		15-16		37-38	7	182-188	1.9
2.0	71-72	9	80-81	29-30	32	60-62		17		39-40	8	189-195	2.0
2.1	73-74		82-83	31-32	33	63-64		18	13	41		196-201	2.1
2.2	75-76	10	84-85	33	34	65-67		19-20		42-43	9	202-208	2.2
2.3	77	11	86-88	34	35	68-69	10	21		44-45	10	209-215	2.3
2.4	78-79	12	89-90	35	36	70-71		22	14	46		216-221	2.4
2.5	80-81	13	91-94	36	37	72-73		23		47-48	11	222-228	2.5
2.6	82	14	95-96		38	74-75		24		49	12	229-234	2.6
2.7	83	15	97-100	37	39	76		25		50-51		235-241	2.7
2.8	84	16	101-102	38	40	77-78		26	15	52	13	242-247	2.8
2.9	85	17	103			79	11	27		53		248-252	2.9
3.0		18	104-105		41	80		28		54	14	253-257	3.0
3.1	86		106	39		81		29		55	15	258-261	3.1
3.2	87	19	107		42	82				56		262-265	3.2
3.3		20	108			83		30	16	57	16	266-268	3.3
3.4	88		109	40	43		12	31		58		269-270	3.4
3.5						84				59	17	271-273	3.5
3.6	89	21	110		44	85		32				274-275	3.6
3.7										60		276	3.7
3.8			111								18	277	3.8
3.9						86		33		61		278-279	3.9
4.0	90								17			280	4.0
4.1		22	112		45	87		34		62		281	4.1
4.2											19	282	4.2
4.3										63		283	4.3
4.4	91							35		64		284	4.4

Table 7.6 shows what a grade-equivalent conversion table looks like. The table is used in the following way. The student's raw score on a subtest is located in a column in the body of the table. From that score, look along the row of raw scores to the margin of the table. The number in the margin is the grade-equivalent of that raw score. For example, if a pupil received a raw score of 33 on the Computation subtest, this raw score would convert to a

grade-equivalent of 2.2 for this subtest. Notice several things about this table. Sometimes several different raw scores convert to the same grade-equivalent score. For example, for Vocabulary a raw score of either 73 or 74 converts to a grade-equivalent of 2.1. Also note that sometimes a difference of one raw score point can lead to relatively large differences in grade-equivalent scores. For example, a pupil who obtains a raw score of 10 on the Auding subtest receives a grade-equivalent score of 2.3. However, a pupil who receives a raw score of 11 on this subtest receives a grade-equivalent score of 2.9.

One important caution should be observed in interpreting grade-equivalents. Remember always that they refer to average performance with respect to the content covered by the test. If, for example, a second-grade student has a grade-equivalent of 4.7 on a second-grade arithmetic test, this does not mean that the student has mastered the content of third- and fourth-grade arithmetic. This content is probably not covered by the second-grade arithmetic test. The score means that this student does as well with the content of second-grade arithmetic as the average person who is seven-tenths of the way through the fourth grade does *with this same* (second-grade) *content.*

It must also be remembered that grade-equivalents are based on the *average* score for pupils at a given grade placement. Even if we have a class typical with respect to pupil competence in the content covered by a test, we should not expect all students to have a grade-equivalent equal to grade placement. By definition, some will have grade-equivalents above and some below.

The Test Manual and Associated Materials Accompanying the Published Test

One of the final steps in the production of a standardized test is the development of a manual or manuals that contain information on administering and scoring the test as well as data concerning its development, standardization, validity, and reliability. In some cases all the information is included in one booklet, while in others it appears in several booklets. These publications are given a variety of names such as "directions for administering and scoring," "technical manual," "directions for interpreting scores." Many of the illustrations used in this chapter and in Chapter 6 represent some of the types of data found in such manuals. Readers not already familiar with test manuals should secure a few to study.*

In addition to information on the quality of a test, test publishers often provide a variety of suggestions and materials to aid in the use and interpretation of test scores. These materials are usually quite well prepared and con-

---

* Samples of tests are ordered from test publishers as "specimen sets." A specimen set includes a copy of the test, the scoring key, manual, and other technical and promotional material related to the test. Test orders are usually restricted to qualified persons.

tribute greatly to professional test use by teachers, supervisors, counselors and administrators.

Types of Standardized Achievement Tests

Anyone planning to use standardized achievement tests must recognize that there are different types of tests and test batteries. The following sections describe some of these.

ACHIEVEMENT TEST SURVEY BATTERIES

Achievement batteries differ both in the grades covered and in the nature of their subtests. Persons selecting such tests will have to take into consideration the rationale underlying the test as well as its specific content. Survey achievement batteries are useful in providing an overall survey of pupil attainment and are helpful in determining an individual student's relative standing in different areas. They can be diagnostic to the extent of identifying broad subject areas or skill areas in which he or she may be weak. This type of diagnosis may also be useful in investigating the strengths and weaknesses of an entire class or of a total school program, or in other situations where the concern is relative achievement in different content or skill areas.

1. *California Achievement Tests, 1970 Edition*[6]—Five battery levels span grades 1.5* through 12 as follows: (1) Level 1, for grades 1.5–2, (2) Level 2, for grades 2–4, (3) Level 3, for grades 4–6, (4) Level 4, for grades 6–9, and (5) Level 5, for grades 9–12. Each level, except Level 1, contains seven subtests: (1) Vocabulary, (2) Reading Comprehension, (3) Mathematics Computation, (4) Mathematics Concepts and Problems, (5) Language Mechanics, (6) Language Usage and Structure, and (7) Spelling. Level 1 has an additional subtest called Auding that attempts to measure the student's listening comprehension. Each level is contained in a separate booklet. Separate test booklets for the three general subject areas (Reading, Mathematics, and Language) at each grade level are also available.

2. *Iowa Tests of Basic Skills (Levels Edition)*[7]—The Primary Battery may be used in grades 1.7 through 3.5. The complete battery includes fifteen subtests: (1) Listening, (2) Reading Comprehension: Picture Interpretation, (3) Reading Comprehension: Sentence Comprehension, (4) Reading Comprehension: Story Comprehension, (5) Spelling, (6) Capitalization, (7) Punctuation, (8) Language Usage, (9) Word Analysis, (10) Vocabulary,

---

* Here we refer to grade levels in "grade-equivalent" notation. Thus, we say "grade 1.5" for "the middle of grade five."

[6] Published by CTB/McGraw-Hill, Monterey, California.

[7] Published by Houghton Mifflin Company, Boston.

(11) Map Reading, (12) Reading Graphs and Tables, (13) Knowledge and Use of Reference Materials, (14) Mathematics Concepts, and (15) Mathematics Problems. A shorter version containing eight of the subtests is also available. The Levels Edition may be used in grades 3 through 8 and includes eleven subtests: (1) Vocabulary, (2) Reading Comprehension, (3) Spelling, (4) Capitalization, (5) Punctuation, (6) Language Usage, (7) Map Reading, (8) Reading Graphs and Tables, (9) Knowledge and Use of Reference Materials, (10) Mathematics Concepts, and (11) Mathematics Problem Solving. The tests in these batteries are concerned with the "basic skills" areas and do not attempt to measure a pupil's achievement in all subject areas. The tests are designed so that within a given classroom different pupils can be given different levels of the tests; thus all pupils can be tested simultaneously. This is accomplished by relating the various levels of the battery (Levels 7 and 8 for the Primary Battery—Levels 9 to 14 for the Levels Edition) to the age of the pupil rather than to grade level. This may be an advantage to school systems using ungraded or individually paced instruction. The multi-level format of the Levels Edition is such that tests for all levels are contained in one booklet, and items are arranged in order of degree of difficulty. Each level starts and stops at different points in this sequence of items.

3. *Iowa Tests of Educational Development*[8]—This battery of tests is designed to be used in grades 9 through 12, and it includes eight subtests: (1) Reading Comprehension, (2) Vocabulary, (3) Language Usage, (4) Spelling, (5) Mathematics, (6) Social Studies, (7) Science, and (8) Use of Sources of Information. These tests are specifically designed to avoid measuring content that might belong to a particular course of study in high school (e.g., a college preparatory curriculum). Rather, they attempt to test educational content that is appropriate for all high school students. This means, for example, that the content of certain highly specific advanced courses in science and mathematics is not covered by the tests.

4. *Metropolitan Achievement Tests*[9]—These tests are published in six different batteries: (1) Primer, for grades K.7–1.4 (three subtests), (2) Primary I, for grades 1.5–2.4 (five subtests), (3) Primary II, for grades 2.5–3.4 (seven subtests), (4) Elementary, for grades 3.5–4.9 (seven subtests), (5) Intermediate, for grades 5.0–6.9 (nine subtests), and (6) Advanced, for grades 7.0–9.5 (nine subtests). As indicated, the number of subtests increases with grade level. For example, the Primary I battery has these subtests: (1) Word Knowledge, (2) Word Analysis, (3) Reading, (4) Mathematics Computation, and (5) Mathematics Concepts, while the Advanced battery has these subtests: (1) Word Knowledge, (2) Reading, (3) Language, (4) Spelling,

---

[8] Published by Science Research Associates, Chicago.
[9] Published by Harcourt Brace Jovanovich, New York.

(5) Mathematics Computation, (6) Mathematics Concepts, (7) Mathematics Problem Solving, (8) Science, and (9) Social Studies. The norms for each battery were developed in such a way that they can be used in grades above and below those for which they are primarily intended. For some of the levels, the reading and mathematics subtests are published as separate booklets.

5. *Stanford Achievement Test Series*[10]—The latest edition of this series includes eight batteries for grade 1 through the first year of college: (1) Primary Level I, for grades 1.5–2.4 (seven subtests), (2) Primary Level II, for grades 2.5–3.4 (ten subtests), (3) Primary Level III, for grades 3.5–4.4 (eleven subtests), (4) Intermediate Level I, for grades 4.5–5.4 (eleven subtests), (5) Intermediate Level II, for grades 5.5–6.9 (eleven subtests), (6) Advanced, for grades 7.0–9.5 (nine subtests), (7) TASK Level I, for grades 9–10 (three subtests), (8) TASK Level II, for grades 11–12 (three subtests). A TASK Level II College Edition for grade 13 is available. The first six batteries listed above are called the *1973 Stanford Achievement Test* and the other battery levels are called the *1973 Stanford Test of Academic Skills* (Stanford TASK). As an example of the subtests, the Primary Level III through the Intermediate Level II batteries have the following subtests: (1) Vocabulary, (2) Reading Comprehension, (3) Word Study Skills, (4) Mathematics Concepts, (5) Mathematics Computation, (6) Mathematics Application, (7) Spelling, (8) Language, (9) Social Science, (10) Science, and (11) Listening Comprehension. Each level is published as a separate booklet. Separate booklets in mathematics and reading for Primary Level I through Advanced are available for those wishing to test in only one of these areas. The Stanford TASK levels have only three subtests: Reading, English, and Mathematics.

    This listing of tests is not intended to be at all comprehensive nor to suggest that those described here are superior to others available but not mentioned here. It merely illustrates the composition of some typical achievement survey batteries. Descriptions of many other tests of this type will be found in the catalogs of major test publishers as well as in *The Seventh Mental Measurements Yearbook*.[11]

TESTS IN SPECIFIC SUBJECT AREAS

For many purposes it is helpful to have a published achievement test that confines itself to one content area. A teacher of a given subject such as chemistry, algebra, or geometry may be interested only in how well students are doing in that subject. To employ an entire battery would be wasteful. Furthermore, because no battery is so comprehensive as to include all subjects, many

---

[10] Published by Harcourt Brace Jovanovich, New York.
[11] Oscar K. Buros, ed., *The Seventh Mental Measurements Yearbook* (Highland Park, N.J.: Gryphon Press, 1972).

teachers at the junior and senior high levels find that their subjects are often not covered by the batteries used in their schools. Also, in a comprehensive achievement battery, no subtest can be long enough to afford much basis for diagnosis of specific strengths and weaknesses within any one subject. These are some of the reasons teachers wish to have tests that are limited to one subject.

If one consults the standard sources for the listings of published tests, one will find that there are a great number of tests available in most subject areas. Since they are so numerous and since they differ greatly in their provision for subscores within an area, it would be of little use to list here the available tests or to give examples. The only way a teacher can become familiar with what is available in a given area is to consult such sources as the *Mental Measurement* yearbooks,[12] the *Test Collection Bulletin,*[13] or test publishers' catalogs and then make a detailed analysis of the content and technical quality of the tests by actually securing copies of them.

Often the goal of testing in specific subject areas is to diagnose pupil strengths and weaknesses so that instruction can be planned. Criterion-referenced tests will be more useful than norm-referenced tests for this purpose since they are developed for specific instructional objectives and usually contain several items testing each objective. The importance, for diagnosis, of having several items testing each curriculum objective should be emphasized. A single test item is a poor basis for any inference about achievement of an instructional objective. A recent survey by Klein and Kosecoff[14] indicated a number of criterion-referenced test development efforts that may be useful to schools. The teacher interested in any of these test development efforts should contact the agencies listed there in order to determine the nature of the various tests and their availability. This listing is neither comprehensive nor complete. The names of other criterion-referenced tests can be found in the *Test Collection Bulletin* published by Educational Testing Service and in the catalogs of several test publishers.

Using a Published
Achievement Test

Preceding sections of this chapter and sections of Chapters 5 and 6 have contained many suggestions for the selection and use of achievement tests. However, additional important suggestions should be made, and certain points should be reemphasized.

---

[12] Ibid., and Oscar K. Buros, ed., *The Sixth Mental Measurements Yearbook* (Highland Park, N.J.: Gryphon Press, 1965) and *The Fifth Mental Measurements Yearbook* (1961).

[13] Published by Educational Testing Service, Princeton, New Jersey.

[14] S. P. Klein and N. Kosecoff, "Issues and Procedures in the Development of Criterion-Referenced Tests," ERIC/TM Report 26, 1973 (Princeton, N.J.: ERIC Clearinghouse on Tests, Measurement, and Evaluation, 1973).

SELECTING A TEST

The first step in selecting a test is to determine exactly what purpose it should serve. This means determining what decisions are to be made on the basis of the results of the test. One should consider whether norm-referenced information, criterion-referenced information, or both are needed for a given decision. If both types of information are needed, one should decide on the priorities of the information needed, since most published tests will emphasize one or the other type.

The second step is to discover what tests are available in the area of concern. Recent editions of the Buros Mental Measurements yearbooks will help here. These yearbooks include descriptions and reviews of essentially all published norm-referenced tests of achievement, aptitude, interest, personality, and other qualities. In addition to a detailed description of the test, there are critical reviews of tests in each area by at least one expert in that area. Such reviews must be looked upon as presenting the judgment of one person, and they are often several years behind the publication of new tests. Some of the newest and most recently published tests will not be reviewed here at all. Nevertheless the reviews are helpful as a starting point for the assessment of any test. Also of help in this step are the catalogs put out by the various test publishing agencies.

Another source of information about tests is the *Test Collection Bulletin* published quarterly by Educational Testing Service and available on a subscription basis. This publication lists all tests contained in the Test Collection of Educational Testing Service. Each issue lists the recent acquisitions of this extensive library and includes the titles of the tests, their authors, their publishers, an identification of the persons for whom the tests are intended, and a very brief description of the tests. Reviews of the tests are not provided. However, some references to test reviews are given so that the reader can look them up in the appropriate professional journals. Sources like test publishers' catalogs, the *Test Collection Bulletin,* and the reviews found in professional journals and in the Buros volumes will help identify tests that should be considered for use in a particular decision context.

Once the tests have been identified, the next step is to obtain sample copies of each, along with manuals and other related materials. The tests themselves should be analyzed, item by item, for *content validity* and *relevance to the curriculum.* Teachers can gain much insight into tests by actually taking them and thus stepping into the student's shoes. Teachers should study the test manual carefully to determine *reliability* and the adequacy of procedures used in the *development and tryout* of the instrument. If the test is designed to yield norm-referenced information, then the *standardization program* should be studied, and consideration should be given to whether the *types of norms* provided will be the ones most useful for the decisions that have to be made. Examination of criterion-referenced tests should be made to determine whether the *behaviors tested* are those the user wishes to test and whether there are *enough items on the test* to warrant generalization from the test performance of a pupil to the behavior domain implied by the objectives being tested. Another important consideration for either norm-referenced or criterion-referenced tests is the *time required for administering* the test. Does the latter make it feasible to use the test in the given circumstances? Less important qualities include probable *ease of administration, ease of scoring, scoring services available,* and *cost.*

When several tests are being considered for a given purpose, they can be compared and judged as to their relative standings on each of the above characteristics. The potential test user should also employ the standards of test quality implied in the discussions in preceding sections of this book. Sometimes the promotional materials a test publisher provides may give misleading impressions about the quality of a test. The teacher's careful study of the test, knowledge of basic measurement principles, and professional judgment should outweigh promotional promises in the test selection decision.

USING THE RESULTS FROM PUBLISHED
ACHIEVEMENT TESTS

In describing various types of published norm-referenced achievement tests and their development, we have touched on some of the uses of these instruments. These and a few other uses can be summarized as follows:

1. Scores from published tests provide an outside definition of achievement, independent of the local school system and of teacher judgment, that can be useful in several ways. Criterion-referenced tests help to define categories of specific behaviors and provide information about how well pupils perform these behaviors. Norm-referenced tests permit comparison of a teacher's class with classes in a large representative group of schools; and, although test norms must never be used as standards, the teacher can use the norms to make judgments about the relative performance of the class, and therefore about the effectiveness of the local instructional program, provided that the initial ability of the pupils and the character of the local instructional program are taken into account. Scores on published tests also provide pupils, parents, and others with a source of objective information that is not affected by the idiosyncrasies of a particular teacher.

2. Because many published achievement tests, particularly the comprehensive norm-referenced batteries, provide successive grade-level forms that can be given each year, it is possible to examine patterns of pupil growth in yearly spans. This is difficult, if not impossible, to do with the scores obtained from teacher-made tests.

3. With norm-referenced achievement batteries for which scores on all subtests are based on the same standardization samples, it is possible to make comparisons, using appropriate norms, of relative achievement in different subject areas both for individual students and for a whole class. This permits

a certain amount of profiling of student strengths and weaknesses. Specific diagnosis in subject areas is better accomplished with criterion-referenced tests tailored to the local school's curriculum than with norm-referenced tests.

4. Scores from published tests are useful when students transfer from one school district to another. Because the meaning of teacher-assigned grades and evaluations differs markedly from school to school, scores from a published test have the value of providing a constant, consistent basis for interpretation. Norm-referenced or criterion-referenced tests may be useful in making decisions about transfer students, depending on whether the decision will be based on relative achievement or specific accomplishments.

5. Scores from norm-referenced achievement tests have been found to be useful predictors of future academic success when instructional procedures are relatively fixed and when the student must adapt to them. Their comprehensiveness and reliability have led to their use, particularly at the secondary school level, as supplementary sources of information that can be combined with grade-point averages and scholastic aptitude test scores to predict achievement in college or in other types of post-secondary training.

USES TO BE AVOIDED

In some instances, results from norm-referenced achievement tests are used in ways not warranted by the type of information they provide and not intended by the test producer. Here are some of the uses that should be avoided.

1. Test norms should not be used as standards that determine the level of satisfactory achievement. For example, if a test is given to a class that is midway through the third grade, a grade-equivalent of 3.5 should not automatically be considered as defining the level these students should achieve. This score does represent the average achievement on this test for typical pupils who are halfway through grade three, but the chances are that few single classes are truly average. If pupils in this hypothetical class are above average in scholastic aptitude or have better than average instructional facilities, then one will probably expect their average grade-equivalent to be better than 3.5. Of course, the reverse will be true if they are below average in scholastic aptitude or do not have adequate instructional facilities. One must always remember that grade-equivalent norms are based on performance of average students and cannot be considered to define the standards that all classes or students should attain.

2. Scores from norm-referenced achievement tests should not be used as the basis for assigning pupils grades or marks. Tests and other evaluation devices that have been developed by the teacher and used regularly throughout the term generally provide a much more comprehensive and valid assessment of overall pupil achievement. Results from such procedures should provide the major basis for determining a pupil's grade or mark.

3. Test results cannot be used to judge the effectiveness of a teacher.

The factors that affect pupil learning are so numerous and their interaction so complex that no attempt to ascribe the amount of learning that takes place within a class to any one factor (such as teacher performance) is entirely unrealistic. Also, norm-referenced tests measure only certain types of academic achievement and are not intended to provide a complete assessment of all that a pupil has gained as a result of being in a classroom. Perhaps the most important reason for not using pupil test scores to evaluate teachers is that, where this has been tried, the inevitable result has been that teachers have been tempted to lose sight of the broad variety of goals toward which they should be guiding their pupils and merely to "teach for the test." Teaching for the test can be done in two ways. One way is to teach only the specific items on a test. This is short-sighted and professionally irresponsible, since the test is only a sample of the broad domain of performances toward which only a part of an educational program is directed. A second way is to direct teaching efforts toward the broad classes of behavior the test is designed to measure without teaching the particular items that appear on the test. Criterion-referenced testing implies the second approach. However, the professionally responsible teacher will be certain to check whether the classes of behavior measured by a test match the curriculum objectives in a comprehensive way and will not restrict teaching to a narrower set of objectives than is required by the school system's curriculum.

ADMINISTERING THE TEST

A rather common point of discussion concerning the use of published achievement tests is whether such tests should be given at the beginning or at the end of the school year. Actually, because of the many different types of tests that are available and the variety of purposes for which they can be used, tests could be used at almost any time during the school year. The information that different tests provide will be useful at different times, depending on the uses to which it is to be put. Decisions as to when particular tests might best be administered should be made on the basis of the overall plan for testing and evaluation.

Strong arguments can be made for giving comprehensive achievement test batteries near the beginning of the school year rather than in the spring. The basic use for such test results should be as aids in the improvement of instruction, and tests given at the start of the year provide up-to-date information on all students enrolled for the first term. These data would seem to be essential for planning instructional programs for individual pupils as well as for the whole class. There is general agreement that standardized test scores should not be used to grade pupils or to evaluate the effectiveness of a teacher, and giving such tests at the start of the year reduces the likelihood of their being used in these ways.

An essential part of the meaning of the term "standardized test" is that such a test is to be administered under carefully specified standard conditions.

If the norms are to have a valid meaning for any given situation, the test must be administered according to the procedures used with the norm sample, those prescribed in the test manual. The instructions to the student must be read exactly as specified, time limits must be rigidly followed, and other conditions must be arranged as stipulated in the directions. Fortunately, the manuals for most tests contain clear and complete specifications. These should be followed exactly; the teacher must resist any temptation to depart from them. Departure from the stipulated directions changes the meaning of the test scores and, in effect, makes a new test.

Obtaining More Information from Standardized Achievement Tests

As has been explained, most standardized achievement tests are norm-referenced and report scores such as percentile ranks, standard scores, stanines, or grade-equivalents. The notion of referencing test scores to specific performance criteria, like behavioral objectives, has been discussed in the context of criterion-referenced testing (pp. 74–78). Often, however, teachers in a school system that uses a norm-referenced standardized testing program do not have such tests readily available. There are ways to obtain a certain amount of specific criterion-referenced information from norm-referenced tests. This will allow the teacher to make some judgment about whether curriculum objectives have been attained by individual pupils.

Such a procedure has been proposed by some test developers[15] and has been made explicit by Cox and Sterrett.[16] The steps of the procedure are outlined below.

1. Obtain or specify the objectives of the curriculum for the class of pupils at hand.
2. Record for each pupil the number of objectives on which the pupil has received instruction.
3. Analyze the items of the standardized test and code each item to the appropriate curriculum objective.
4. Score the standardized test in two ways: (a) record the percentage of items the pupil got correct that test those objectives on which the pupil received instruction, and (b) record the percentage of items the pupil got correct that test objectives on which the pupil did not receive instruction or that are not part of the curriculum.

With regard to the first step, many schools either have developed their own objectives or have adopted curricula or programs that have specific

---

15 For example, E. F. Lindquist and A. N. Hieronymus, *Iowa Tests of Basic Skills: Manual for Administrators, Supervisors, and Counselors* (Boston: Houghton Mifflin Company, 1964).

16 R. C. Cox and B. G. Sterrett, "A Model for Increasing the Meaning of Standardized Test Scores," *Journal of Educational Measurement*, 7 (1970), 227–28.

objectives already defined. If a school system does not have specific objectives defined, teachers may have to develop their own.

With regard to the second step, teachers are likely, because of the trend toward individualization of instruction, to have a cumulative record of the number of objectives on which each pupil has received instruction from the beginning of the year until the time of administering the standardized test. If instruction is not individualized but paced, say with smaller groups of pupils within the class, then all members of the group will probably have been instructed on the same objectives.

The third step is to code the test items to the curriculum objectives. This requires careful attention. Often minor changes in wording, the numbers in an arithmetic item, or the format of test items alter their meaning and hence their location with respect to curriculum objectives. There are many ways to write items for a specific instructional objective. A very useful way to decide whether a test item matches an instructional objective has been devised by Mager.[17] This procedure is easy to learn and apply.

Sometimes a test item will not match any of the curriculum objectives at a given grade level; or there will be curriculum objectives that are not covered by the standardized test being used. Some degree of such discrepancy is to be expected since no standardized test attempts to specifically favor one particular curriculum. However, if a majority of important curriculum objectives are not covered by the test items, then the test may lack validity for that local school system.

A further point mentioned by Cox and Sterrett that is worth considering here, especially in regard to individualized instructional programs, is the matching of the test items to the actual objectives for which the individual pupils have received instruction. It sometimes happens that the curriculum objectives are covered by the test's items, but that a particular group of pupils may not have covered much of the curriculum at that point in time. The test would then lack some validity for these pupils in the sense that it would test objectives that they had not covered. The test would nevertheless be a valid measure of the school's curriculum objectives.

The fourth step of the procedure is to score the individual pupils' tests in light of their curriculum placement. One type of score is the percentage of items correct out of those items on the test that match the curriculum objectives that a student has covered. For example, a particular test may have 30 items. Of the 30 items, 20 may match curriculum objectives the student has worked on during the year.* If the pupil answered 16 of these 20 items cor-

---

[17] Robert F. Mager, *Measuring Instructional Intent: Or, Got a Match?* (Belmont, Calif.: Fearon Publishers, 1973).

* Note that the total number of objectives a student has learned during the year is not taken into account by this procedure. Thus, the information provided by this procedure cannot be used to determine the student's absolute level of mastery. The information obtained is specific to those objectives that happen to be included on the published test.

rectly, he or she would receive a score of 80 percent. A second score could be obtained by determining the percentage of items a pupil answers correctly that do not match the curriculum objectives on which the pupil has received instruction. Thus, for example, if 10 items corresponded to objectives not taught and the pupil got 5 of these items right on the test, then the pupil's second score is 50 percent. These two scores: 80 percent of the items the pupil was expected to know, and 50 percent of the rest of the items, are additional pieces of information that would not be obtained from the usual norm-referenced scoring procedure.

Test publishers often have available an item analysis service that test users can purchase. What is provided is a pupil-by-item matrix in which the responses of the pupils to the test items are recorded. An example of such an item analysis matrix is shown in Figure 7.3. This figure shows the item performance of one class on one subtest of the test battery. The items have been grouped according to subject area topics, which are listed at the top of the item report form. In the body of the report are symbols indicating each pupil's response. (A key to these symbols appears at the bottom of the figure.) The percentage of students in this class passing each item is shown in the row labeled "CLASS %." While such computer-prepared item analysis reports can save the teacher a great deal of clerical labor, the same reports can also be prepared by hand.

The teacher should be aware that often a test may contain only one item that matches a curriculum objective. One test item is a very shaky basis for an inference that an objective has or has not been mastered. Further, since standardized test developers often try to provide a mixture of easy and difficult items, the one item that matches a particular objective may be one of the easiest or one of the most difficult items out of all items that could be constructed to measure that objective. Neither a correct response on the former, nor an incorrect response on the latter, would give satisfactory information on a student's level of achievement for that objective. Hence, the Cox/Sterrett procedure outlined above cannot be recommended as a substitute for more extensive single objective mastery tests of the type described in Chapter 9. The procedure does, however, help the teacher examine a pupil's standardized test performance in relation to the objectives on which the pupil was instructed (when the test happens to contain items measuring them), and thereby it can broaden the interpretation of the pupil's test scores.

Summary

Published achievement tests can be important tools for the professional teacher who knows how to select and use such instruments. In general, these tests are produced by experienced personnel, meet rather high technical standards, and have an established degree of reliability. Norm-referenced tests permit a comparison of the achievement of students in any local school or

Figure 7.3

A COMPUTER-PREPARED PUPIL ITEM REPORT FOR THE METROPOLITAN ACHIEVEMENT TESTS, INTERMEDIATE BATTERY, MATHEMATICS COMPUTATION SUBTEST, FORM F

METROPOLITAN ACHIEVEMENT TESTS

ITEM REPORT

GRADE 5   DATE TESTED 10/71   NORM PERIOD BEG   LEVEL INTERMEDIATE   FORM F   PROCESS NO

••MATHEMATICS COMPUTATION••••••••••••••••••••••••••••••••••••••

KEY FOR TOPIC SYMBOLS—
NATURAL NUMBERS
NA – ADDITION
NS – SUBTRACTION
NM – MULTIPLICATION
ND – DIVISION

FA – ADDITION
FS – SUBTRACTION
FM – MULTIPLICATION
FD – DIVISION

FRACTIONS
FR – REDUCTION
D – DECIMALS
PR – PERCENT
RD – ROUNDING

AV – AVERAGE

	NANANANANANA	NSNSNS	NMNMNMNMNH	NDNDNDNDNDND	FAFAFA	FSFSFS	FMFMFMFM	FD	FR	D D D D D	PR	RD	AV
ITEM NUMBER	020611152036	040712	0105212223	03091318 2628	103233	081735	31343740	16	30	14192425 59	27	29	38
CLASS % N= 20	995050506030	604050	9960504030	70704040506 0	500010	603010	40203000	50	20	2020104010	50	40	30
BUILDING % N= 40	906556606530	705060	9560404535	70705050 4040	400020	355010	25102005	45	25	4035305010	30	35	35
SYSTEM % N= 100	887055606328	735558	9063354835	78754043323	350018	303313	23181315	43	20	4330403815	25	38	23
NATIONAL	807575556020	756560	8080355030	756540452015	400510	404015	25252005	50	20	5550355010	30	30	10
AGNEW STEVEN A	+ – – – – –DK	+ +	+ –DK	+ + +DKDK	– – –	– –DK	+ – –	0	DK	+ –DK –DK	+	+	+
CLINTOCK ALAN E	+ – – – + –	+ – –	+ – +DKDK	+ – – – –	DKDK	+DK –	– – +DK	+	–	DK – + –	+	–	–
DUNHILL ARNOLD G	+ + – – + +	+ – –	+ + –DK	+ + – – +	– – –	+ – 0	– – 0 –	+	0	– – – –	–	–	I –
GOLDEN CYNTHI I	+ + + + + 0	+ + +	+ + –DK	+ + + +DK	+ –DK	+ + I	DK – –	+	–	+ + – –	+	DK	0 I
HUNTER BILLEY K	+ + + + +	+ + +	+ + – +	+ + + +DK	+ –DK	+ + +	– + +	+	+	+ + + +	+	+	+
MORTON SUSAN P	+ + – + +	+ + –	+ + + + +	+ + – + +	– – –	DKDKDK	+ – – –	+		– – – +	–	DK	DK
NOVAK CHRIS Q	+ – –DK –	– –DK	+ –DKDK	DK ODK – – –	– – +	– –DKDK	– –DK –	+	DK	DK – – –	DK	DK	DK
RICHOFF SANDRA S	+ + + + + +	+ + +	+ + + + +	+ + + + – +	– – –	+ + + I	+ – + +	–	I	– – – +	+	+	+
SCHROOK AARON	+ + + + + +	+ + +	+ + + + +	+ + + + +	– – –	+ + + +	+ I + +	–		+ + – +	–	+	+
STRONGMAN LAREEN	+ + + + + +	+ + –	+ + + + +	+ + + + +	– – –	+ + +	DKDK –DK	+	DK	+ + + +	+	+	+

CODE: "+" = Right   "—" = Wrong   "O" = Omit   "DK" = Don't Know

classroom with that of a large national sample of students at the same grade level. Norm-referenced tests also provide a relative basis for profiling pupil strengths and weaknesses, for the study of yearly growth, and for many other comparisons. However, criterion-referenced tests can provide more specific diagnosis of pupil strengths and weaknesses since they are oriented toward specific instructional objectives and often have more items per objective than broad survey batteries. While educators should recognize these important uses of standardized test results, they should nevertheless be alert to some of the common misuses, such as treatment of the norms as standards, or use of the scores to grade pupils or to assess teacher effectiveness. The teacher who is aware of how published tests are developed, who is acquainted with the criteria that should be used in the evaluation of such instruments, and who knows the sources to use in investigating available tests should be able to locate standardized achievement tests that will be of major assistance in providing important information concerning students.

SUGGESTIONS FOR CLASS DISCUSSION
AND FURTHER INVESTIGATION

1. Secure copies of tests and test manuals for several standardized achievement tests.* Study each manual to determine what each publisher feels a given test is designed to measure and then study the test itself to determine how well it covers what it is intended to measure. Compare your judgments with those of your classmates.

2. For each test investigated in Suggestion 1, note also such things as the publication date, the composition of the standardization group, the size of the reported reliability coefficients, and the method used to determine reliability. Rank the tests with respect to their adequacy on each of these points. Discuss your rankings with your classmates.

3. Consult the *Mental Measurements Yearbook* (fifth, sixth, and seventh) and note what the reviewers say about each of the tests you examined in Suggestions 1 and 2. Do you agree with the assessments of the reviewers?

4. The use of published tests is sometimes criticized on the basis that it may tend to dictate what is taught in a school. Under what conditions might this happen? How might this be avoided even though standardized tests were used? Are there any conditions under which some degree of "dictation" of this type might be helpful?

5. Assume that you are responsible for developing a testing program for kindergarten through twelfth grade in a given school system. Outline what you would consider to be the most desirable testing program and show exactly when and where you would use specific types of achievement tests.

---

* See the footnote on page 152. Your instructor or your school administrator may have to countersign your order.

SUGGESTIONS FOR FURTHER READING

An essential supplement to this chapter will be the reading of a variety of published achievement tests and their accompanying manuals. Test catalogs and the tests themselves can be obtained from the major test publishers, which are:

> American Guidance Services, Inc., Publishers' Building, Circle Pines, Minnesota 55014.
>
> CTB/McGraw-Hill, Inc., Del Monte Research Park, Monterey, California 93940.
>
> Educational Testing Service, Princeton, New Jersey 08541.
>
> Harcourt Brace Jovanovich, Inc., Test Department, 757 Third Avenue, New York, New York 10017.
>
> Houghton Mifflin Company, 110 Tremont Street, Boston, Massachusetts 02107.
>
> The Psychological Corporation, Test Division, 304 East 45th Street, New York, New York 10017, and 757 Third Avenue, New York, New York 10017.
>
> Science Research Associates, Inc., 259 East Erie Street, Chicago, Illinois 60611.

Extensive reading should also be done in the *Mental Measurements Yearbook,* discussed briefly in this chapter, edited by Oscar K. Buros: *The Seventh Mental Measurements Yearbook* (1972), *The Sixth Mental Measurements Yearbook* (1965), and *The Fifth Mental Measurements Yearbook* (1961), all published in Highland Park, New Jersey, by Gryphon Press.

Good discussions of standardized norm-referenced achievement tests and of their uses are to be found in: Robert L. Ebel, *Essentials of Educational Measurement* (Englewood Cliffs, N.J.: Prentice-Hall, 1972), chapters 17 and 18; William A. Mehrens and Irvin J. Lehmann, *Standardized Tests in Education* (New York: Holt, Rinehart and Winston, 1969), chapter 3; Victor H. Noll and Dale P. Scannell, *Introduction to Educational Measurement, Third Edition* (Boston: Houghton Mifflin Company, 1972), chapters 9 and 10; Robert L. Thorndike and Elizabeth Hagen, *Measurement and Evaluation in Psychology and Education, Third Edition* (New York: John Wiley, 1969), chapters 8 and 9.

8

Tests of
Scholastic Aptitude

It is generally recognized that the best predictor of a student's future success in any type of course work is the student's record of past achievements in the area. The best indicator of success in college is the high school scholastic record. The scores that students make on mathematics achievement tests covering their seventh- and eighth-grade work are good predictors of success in high school algebra. Since the same factors that have influenced past performance are likely to be the major determiners of future achievement, it is not surprising that teachers depend primarily on past school records to determine the aptitude of students for almost any type of school work.

However, there are occasions when supplementary evidence is needed. The teacher who wants to determine the scholastic aptitude of a beginning first-grade student has no records on which to base a judgment. At any grade level, the records of many students present conflicting evidence as to their aptitudes for a particular type of study. A student's progress in a given field may show an uneven pattern marked at times by success and at times by failure. The teacher, then, is concerned with the real aptitude of a particular student for a certain type of work. Also, the meaning of past academic performance in the form of grades varies greatly from school to school, causing confusion when students transfer from one school to another or when they move from high school to college. For such reasons as these, standard tests of scholastic aptitude are considered important tools for teachers and school officials.

It is important to realize that aptitude and intelligence tests are not designed to measure a capacity that is purely innate and entirely independent of previous experience or schooling. A person's intelligence or mental ability, as measured by testing devices, depends to a great extent on environment, the influence of other people, and experience. Tests of scholastic aptitude, including the so-called tests of readiness, intelligence, and general mental ability, as well as various other tests that include the word *aptitude* in their titles, measure aptitude indirectly by measuring what the pupil has actually learned. This method of testing is based on the common-sense assumption that the only way in which aptitude can be measured is by determining the extent to which a student has actually applied that aptitude in acquiring a certain amount of knowledge by a given stage in his or her career. As a result, many of the items found on aptitude tests resemble the items found on achievement tests.

The essential difference between achievement tests and aptitude tests is that an achievement test attempts to measure abilities a student is to have acquired as a result of a specific amount of study in a given instructional sequence, while an aptitude test attempts to measure what a pupil has learned as a result of more general experience and is not centered on the specific objectives of instruction for a particular course. For example, an achievement test given at the end of the first grade or at the start of the second grade would be based on subject area knowledge and skills that the pupil has acquired during the first year in school, but the items found on an intelligence or an aptitude test given at that same time would be based on material that the typical child of that age would have been expected to learn as a result of everyday experience.

The fact that the contents of aptitude tests are based on what the typical person of a given age is expected to have learned as a result of everyday experience should serve as an immediate caveat to the test user. Test developers have attempted to take into account the variety of everyday experience and have tried to base test items on only those experiences that are common to the majority of persons. Naturally, persons who do not belong to the majority and have not had the experiences assumed to be common to the majority will score poorly on tests of scholastic aptitude. The low scores of such persons do not have the same meaning as the low scores of persons who have had the opportunity to learn. Although easy enough to ask, questions like the following are difficult to answer:

> What do any test results signify, in the case of persons from a deprived group, so far as future achievement is concerned? Are the relationships between measures of present ability and future outcomes as high for pupils from limited backgrounds as for the generality of pupils? For a given score, how should the prognosis be modified, if at all, by knowledge that the score was earned by a pupil from a meager environment? Since his score may

have been held down by his environmental limitations, should we predict a higher school or job performance for him than for his more favored classmate who matches him in initial score? Should we predict essentially the same outcome for both? Or does experience indicate that the child from the more limited background will lapse back to a lower final level?[1]

Some educational psychologists believe that to a considerable extent the traditional measures of scholastic aptitude serve to predict how well a pupil can adapt to a fixed set of instructional procedures.[2] Their view is that scholastic aptitude tests should be designed and validated so that the scores can help educators make the decision as to which type of instructional procedure will optimize each pupil's learning of a given set of skills and knowledges. Aptitude tests such as these would function as placement tests, rather than selection tests (see Chapter 6). In the past, scholastic aptitude tests have been developed along the lines of selection. A rising view, however, is that schools should not function selectively. This view holds that every child has a right to be educated to his or her fullest capacity. One implication of this is that if a type of instructional procedure is not effective for a given pupil, then another procedure needs to be found that will be. In this way, different instructional methods will be used with different pupils. Instruction is adaptive to the pupil, rather than being a fixed procedure to which all pupils must adapt.

Aptitude tests for predicting successful learning in different kinds of instructional methods are not now readily available to teachers. The scholastic aptitude tests that are available generally have not been validated for use in assigning pupils to different kinds of instructional methods that teach the same skills. They do, to some degree, predict how well a student will perform in nonadaptive instructional settings and in this context may be useful. In this chapter we review these types of traditional scholastic aptitude tests. They may be placed in four major categories: (1) general scholastic aptitude or intelligence tests, (2) readiness tests, (3) aptitude test batteries, and (4) tests for measuring aptitude for some one subject. Since general scholastic aptitude or intelligence tests are by far the more frequently used of the four types, our discussion of aptitude tests will begin with them.

General Scholastic Aptitude or Intelligence Tests

Since present-day intelligence tests are very much a product of the historical development of testing in this area, it is essential that the person who uses such tests have a general understanding of the history of intelligence testing.

---

[1] R. L. Thorndike and E. Hagen, *Measurement and Evaluation in Psychology and Education, Third Edition* (New York: John Wiley, 1969), pp. 329–30.

[2] See, for example, L. J. Cronbach, "How Can Instruction Be Adapted to Individual Differences?" in Robert M. Gagne, ed., *Learning and Individual Differences* (Columbus, Ohio: Charles E. Merrill, 1967), pp. 23–39; R. Glaser, "Individuals and Learning: The New Aptitudes," *Educational Researcher* (1972), 1(6), pp. 5–13.

This history can be considered as beginning with the work of Alfred Binet, the French physician and psychologist who was active in the late nineteenth and early twentieth centuries in the study of mental traits. During the early part of his career, Binet was interested in studying and identifying factors that might be predictive of a person's ability to carry out simple tasks. Among the variables he tested in seeking a predictor of this type were such things as the size of a person's head and the amount of food the person eats in a given period of time. Early in the 1900's, the Paris school system chose Binet, because of his interest in this problem, to be a member of a committee formed to develop a procedure for identifying children who could be expected to profit from instruction in the first grade. The job of the committee was to develop some type of measure of general scholastic aptitude.

The result of the committee's work was the scale published in 1905 by Alfred Binet and Theodore Simon. This first scale consisted of thirty different simple tasks or tests arranged in order of increasing difficulty. Experiments with this first scale on normal and subnormal children enabled Binet to determine a point on the scale that divided the students who could profit from normal classroom instruction from those who probably would not be able to succeed in the average classroom.

In 1908, Binet revised his earlier scale to include fifty-nine tasks and assigned each task to an age level (ages three to thirteen), thus introducing the concept of "mental age." The tests on these scales were administered individually by an examiner. Examples of the tasks on Binet's scale would include asking the examinee to point to the different parts of the body, repeat a certain number of digits, count coins, repeat a sentence, name colors, define words, and use words in a sentence.

The Binet-Simon scale seemed to show great promise and attracted considerable attention in several other countries. Although several persons worked on translations and adaptations of the Binet scale for use in this country, by far the most successful of these persons was Lewis M. Terman of Stanford University. Terman's first Stanford revision of the Binet scale appeared in 1916 and was followed by revisions in 1937, and 1960. In 1972 the Stanford-Binet was re-normed.[3]

The person administering the Stanford-Binet test must be given special training typically offered in graduate courses in psychology. In using the test the first attempt is to determine the examinee's "basal age," the highest age level at which he or she can pass all six tasks assigned for that age. With the average student the examiner will probably start testing at the age level one year below the examinee's chronological age. If the student cannot pass all tasks at this level, the examiner will then work downward through the age levels to find the age level at which the student can pass all tasks. The tester

---

[3] L. M. Terman and M. A. Merrill, *Stanford-Binet Intelligence Scale: Manual for the Third Revision, Form L–M* (*1972-Norm Edition*) (Boston: Houghton Mifflin Company, 1973).

works upward from the student's basal age in administering all tasks at age levels above that, recording the number of tasks successfully performed by the student at each age level, until an upper level is reached at which the examinee can answer none of the tasks correctly. When this level is reached, the examining stops. A basic type of score in intelligence or general scholastic aptitude testing is the *mental age score*. On the Stanford-Binet test, mental age is determined by adding to a student's basal age two months* of credit for every task passed above the level of the student's basal age. What this involves can be illustrated by the following hypothetical results:

Subject's performance	Credit received
Passes all tasks at year 10	10 years (basal age)
Passes 3 of 6 tasks at year 11	6 months
Passes 2 of 6 tasks at year 12	4 months
Passes no task at year 13 (testing stops)	
	MA = 10 years 10 months

Suppose the student in the above example has an actual age of 9 years 1 month. Having passed all items at year 8, the student took the tests indicated above and eventually, at year 13, passed none of the items. The student was given a mental age (MA) of 10 years 10 months, receiving 2 months' credit for each item above year 10 (basal age) answered correctly.

Another type of score obtained from scholastic aptitude tests is the IQ score. The IQ score is a norm-referenced score. Originally, IQ was thought of as an *intelligence quotient* defined to be the ratio of the MA score to the person's actual chronological age (CA) multiplied by 100. This is shown in the formula below:

$$IQ = \frac{MA\ Score}{CA} \times 100$$

For a number of technical as well as interpretative reasons, this notion of intelligence quotient has been abandoned in current testing. The IQ score now obtained from the Stanford-Binet is a *standard score* (see Chapter 5) in a normal distribution with a mean of 100 and a standard deviation of 16. Thus, an IQ score of 100 means that a child's MA score is at the average of the distribution of all norm-group children that have the same CA as this child. An IQ score of 116 is one standard deviation above the mean of a person's age group. An IQ score of 84 is one standard deviation below the mean of the age group. Notice that IQ scores have a norm-referenced interpretation and that the norm group for each examinee is composed of persons who have the same CA as the person tested.

With the introduction of the IQ score as a standard score, the older notions about the relationships between mental age, chronological age, and IQ that are shown by the formula above no longer apply. For example, if you

---

* Applies to ages 6 through 14 only.

Table 8.1

ESTIMATES OF THE AVERAGE 1972 IQ SCORES WHEN THE
1972 STANFORD-BINET TEST PERFORMANCE IS REFERENCED
TO THE 1937 NORMS

Age	Mean IQ score	Age	Mean IQ score
2–0	110.4	8–0	103.3
2–6	110.6	9–0	102.1
3–0	110.7	10–0	101.9
3–6	110.8	11–0	102.2
4–0	110.7	12–0	102.5
4–6	110.4	13–0	102.9
5–0	109.7	14–0	103.3
5–6	108.4	15–0	103.9
6–0	107.1	16–0	104.7
7–0	105.0	17–0	105.7
		18–0	106.9

From L. M. Terman and M. A. Merrill, *Stanford-Binet Intelligence Scale: Manual for the Third Revision, Form L–M (1972 Norms Edition)*. Published by Houghton Mifflin Company, 1973. Used with permission.

were to apply the formula on p. 171 to the scores of a child who was tested at CA = 5 years and 0 months and who had a MA of 5 years and 0 months, you would obtain an intelligence quotient of 100. However, since the IQ score in current testing is a standard score,

> a child on his fifth birthday who achieves a MA of 5–0 does not receive an IQ of 100, but rather one of 91. In order to be credited with an IQ of 100, he must achieve a MA of 5–6.[4]

The idea that the IQ is a norm-referenced score that is subject to change as the norm group changes can also be seen from Table 8.1. This table shows the average 1972 IQ's when they are referenced to the 1937 norm group. When the persons tested in 1972 are referenced to their own group, the average IQ scores would be around 100 for each age instead of the values shown in this table. The differences between the 1937 and 1972 IQ's not only reflect changes in composition of the two norm groups (the 1937 norm group was limited to primarily English-speaking and white persons) but also reflect significant social and cultural changes that have occurred during the intervening years.

> This shows up most acutely in the case of preschool children, whose cultural environment has probably changed the most radically. In the 1930's,

---

[4] L. M. Terman and M. A. Merrill, *Stanford-Binet Intelligence Scale: Manual for the Third Revision, Form L–M (1972-Norm Edition)* (Boston: Houghton Mifflin Company, 1973), pp. 360–61.

radio was new and relatively limited in its impact on small children, whereas in the 1970's television is omnipresent and viewed for hours each day by the typical preschooler. The impact of television and radio, the increases in literacy and education of parents, and the many other cultural changes of almost 40 years would appear to have had their most impressive impact on the preschool group. Furthermore, the tendency to persist in schools through the end of secondary education has continued to grow, and the number of 15-, 16-, and 17-year-olds who are still in school in the 1970's is clearly higher than it was in the 1930's. This is perhaps the reason for an apparent modest rise in the curve at the upper ages.[5]

An examiner must be prepared through extensive training and practice before administering individual intelligence tests such as the Stanford-Binet. One cannot expect to become prepared for this merely by taking a general course in testing. Hence, the present discussion of individually administered tests is not intended to be complete but is merely a brief introduction to one test, the Stanford-Binet. One reason for providing this introduction is that the Stanford-Binet is widely used, and many teachers will have access to results from this test where the actual testing has been done by a school psychologist or some other trained person.[6] Perhaps the more important reason, however, is that since the Stanford-Binet was the first widely used test of intelligence, and since it has maintained its position as in many ways the standard measure of intelligence for so many years, one can understand other tests better when they are related to the Stanford-Binet. Many tests are descendents of this scale in the sense that they attempt to measure the same thing. Test manuals often discuss the similarity of a given test to the Binet and in many cases present correlations between scores from the two tests. In other cases a test manual may describe how that test is different from the Binet. In either case it is used as a point of reference.

GROUP TESTS OF SCHOLASTIC APTITUDE

The Stanford-Binet is an individually administered test requiring a trained examiner to administer the test to one person at a time. Group tests, on the other hand, can be administered to many persons at the same time. The development of group tests was accelerated during World War I when a number of persons collaborated to produce tests that could provide quickly and easily a measure of the aptitude of the many armed forces recruits. The results of this effort were the two tests known as the Army Alpha and the Army Beta. The Army Alpha was used for the general testing of recruits, while the Army Beta was used for testing illiterate recruits and non-English-speaking recruits. After this breakthrough, the years immediately following the war saw the development of a number of these paper-and-pencil tests,

---

[5] Ibid., p. 360.

[6] Other widely used individual tests are the *Wechsler Intelligence Scale for Children,* WISC, and the *Wechsler Adult Intelligence Scale,* WAIS, both published by the Psychological Corporation, New York.

and their popularity has resulted in the continuing development of such instruments. Group tests can be given much more economically, in terms of both time and money, than individual tests; they can be administered easily by the typical classroom teacher, and they have been shown to produce essentially the same results as individual tests, so it is not surprising that they have come to be the most widely used measures of intelligence.

TYPES OF GROUP TEST

The *omnibus* test is perhaps the most common of the group scholastic aptitude or intelligence tests. It does not measure aspects of aptitude separately, but combines in one test items that seem to be measuring abilities of a number of different types. This procedure is like that of the Stanford-Binet test,

Table 8.2

NUMBER AND PERCENT OF ITEMS, CLASSIFIED BY TYPE,
IN EACH FORM OF OTIS-LENNON ELEMENTARY II,
INTERMEDIATE, AND ADVANCED LEVELS

Item type	Elementary II level		Intermediate level		Advanced level	
	Number	Percent	Number	Percent	Number	Percent
Verbal Comprehension	20	25	20	25	25	31
Synonym-Definition	8		8		9	
Opposites	6		6		12	
Sentence Completion	3		3		3	
Scrambled Sentences	3		3		1	
Verbal Reasoning	32	40	32	40	25	31
Word-Letter Matrix	4		4		3	
Verbal Analogies	15		15		13	
Verbal Classification	4		4		0	
Inference	6		6		5	
Logical Selection	3		3		4	
Figural Reasoning	15	19	15	19	15	19
Figure Analogies	7		7		5	
Series Completion	4		4		5	
Pattern Matrix	4		4		5	
Quantitative Reasoning	13	16	13	16	15	19
Number Series	7		7		7	
Arithmetic Reasoning	6		6		8	
Total	80	100	80	100	80	100

which also combines performance on a variety of tasks to yield one general measure of mental ability. An example of a group test of the omnibus type is the Otis-Lennon Mental Ability Test.[7] Table 8.2 shows the number and types of items included on three of the levels of this test. Figure 8.1 illustrates a few of these item types: sentence completion, verbal analogy, synonym definition, and figure analogy. Considering all of the items on the test on a logical basis, it would appear that some of these items should be most highly related to achievement in verbal types of learning, others to numerical types of learning, and others to learning involving figures. However, an omnibus test does not involve the separation of items and the reporting of scores on such a basis. Instead it is built on the assumption that combining items that measure a variety of abilities so as to produce one test score will provide a broad and reliable measure of a pupil's general aptitude for school work.

Figure 8.1

ILLUSTRATION OF SOME OF THE TYPES OF ITEMS FOUND
ON THE OTIS-LENNON MENTAL ABILITY TEST,
ELEMENTARY II LEVEL, FORM J

30. Choose the word that *best* completes this sentence:
Nothing can _____ such a loss.
  f rebuke   g accept   h replace   j invent   k provoke

31. **Governor** is to **state** as **general** is to –
  a army   b war   c king   d captain   e commander

32. **Timber** means –
  f fall   g fear   h music   j wood   k glass

33. 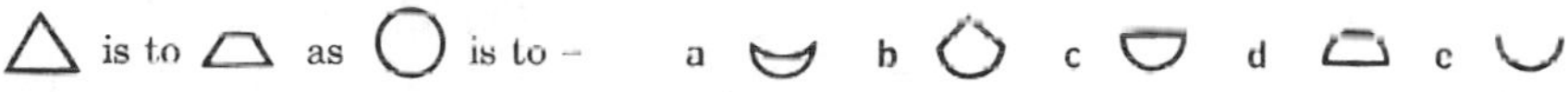 △ is to ◁ as ◯ is to – a ◡ b ◌ c ▽ d ◻ e ◡

Most omnibus tests provide only one raw score. This raw score is then referenced to norms in a number of ways. The Otis-Lennon Mental Abilities Test, for example, provides a deviation IQ score (DIQ). The DIQ is a standard score much the same as the IQ score of the Stanford-Binet. Although these are both standard scores, they are not directly comparable, since the norm-referencings are based on different standardization samples. A pupil's IQ score on the two tests will be different.

Norms for the Otis-Lennon are provided for age groups and also for grade groups. The norms for age groups are based on a sample of pupils who

[7] A. O. Otis and R. T. Lennon, *Otis-Lennon Mental Ability Test* (New York: Harcourt Brace Jovanovich, 1967).

have the same age but are in different grades. The norms for grade groups are based on a sample of pupils who are at the same grade level but who are of different ages. A pupil's test score can be referenced to either or both norm groups. For pupils of average age for their grade level, the two norm-referenced scores will be quite close. Somewhat larger differences between the age group norm-referenced score and the grade group norm-referenced score will occur for pupils who are older or younger than the bulk of pupils at their grade level. For these pupils, there will be a tendency for their test score to be closer to the average test score of their *grade level* group than to the average test score of their *age* group. This comes about because the older or younger pupil's age group will tend to be concentrated at a grade level above or below the one in which this pupil is located. That is, two pupils, whether or not they are the same age, are more likely to get similar scores if they are in the same grade level than if they are in different grade levels. The publishers of the Otis-Lennon recommend that both norms be used to interpret a pupil's score. Besides DIQ scores, this test, like most others of its type, provides two other norm-referenced scores: percentile ranks and stanine scores.

While most omnibus tests provide only a single raw score, that is, a single number that can then be transformed into a variety of norm-referenced scores (DIQ's, percentile ranks, stanines, etc.), some tests of this type provide two subtest scores: verbal and nonverbal. Items are placed in one of the two subtests on the basis of whether they involve primarily the use of words or primarily the use of figures and numbers. In some cases such separate subtest scores can provide interesting and useful information. They may help to identify students whose lack of verbal facility is making them appear to have less ability than they actually have. One score may provide a check on the other. However, verbal and nonverbal scores are usually quite highly correlated, and for many students there is little difference between the two measures. It should also be recognized that nonverbal tests are actually dependent in certain respects on the student's verbal ability. Because the directions in almost all cases are given through the printed or spoken word, the student who has a weakness in verbal comprehension will be handicapped even on the nonverbal test. When verbal and nonverbal scores are compared as to their predictive validity for school subjects, the nonverbal scores are generally found to have somewhat lower correlations for most types of schoolwork. This is to be expected since most subjects are verbally oriented.

In contrast with the omnibus type of aptitude test, a few tests do in fact group items measuring the same ability into a subtest and provide for several subtest scores of separate mental abilities through the use of such subtests. These tests are generally referred to as *multiple aptitude batteries*. One such multiple aptitude battery is the Differential Aptitude Test[8] (DAT). The DAT

---

[8] G. K. Bennett, H. G. Seashore, and A. G. Wesman, *Differential Aptitude Tests* (New York: The Psychological Corporation, 1973).

is designed for use with students in grades eight through twelve. This multiple aptitude battery reports scores for eight subtests: Verbal Reasoning, Numerical Ability, Abstract Reasoning, Clerical Speed and Accuracy, Mechanical Reasoning, Space Relations, Spelling, and Language Usage. Since the DAT is a norm-referenced test, interpretation of the raw scores on each subtest is made through the use of percentile rank norms and stanine norms. The test publishers provide separate norms for fall and spring testing and also provide separate norms for boys and for girls.

The separation of norms for boys and for girls in order to interpret test scores reflects some of the problems inherent in norm-referenced testing that come about when a culture, a curriculum, or a vocational area are dominated by one group. In the past, for example, women have not dominated mechanical fields. Thus the lack of experience with mechanical things (at least those that appear on tests) has become characteristic of females as a group, even though this may not be true for specific individuals. As a result, boys and girls score differently on a test like the DAT's Mechanical Reasoning, and separate norms become necessary. The authors of the DAT say it this way:

> In counseling a girl who wishes to enter a mechanical field, her raw score on *Mechanical Reasoning* should be compared with the boys' norms for the same grade level. To indicate real promise in this field, she would need to score very high in relation to other girls. Assuming that she was tested in grade 10, in the fall semester, she would need to be at the 95th percentile for girls in order to equal the 75th percentile for boys. We may anticipate, however, that with the present day trend of girls showing interest in subjects and fields previously associated mainly with boys, the difference in scores obtained by the two sexes will gradually diminish.[9]

USING SCHOLASTIC APTITUDE TEST RESULTS

Scholastic aptitude test scores are easily misinterpreted and sometimes misused. They are not pure measures of innate ability or latent capacity. The foregoing discussion should have made it clear that aptitude tests attempt to measure what a person can do. They examine a person's capacity by measuring how he or she has used that capacity to learn certain things. The test items call for the student to display knowledge or abilities that the typical person has had the opportunity to acquire. As a result, performance on the test will depend on the environment in which the person has been raised and the experiences that he or she has had. Someone who has been raised in an impoverished environment or in an environment that differs to any extent from that of the majority of children will be handicapped as far as performance on the test is concerned. For example, it has been shown that children from slum areas of large cities, from isolated Indian reservations, and from families

[9] G. K. Bennett, H. G. Seashore, and A. G. Wesman, *Differential Aptitude Tests: Administrator's Handbook, Forms S and T* (New York: The Psychological Corporation, 1973), p. 52.

where a foreign language is the usual means of communication have higher abilities than their scores on aptitude tests would indicate. It might be said that the tests discriminate against such persons. However, to the extent that instruction is based on the assumption that children come to school with certain common background experiences that have a bearing on test performance, it would be more correct to say that society or the schools discriminate against such culturally different pupils. Efforts have been made to develop "culture-free" or "culture-fair" tests, but they have not been used very widely.

It should also be reemphasized that scholastic aptitude tests are intended to measure aptitude for typical schoolwork. Scores on these tests do not indicate aptitude for artistic tasks, creativity, social adaptability, or any of a great number of other abilities. They are measures of a limited type of aptitude—that required for predicting performance in tasks of an academic nature under relatively fixed instructional conditions. However, information on this type of aptitude can be very useful to the teacher if it is recognized for what it is and used properly.

THE MEANING OF APTITUDE TEST SCORES

The scholastic aptitude tests we have discussed in this chapter are norm-referenced tests. The meaning of the scores resulting from these tests comes from referencing the raw scores to specific groups and then reporting certain norm-referenced scores such as percentile ranks, deviation IQ scores, or stanines. As was stated in reference to Table 8.1 and in the discussion of the DAT, the meaning of these norm-referenced aptitude scores depends on the particular group to which they are referenced. Further, groups, as a reflection of social and cultural conditions, change over time. Frequent or periodic re-norming of a test results in redefining what is average for a group. While this process helps to keep the relative perspective of test performance in line with the current performance of a group, it should be recognized that there is a general tendency for groups as a whole to improve their performance over time due to improvement in education and in society generally. Thus, what is considered average by today's norms was usually above average several years ago.

The normal curve model is often used to obtain norm-referenced interpretations from aptitude tests. We have already discussed how percentile ranks and stanines relate to a normal curve (see pp. 90–93). Figure 8.2 is an example of how deviation IQ scores relate to a normal curve model.

In this section on the meaning of scholastic aptitude test scores, we have emphasized the norm-referenced character of such tests. This concern echoes that of the *Standards for Educational and Psychological Tests*[10] in its

---

[10] Joint Committee of the APA, AERA, and NCME. *Standards for Educational and Psychological Tests* (Washington, D.C.: American Psychological Association, Inc., 1974).

Figure 8.2

RELATIONSHIP AMONG OTIS-LENNON DIQS, PERCENTILE RANKS, AND STANINES

Verbal Description	Range of O-L DIQs	Range of %ile Ranks	Stanines	
Superior 4%	128 and above	96 and above	4%	9
Above Average 19%	120-127	89-95	7%	8
	112-119	77-88	12%	7
Average 54%	104-111	60-76	17%	6
	96-103	40-59	20%	5
	88-95	23-39	17%	4
Below Average 19%	80-87	11-22	12%	3
	72-79	4-10	7%	2
Low 4%	71 and below	Below 4	4%	1

Reproduced from the Otis-Lennon Mental Ability Test, Elementary II, Intermediate, and Advanced Levels, Forms J and K, Manual for Administration, copyright © 1967, by Harcourt Brace Jovanovich, Inc.. Reproduced by special permission of the publisher.

section on the interpretation of test scores. Among the points considered to be essential to the interpretation of test scores, the following are listed:

A test score should be interpreted as an estimate of performance under a given set of circumstances. It should not be interpreted as some absolute characteristic of the examinee or of something permanent and generalizable to all other circumstances [p. 68].

A test user should consider the total context of testing in interpreting an obtained score before making any decisions (including the decision to accept the score) [p. 68].

In general, test users should avoid the use of descriptive labels (e.g., retarded) applied to individuals when interpreting test scores [p. 69].

In norm-referenced interpretations, a test user should interpret an obtained score with reference to sets of norms appropriate for the individual tested and for the intended use [p. 70].

It is usually better to interpret scores with reference to a specified norm group in terms of percentile ranks or standard scores than to use terms like IQ or grade equivalents that may falsely imply a fully representative or national norms group [p. 70].

Test users should avoid the use of terms such as IQ, IQ equivalent, or grade equivalent where other terms provide more meaningful interpretations of a score [p. 70].

A test user should examine differences between characteristics of a person tested and those of the population on whom the test was developed or norms developed. His responsibility includes deciding whether the differences are so great that the test should not be used for that person [p. 71].

THE STABILITY OF SCHOLASTIC APTITUDE TEST SCORES

One question about scholastic aptitude test scores concerns the extent to which a person's score will remain constant over the years. There is some definite tendency toward constancy; that is, most persons maintain a somewhat stable level of relative aptitude for schoolwork throughout their school careers. This stability of aptitude scores is more characteristic of groups of individuals rather than of specific individuals. For specific individuals there are often large fluctuations in scores over time.

The stability of aptitude scores for groups is often interpreted to mean that scholastic aptitude is innate and fixed. However,

> group data on the constancy of the IQ . . . have often been misconstrued as supporting this interpretation. . . . The observed constancy of the IQ on such tests as the Stanford-Binet can be explained in terms of: (1) the cumulative nature of intellectual development, with the resulting overlap of intellectual skills tested at successive ages; (2) the fact that most children remain in the same general environment as they grow up; and (3) the influence of prerequisite intellectual skills on subsequent learning. Moreover, there is evidence that dramatic rises in IQ do in fact occur as a result of special educational programs and other environmental interventions.[11]

Several factors influence aptitude test scores so that we cannot expect an individual's score to be exactly the same from one testing to the next.

1. Even if a person's "true" aptitude test score did remain constant from one testing to the next, there would be some variation in measured aptitude due solely to the less-than-perfect reliability of the test. Often these differences in observed scores can be substantial.
2. If scores are obtained at two testings through the use of two different tests, we can expect some variation due to the differences in the

---

[11] A. Anastasi, *Psychological Testing, Third Edition* (New York: Macmillan, 1968), p. 565.

content of the tests and the differences in the composition of the norm groups through which the norm-referenced scores are obtained.

3. A third reason why a person's score might change from one occasion to the next is that the person may actually have changed. Previous sections have emphasized that performance on aptitude tests is affected by the background of the student and the type of experience he or she has had. A student who comes from a home life and general environment quite different from that of the typical family could be expected to be handicapped in taking an aptitude test upon first entering school. If, during the ensuing years, however, the home environment changes, or if the school environment is such as to provide an enrichment of background, the student's measured scholastic aptitude will probably increase. That is, with some students there will be significant changes in measured aptitude produced by fundamental changes in the culture to which the student is exposed.

In summary, a person's scholastic aptitude test scores may vary from one testing to the next solely on the basis of the unreliability of the scores or changes in the test being used. Variations due to unreliability, then, probably do not indicate any change in actual aptitude, and for the majority of persons changes over time will be only of a magnitude that can be attributed to unreliability. However, for some persons significant changes in the experiences to which they are exposed or in their physical or mental health may produce much larger shifts in measured aptitude.

SPECIFIC USES FOR SCHOLASTIC APTITUDE TESTS

Measures of scholastic aptitude may be useful to teachers in a variety of ways and at a number of stages in a pupil's career. In general such measures can be helpful whenever it is important to predict something about a pupil's potential for academic success in a relatively nonadaptive instructional setting.

The uses of scholastic aptitude tests, like the uses of all tests, must be integrated into the overall instructional program and must be evaluated in a decision context. The uses to which scholastic aptitude tests are to be put need to be clearly specified before such tests are employed. In this way, the tests can be validated *for these uses* in the local decision context in which they are employed. A rather prominent use of scholastic aptitude tests in the past has been to group pupils for the purpose of instruction. The assumptions underlying this practice are, first of all, that students learn better when taught in groups of homogeneous ability and, second, that groups of homogeneous ability can in fact be formed.[12] Both of these assumptions have failed to be supported by empirical evidence.

---

[12] R. W. Tyler, "Using Tests in Grouping Students for Instruction." In R. W. Tyler and R. M. Wolf, eds., *Critical Issues in Testing* (Berkeley, Calif.: McCutchan Publishing Corporation, 1974), pp. 65–69.

Thus, it appears that the usual ways in which test results are employed to group students for instruction neither produce homogeneous groups nor greatly increase student learning. Furthermore, ability grouping is now under attack by those seeking to eliminate school segregation. They point out that as children from different racial and ethnic groups are enrolled in the same school, they are assigned to segregated classrooms on the basis of test results. In this way the effort to facilitate social interaction among racial and ethnic groups is thwarted by the separation of children into different tracks or so-called ability groups.[13]

As pupils progress through school, teachers at all grade levels will find it helpful to know something about their academic aptitudes. Considerable information will be provided by their records of achievement, by their grades, and by their scores on achievement tests. However, in some cases a record of past achievement is not a true indicator of a student's aptitude, and the teacher who wishes to be certain of helping the student to work to capacity may find scholastic aptitude test results a useful source of supplementary information.

An anecdote may serve to illustrate how scholastic aptitude tests might be useful for opening opportunities for some students. The son of one of the authors has a severe congenital hearing loss. The usual educational decision for pupils with this magnitude of hearing loss would result in placement in either a separate special education class or, perhaps, in a residential facility for deaf students. By administering several standardized scholastic aptitude tests (both verbal and nonverbal), it was estimated that this boy was "extremely bright" despite his below average performance on verbal tests. This information, coupled with the parents' insistence and persistence, enabled the boy to be admitted into the public school in a standard classroom. This has been most beneficial to him and he is doing quite well. When this is viewed relative to other pupils with similar hearing losses, his educational progress seems truly amazing.

Anecdotes, however, do not serve as proof for the validity of scholastic aptitude tests for specific educational decisions. Many anecdotes could be cited to illustrate the opposite point—students who could have succeeded but were either denied the opportunity and therefore never did succeed, or those who through determination succeeded in spite of the insistence of others that they could not.

In the junior high and high school years scores from aptitude tests are useful to the teacher and guidance counselor in assisting the student to make career decisions. By this time students who have been enrolled in typical school systems will have taken scholastic aptitude tests at three or four points during their school careers. These records of aptitude test results together with their records of achievement can provide some indication of students' chances for success in specialized types of courses in high school, in various

---

13 Ibid., p. 67.

types of post–high school study, and in different occupations and professions. This information should be weighted together with interests and other factors in making career plans and decisions.

Other Aptitude Tests

Although tests of general scholastic aptitude are much more widely used than any other type of aptitude test, certain other tests are used often and should be mentioned here. These include readiness tests and tests of aptitude for specific subjects.

READINESS TESTS

First-grade teachers frequently find tests of reading readiness or of *general readiness* for school instruction useful supplements in providing information about pupils. Although scholastic aptitude tests can be used to predict reading achievement, instruments that are specifically constructed as reading-readiness tests can focus attention more directly toward skills prerequisite to learning to read. One popular test, the Metropolitan Readiness Tests, has six subtests:

Test 1. Word Meaning, a 16-item picture vocabulary test. The pupil selects from three pictures the one that illustrates the word the examiner names.

Test 2. Listening, a 16-item test of ability to comprehend phrases and sentences instead of individual words. The pupil selects from three pictures the one which portrays a situation or event the examiner describes briefly.

Test 3. Matching, a 14-item test of visual perception involving the recognition of similarities. The pupil marks one of three pictures which matches a given picture.

Test 4. Alphabet, a 16-item test of ability to recognize lower-case letters of the alphabet. The pupil chooses a named letter from among four alternatives.

Test 5. Numbers, a 26-item test of number knowledge.

Test 6. Copying, a 14-item test which measures a combination of visual perception and motor control.[14]

The content of these subtests was derived from the test authors' broader logical analysis of the important components of the construct of first-grade readiness. However, the contents specifically included in the subtests do not necessarily have a direct correspondence to the general conception of readiness. The subtest content represents a narrower definition of readiness and

---

[14] G. H. Hildreth, N. L. Griffiths, and M. E. McGauvran, *Metropolitan Readiness Tests: Manual of Directions* (New York: Harcourt Brace Jovanovich, 1969), p. 2.

cannot form the basis for the development of a complete readiness curriculum such as might be desired for kindergarten. Thus, although there is a correlation between beginning-of-year readiness scores and end-of-year achievement test scores, no causal relationship can be inferred between the test performance and end-of-year success.

> For example, knowledge of the lower-case letters of the alphabet may not be necessary for learning to read under certain methods of instruction, but scores on Test 4, Alphabet, may serve as reflections of the child's early home environment, an important factor in his readiness. Note that . . . Table 8 [of the manual] shows the Alphabet subtest to have the highest correlation with end-of-the-year reading achievement.[15]

This example of a readiness test points out the need for the professional teacher to be careful in the interpretation of the correlation coefficients that are reported as validity evidence for readiness and other tests. If one were to proceed on the assumption that knowledge of the names of the letters of the alphabet was causally related to learning to read, one would erroneously postpone beginning reading instruction for pupils who did not have such knowledge. If beginning reading instruction were based on a method that taught the pupil the *sounds* of the graphemes and how to *blend* these sounds into words, knowledge of the *names* of the individual letters need not be a prerequisite to beginning to read.

Although we have used the Metropolitan Readiness Tests as an illustration here, there are several other tests that are available for either general readiness or reading readiness specifically. Each test is based on its author's own point of view about what constitutes readiness. The professional teacher should study these tests carefully before selecting one for use. In particular, the teacher should consider the uses to be made of the test scores and whether the tests provide evidence for the validity of the scores for such uses.

One way to consider readiness tests is to ask if they can function as placement tests rather than selection tests. Can the test score offer help in the decision about the particular method by which pupils should be given reading (or arithmetic) instruction? Or, can the test scores help in the decision about the type of remedial instruction pupils need that, when combined with the regular reading (or arithmetic) instruction, will lead to higher achievement for these pupils? Schools are not free to select which pupils should be taught to read or to do arithmetic. Rather, they are mandated to teach these skills to all pupils who enroll.

A useful way of examining the concept of readiness is to consider the skills prerequisite for success in the particular instructional method that is used in a school. These prerequisites are derived from an analysis of not only the tasks that have to be learned but also the method by which they will be taught. Pupils who score low on tests of particular prerequisites should do better when instructed specifically on these particular prerequisites (as well

---

[15] Ibid., p. 15.

as being given the regular instruction, either concurrently or subsequently) than similarly low-scoring pupils who have been given only the regular instruction. A truly useful readiness test would be one that provided scores that served this purpose of indicating effective remedial procedures. The important point here is that the concept of readiness seems to affirm that pupils who are "not ready" can be made "ready" through specific remedial instruction. If readiness tests are to be useful in this process of making students "ready," then decisions about remedial instruction made on the basis of these test scores need to be validated. This is done by determining whether the remedial instruction given to pupils, which the test scores "said" they needed, in fact improved the pupils' performance on the final criterion (e.g., reading performance or arithmetic performance). Correlation coefficients between beginning-of-year readiness test scores and end-of-year achievement test scores do not provide strong evidence that readiness tests can be used to prescribe specific remedial instruction.

TESTS OF APTITUDE FOR SPECIFIC SUBJECTS

Traditionally, instructional methods in specific courses have been relatively fixed, especially at the high school and post–high school levels. Thus, for example, there has been one way that a given school (or a given teacher) teaches the content of the Algebra I course. If all pupils in a school are taught Algebra I by this method, some will do well and some will do poorly. The solution to this problem has been to try to predict which students will not do well in the course and to encourage them to enroll in another course, such as a different kind of mathematics (for example, general mathematics).

In this context, the mathematics instruction is viewed as a fixed procedure. Some pupils will learn under this procedure. Those who cannot are advised to learn something else. This, of course, is not the adaptive instructional approach we described at the beginning of this chapter.

In the context of fixed instruction, such questions as the following will be raised: Can this student be expected to master a foreign language? Does this student have the aptitude needed in typing and shorthand? Should this student enroll in algebra or should the student be encouraged to take a general mathematics course? To help answer these questions, the student's record in related courses that have already been taken will be useful, but a test of aptitude for the specific subject may also be of considerable help.

One interesting test of aptitude for specific subject areas is the *Modern Language Aptitude Test* (MLAT).[16] This test is clearly designed to serve as a selection test. The complete test consists of five parts that are administered with the help of a tape recorder: (1) Number Learning, (2) Phonetic Script, (3) Spelling Clues, (4) Words in Sentences, and (5) Paired Associates. The

---

[16] J. B. Carroll and S. M. Sapon, *Modern Language Aptitude Test* (New York: The Psychological Corporation, 1959).

first two parts test the examinee's ability to learn numbers that are orally presented and to learn correspondences between sounds and printed words, both of which are presented via the tape recorder in an artificial language. In part three the student is presented with an approximate phonetic spelling of an English word and asked to find an English synonym for the word from among several options. Part four deals with English grammatical structure, requiring the examinee to select a word in a sentence that has the same function as words in another sentence. In part five, the examinee is given time to study pairs of words where one member of the pair is English. After two minutes the examinees are tested on how well they have learned these pairs. The MLAT is designed for high school and college students and adults. An elementary school version has been developed also.

The use of this special subject-matter aptitude test for selection decisions is described by its authors in this way:

> The MLAT does *not* predict *whether* an individual can learn a foreign language if he is given enough time and opportunity to do so; what it *does* predict is how well he can learn a foreign language in typical foreign language courses in the usually allotted time. The use of the MLAT in selecting students for foreign language courses, therefore, is based on the premise that only students with reasonable promise of rapid learning and success at a high level of proficiency are worth the time and expense of training. This premise will hold true for many situations in the government, in industry and business, and in education, particularly where individuals are being trained in a foreign language with a view to immediate practical use.[17]

Its authors also feel that the test may be useful in helping to diagnose the particular learning difficulties that the student may have when studying a foreign language.

> Thus, low scores on Part II tend to mean that the individual will have difficulty learning the phonology (sound system) of a foreign language and also difficulty in mimicking spoken sentences accurately. Low scores on Part IV probably mean . . . difficulty in learning the grammar and structure of the foreign language, and low scores on Part V may suggest that the individual may have to spend more time with the rote memory aspects of learning a foreign language.[18]

Although we have briefly considered only the MLAT in this section, a number of tests for aptitudes for specific subject areas have been developed. The manuals for these tests present validity data indicating how scores correlate with a variety of measures of achievement. The school or the individual teacher using any of these instruments should make a study of how valid it is in the *local situation*. In some cases they have been found to be quite valid as predictors of success. In many situations, however, they have

---

[17] J. B. Carroll and S. M. Sapon, *Modern Language Aptitude Test: Manual (1959 Edition)* (New York: The Psychological Corporation, 1959), p. 20.

[18] Ibid.

been found to be no more useful than the already available measures of general scholastic aptitude or achievement.

Summary

Aptitude tests have been found to be of greatest use in selection situations. Whether schools should operate as selection situations is very much an open philosophical issue. The trend appears to be away from selection and toward placement, that is, providing optimum educational opportunity for all pupils regardless of their general scholastic aptitudes. This chapter has discussed the general area of scholastic aptitude in this context.

Among the most widely used measures of aptitude are the tests of general scholastic aptitude. Such tests include both individual and group tests. Some of these tests yield a total test score that is referenced to norms through the use of deviation IQ scores, percentile ranks, or stanines. Others yield both verbal and nonverbal scores that are then referenced to norms, while still others provide scores for a number of separate abilities. Which instruments are most valuable as sources of information for decision-making can be investigated by a study of the validity and reliability data published with the tests and by interpretation of these data in terms of the explicitly stated purposes for which test information will be used in the local situation. Final answers to this question can be obtained only after the test has been used and the validity of the scores for the local situation and decision context has been determined.

In addition to general scholastic aptitude tests, certain other aptitude tests may be used in the schools. These include readiness tests, tests of aptitude for specific subjects, and aptitude test batteries. The same cautions offered with respect to the use of general scholastic aptitude tests are also applicable to the use of these instruments. It is important to remember that all of these tests measure only a limited aspect of a student's developed ability and that many other sources of information must be given equal consideration.

It must be remembered that aptitude tests are developed on the basis of the assumption that the individuals being tested have had common experiences and, thus, they test what these individuals have learned from these common experiences. Further, aptitude test scores derive their meaning from norm-referenced interpretations. To the extent to which a given pupil does not have the common experiences and opportunities assumed by the tests, to that extent will the norm-referenced interpretation of the test score be misleading unless such factors are taken into account. While test abuses are not restricted to aptitude tests, these abuses tend to occur much more frequently in the aptitude area. Therefore, the professional teacher will make every effort to guard against erroneous test interpretation and use. If aptitude tests are to be used and discussed by teachers, then there is a professional and ethical obligation to acquire the technical knowledge and skill needed to understand the evidence supporting the claims made by test publishers in their manuals and other literature.

SUGGESTIONS FOR CLASS DISCUSSION AND FURTHER INVESTIGATION

1. Study the manuals for several tests of scholastic aptitude, giving particular attention to the purposes and uses of the test scores claimed by the tests' publishers.* Check the manuals carefully to see if there are data presented that validate these claimed purposes and usages. What evidence would you have to provide in order for these same purposes and usages to be validated in a local school system? What other types of data might be helpful to you if you were considering using one of these tests?

2. Make a careful study of the content of the test items of a given test of general scholastic aptitude. Where would an examinee have acquired the abilities required by these items? What types of background and experience might handicap an examinee in making a good score on this test? What types would give him or her an advantage?

3. In Chapter 6, construct validation was discussed. Review your answer to Questions 1 and 2 above in light of the notions of test score interpretations discussed in connection with construct validation. Propose counter-hypotheses to explain why your interpretations of test scores in Questions 1 and 2 might be erroneous. Then describe the kinds of studies and the kinds of empirical evidence resulting from these studies that would refute or support these counter-hypotheses. Finally, reexamine the test manuals to see if these studies have been done and if there is any evidence to support or refute your counter-hypotheses.

4. All members of the class should give their own definitions of *intelligence* and *scholastic aptitude*. Discuss what each person's definitions mean in terms as precise as possible. How many different definitions for each term has the class given? If most students give different definitions, what problems might one expect them to have in communications involving these terms? What problems would arise when different persons talk about a pupil's potential success in school?

5. Review the statement by Goslin that was cited in Chapter 5. Discuss his findings in light of your own experiences concerning decisions made about pupils. Does the class agree with his findings?

6. Review the citations from the *Standards for Educational and Psychological Tests* that were presented in this chapter. Discuss these in class in light of your answers to Questions 1 through 5 above.

7. Analyze a unit of instruction in terms of the behaviors to be learned and what additional behaviors are required of the student by the way in which

---

* See the footnotes on pages 152 and 165. Your instructor or school administrator may have to countersign your order.

the unit is to be taught. In your analysis of the way in which the student is to be taught make no assumptions about the pupil. Rather, consider the situation in which there is an instructor and a pupil and certain behaviors to be learned. What is the first thing the pupil has to do? The next? and so on; all of this in light of the method of instruction that you are using. Review your list of additional behaviors required of the student and determine the kinds of abilities and prerequisites that your method of instruction requires of each pupil. Discuss your findings with regard to the readiness testing ideas presented in this chapter and also in terms of how different instructional methods could be used to adapt to pupil differences in these abilities and prerequisites.

SUGGESTIONS FOR FURTHER READING

Rather complete discussions of various types of scholastic aptitude and specialized aptitude and specialized aptitude tests are found in these widely used texts: Anne Anastasi, *Psychological Testing, Third Edition* (New York: Macmillan, 1968) and Lee J. Cronbach, *Essentials of Psychological Testing, Third Edition* (New York: Harper & Row, 1970).

A useful discussion of the assumptions and rationales behind the use of prediction tests of aptitude is found in Paul A. Schwarz, "Prediction Instruments for Educational Outcomes," chapter 11 in R. L. Thorndike, ed., *Educational Measurement, Second Edition* (Washington, D.C.: American Council on Education, 1971), pp. 303–31.

A discussion of selection testings and placement testing in a decision-making context and the problems inherent in these procedures is found in a number of sources, one of which is John R. Hills, "Use of Measurement in Selection and Placement," chapter 19 in R. L. Thorndike, *Educational Measurement, Second Edition* (Washington, D.C.: American Council on Education, 1971), pp. 680–729.

The teacher would also benefit from reading a copy of the *Standards for Educational and Psychological Tests* (Washington, D.C.: American Psychological Association, 1974).

Essential materials for study with this chapter are tests and manuals for a number of group-administered scholastic aptitude, special aptitude, and readiness tests. These can be secured from a school's test library or by ordering specimen sets from the publisher. (See the footnotes on pp. 152 and 165.) In reviewing such materials the reader should also have available the *Mental Measurements Yearbooks* edited by Oscar K. Buros listed at the end of Chapter 7.

9

Testing and Evaluation in the Individualization of Instruction

Jan Miller was completing her first year as a third-grade teacher. She felt that teaching had been challenging and that she had learned quite a bit. However, she was planning to do some things differently next year and was looking forward to doing some work on this during the summer. In reviewing her pupils' end-of-year achievement, she was impressed by the need for giving greater attention to the individual differences in ability and interest. When Jan spoke to her principal about her desire to try to individualize instruction, it was arranged for her to visit classes in two neighboring school districts where people were working on this problem.

In the classroom that she visited in the first district, Jan saw a teacher using a plan of individualized assignments. Each pupil appeared to be working at a different point in the curriculum and was following an individual assignment which told what he or she should be studying. Jan noted that most students seemed to be working quite independently with only occasional help from the teacher. A few students appeared to require more frequent assistance. At one point the teacher had five students, who seemed to be having the same kind of difficulty, gather around the chalkboard while a

*particular process was explained to them. When Jan asked the teacher
how each pupil's assignment was developed, the teacher showed her
some of the tests used to diagnose pupil needs and a variety of
evaluation devices used to assess progress.*

*In the second school district Jan visited a class that was
described to her as an "open classroom." Here she noted that several
pairs or small groups of three or four students were working on
projects. However, many students were studying quite independently,
and Jan saw that they were working with such things as arithmetic
textbooks, workbooks, science texts, encyclopedias, and other
reference books. When she asked how these pupils knew what to
study, Jan was told that this was worked out in teacher-pupil
conferences. The teacher further explained that the pupils studying
independently were trying to develop specific skills or acquire a type
of knowledge that they had found essential for proceeding with work
on projects. When a student came to the teacher with the question
"How can I learn this?" they sat down together and worked out
a plan of study that would meet that student's needs. They made
use of a special set of diagnostic tests that helped the student
determine where to start studying. This set of tests was also
of help in keeping a record that permitted both pupil and teacher to
see how the pupil was progressing in acquiring certain basic study
skills.*

The resolve of our third-grade teacher, Jan Miller, to take steps to individualize instruction is probably shared to some degree by most teachers and
prospective teachers. But how does one go from this type of expressed desire to the actual establishment of learning situations such as those described
in our two hypothetical classrooms? As most teachers will affirm, such situations are not easy to achieve. Teachers know how to handle group instruction, how to explain something to the class, how to make a common
assignment, how to maintain some type of control of the total group. But how
can you arrange and manage a classroom situation where each pupil is doing
something different?

Under the general approach to instruction and evaluation that has been
outlined in this book the basic demands for group instruction and individualized instruction are the same. Basic to the operation of both types of instruction is valid and usable information for instructional decision-making.
The differences are in the types of instruments needed for this purpose and in
the structure within which the instruments are used.

A FRAMEWORK FOR INDIVIDUALIZING INSTRUCTION

In outlining the role of evaluation in individualizing instruction, we will center attention on those situations where the concern is for pupil acquisition of

specific skills or understandings that are a part of some organized body of knowledge: for example, principles and procedures for certain aspects of science, reading skills, and skills and understandings in arithmetic. Individualized instruction would seem to be most appropriate in such areas. For many other types of school learning group activities are probably best.

The procedures to be outlined here should be appropriate for any situation in which the pupil is to acquire certain specific abilities. It may be that individual pupils have decided that they need to learn certain things, or it may be that what they are to learn is dictated largely by the curriculum sequence of the school system. The teacher in the "open classroom," faced by pupils asking for assistance in their independent study of particular skills, has much in common with the teacher attempting to individualize instruction in a school with a mandated curriculum content. Their common concerns include the following:

1. Establishing effective sequences of prerequisites
2. Determining what the pupil already knows in the relevant part of a given sequence and what he or she would study next
3. Helping the pupil to secure relevant study materials
4. Assisting the pupil in the study of relevant materials
5. Guiding pupil progress from skill to skill and unit to unit

What is required, then, is material that can help the teacher carry out these tasks. Note that these basic concerns are related to the major aspects of a program for testing and evaluation that have been emphasized throughout this book: identifying and sequencing objectives, developing diagnostic tests, obtaining criterion-referenced information, relating test results to specific instructional activities, and evaluating pupil progress on a continuing basis.

It will help the reader see how the above tasks can be carried out to examine, in some detail, one specific procedure for accomplishing a certain type of individualized instruction. The example used here will be the mathematics curriculum for Individually Prescribed Instruction (IPI). Although other programs could be used equally well for this purpose, the authors have chosen IPI because of their personal involvement in the development of this program.

It should be emphasized that the IPI program is one that has been developed over a period of several years by a relatively large staff and with a considerable financial investment. It is not representative of a program that could be developed by an individual teacher or even by a single school. However, the IPI program does provide a specific example of the type of testing program needed for this form of individualized instruction. The example should be useful, therefore, in illustrating the many purposes that can be served by tests in the management of an individualized system. After this specific procedure has been described, attention will be given to possible modifications in this system that would permit a teacher to develop a local program serving some of the same purposes.

Individually Prescribed
Instruction (IPI)[1]

Individually Prescribed Instruction (IPI) is a procedure that has been applied in the development of a program for individualizing instruction in mathematics and in certain other subjects in the elementary school. Since the IPI Mathematics program is the one that has been developed most completely and used most widely, the examples of program components will be taken from it.

The IPI Math curriculum is defined by carefully specified sequences of instructional objectives organized by topics and units. Each pupil is permitted to work through these sequences and units at a pace determined by his or her own ability and interest. For each objective there are clearly identified instructional materials and learning procedures with which the pupil can, largely through independent study, acquire the specified ability. Just what the individual students use in their study for given objectives is spelled out in their individualized lesson plans or "prescriptions" for those objectives.

An idea as to the overall organization of the IPI Math objectives can be gained from Figure 9.1. Shown here are ten basic topics in mathematics, each of which is studied at successively higher levels of the curriculum. Each of the levels, A through G, can be considered comparable to a grade level to the extent that students typically complete the work on all topics at one level before they move on to the next. Of course, not all topics are appropriate for instruction at the lowest (A) or the highest (G) levels, but once a topic is introduced it is studied again at successive levels until all its prescribed units have been covered. In the IPI curriculum the set of objectives for a given topic at a given level (for example, Level D, Numeration and Place Value) constitute a *unit*. The specific objectives included in four such units are shown in Table 9.1.

PROCEDURES USED IN OPERATING
AN IPI CLASSROOM

Typical use of the IPI curriculum to individualize instruction may be outlined by the following steps.

1. At the start of the school year all students are given a placement test to determine their levels of mastery in each topic. The results for one pupil might be something like those summarized in the *student profile* shown

---

[1] See C. M. Lindvall and John O. Bolvin, "Programed Instruction in the Schools: An Application of Programing Principles in Individually Prescribed Instruction," *Programed Instruction,* 66th Yearbook NSSE, Part II (University of Chicago Press, 1969), pp. 156–88.

Figure 9.1

SIMPLIFIED STRUCTURE OF IPI MATHEMATICS CURRICULUM SHOWING NUMBER OF OBJECTIVES FOR EACH TOPIC AT EACH LEVEL

Topic	A	B	C	D	E	F	G
Numeration/Place Value	15	9	14	5	6	7	4
Addition/Subtraction	17	12	13	10	4	4	6
Multiplication		4	7	9	7	4	3
Division		3	4	7	9	5	6
Fractions	3	3	6	7	11	8	8
Money	1	1	5	5			
Time	1	3	6	4	4	2	
Systems of Measurement		3	6	6	5	5	6
Geometry		3	2	4	6	4	2
Applications		3	8	9	5	4	6

(column header above: Level)

From "IPI Mathematics Continuum Chart" (New Century Education Corporation, 1972). (Developed by Research for Better Schools, Inc., Philadelphia, Pa., and Learning Research and Development Center, Pittsburgh, Pa.) Used by permission.

Table 9.1

INSTRUCTIONAL OBJECTIVES FOR FOUR UNITS IN THE IPI MATHEMATICS CURRICULUM

Level D	Level E

Numeration/Place Value

Level D

1. Completes statements to show that ten ones equal one ten, ten tens equal one hundred, or ten hundreds equal one thousand.
2. Identifies the place-value of a specified digit or writes the digit that is in a specified place. (0–9,999)
3. Writes numerals in short sequences to show counting by ones, fives, tens, or hundreds. (0–9,999)
4. Rounds a number to the nearest ten or hundred. (0–9,999)
5. Writes the standard numeral for a roman numeral. (0–2,000)

Level E

1. Writes the place value name of a specified digit or writes the name of the period of a specified group of three digits. (0–999,999,999)
2. Writes the numeral name for a standard numeral. (0–999,999,999)
3. Writes numerals in short sequences to show counting by ones. (0–999,-999)
4. Writes >, <, or = between two numbers. (0–1,000,000)
5. Writes the number of groups of one thousand, one hundred, ten, or one that are in a number. (0–9,999)
6. Rounds a number to the nearest thousand, ten thousand, or hundred thousand. (0–999,999)

Addition/Subtraction

1. Writes the missing sum or addend in an addition or subtraction sentence. (Sums to 99)
2. Writes the expanded notation for a standard numeral or the standard numeral for an expanded notation. (0–9,999)
3. Adds two numbers and checks using the cummutative property. (Addends 0–99)
4. Adds two numbers. Addends 0–999)

5. Adds as many as four numbers. (Addends 0–999)
6. Adds as many as four numbers. (Addends 0–9,999)
7. Subtracts with no regrouping of hundreds or thousands. (Sums to 9,999)
8. Writes the expanded notation for a standard numeral and renames it by regrouping from one specified place to another. (0–9,999)
9. Subtracts with regrouping in any place. (Sums to 9,999)
10. Adds two numbers and checks by subtracting. (Addends 0–9,999) Subtracts and checks by adding. (Sums to 9,999)

1. Adds or subtracts. (2 addends 0–999,999)
2. Adds four or five numbers listed vertically or horizontally. (Addends 0–9,999)
3. Adds or subtracts to solve a one-step word problem. (2–5 addends 0–999,999; sums to 999,999)
4. Adds and subtracts to solve a one-step word problem. (2–4 addends 0–9,999; sums to 999,999)

From "IPI Mathematics Continuum Chart" (New Century Education Corporation, 1972). (Developed by Research for Better Schools, Inc., Philadelphia, Pa., and Learning Research and Development Center, Pittsburgh, Pa.) Used by permission.

in Figure 9.2. Here the cross-hatched cells identify the units this student mastered on the Level D Placement Test.

2. On the basis of the placement test results a decision is made as to which unit the student should study first. In the case of the results shown above, the student might well be assigned to D-level Addition/Subtraction.

3. Before starting work in this first unit the pupil takes the unit pretest. This is a diagnostic test that tells the pupil and the teacher something about the pupil's degree of mastery of each objective in the unit. Because of the limited number of items that can be devoted to any one unit, the placement test provides information only on the pupil's overall mastery of the basic ability taught in each unit. The unit pretest, however, is long enough to yield a separate score for each objective. Let us assume that our hypothetical

Figure 9.2

STUDENT PROFILE USED IN RECORDING RESULTS
FROM IPI PLACEMENT TESTS

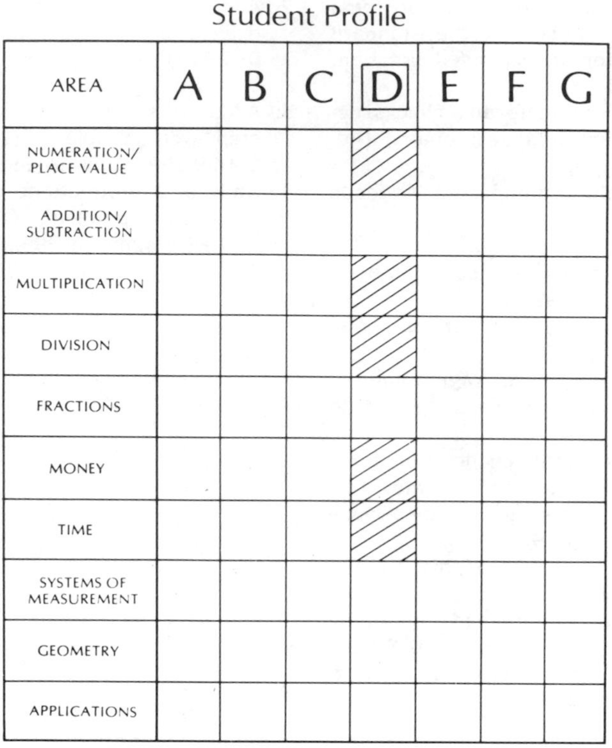

Student Profile

AREA	A	B	C	D	E	F	G
NUMERATION/ PLACE VALUE				▨			
ADDITION/ SUBTRACTION							
MULTIPLICATION				▨			
DIVISION				▨			
FRACTIONS							
MONEY				▨			
TIME				▨			
SYSTEMS OF MEASUREMENT							
GEOMETRY							
APPLICATIONS							

From "Placement Test–D," IPI Mathematics (New Century Education Corporation, 1972). (Developed by Research for Better Schools, Inc., and Learning Research and Development Center.) Used with permission.

student took the D-level Addition/Subtraction pretest and earned the following scores on each objective.

Objective	% Correct
1	100
2	100
3	100
4	100
5	90
6	88
7	22
8	67
9	44
10	20

In this case the pupil probably would not work on Objectives 1 through 6 but would be expected to study the last four objectives and would probably first be prescribed work in Objective 7. (By examining the objectives for this unit as they are listed in Table 9.1, one can see that this pupil's difficulties are in subtraction.)

4. The pupil's work on a given objective is outlined in a *prescription* telling exactly what lesson materials should facilitate mastery of the objective. This prescription may be developed by the teacher or by the pupil, depending upon the pupil's grade level and how the teacher chooses to operate the system. In actual IPI operation the prescription is outlined by means of a special form on which the numbers of the lesson pages to be used are simply listed. It is also noted on the form whether the pupil is to work alone, with one other pupil, in a small group, or with direct teacher instruction. The final item in a prescription calls for the pupil to take a *curriculum-embedded test* (CET), which is a brief quiz assessing mastery of the objective. A pupil who passes this test will move on to the next objective. A pupil who fails will be given more work on this current objective and then will be given the CET again.

5. The pupil who has studied and passed CET's for all the objectives prescribed in a given unit is given a unit posttest. This is an alternate version of the unit pretest and provides a separate score on each objective in the unit. A posttest will show the extent to which the student has retained each skill learned in the unit and, therefore, how ready he or she is to move on to another unit.

6. The student who fails the subtest on any objective on the posttest engages in further study on that objective and then takes a second posttest. When the student passes all such subtests, he or she begins work on the next unit by taking the appropriate pretest and repeating the process outlined in the foregoing steps.

The steps presented above provide a bare outline of what is involved in the individualization of instruction as provided under the IPI procedure. There are, of course, many ways in which a skilled teacher can use this framework to achieve further individualization.

Perhaps the most important aspects of any program for individualized instruction are those contributed by the teacher on the basis of informal knowledge of pupil interests, abilities, and needs for personal attention. However, a successful program must provide a framework that involves a rather systematic and structured procedure for adapting to the more obvious individual characteristics of each student and thereby frees the teacher to think about other more personal contacts that may be necessary. And it is the lack of this structure that is the typical barrier to the individualization of instruction. It is probably safe to say that most teachers have more ideas about how to individualize the classroom than they are ever able to implement, merely because keeping a classroom "running" requires all their time and attention. It is only when a system is established that rather automatically takes care of the simpler demands of individual differences and that places major responsibility on the students for managing their own programs that the teacher is free to implement the more sophisticated tools of individualization of instruction.

In most systems having this necessary structure, testing and evaluation play a key role. For a fuller understanding of this role let us reexamine the IPI testing program in more detail and also consider some variations that might make the general procedure applicable in many other situations.

THE ROLE OF TESTING AND EVALUATION IN IPI

The purposes served by testing in the IPI program can be outlined in terms of four major roles.

1. *Placement Testing*—The general purpose of placement testing is to determine where a student should start studying with respect to an organized framework of content. In the IPI Mathematics program this framework is provided by the units of study, identified by topic and level, as shown in Figure 9.1. Some framework of this general type is essential to placement of pupils. Information must be available about each student that says "This student has mastered this topic up to this level." Such information can be obtained only with reference to a structure that defines a sequence of abilities —each prerequisite for the next—within subject and topic. Tests used to place pupils within such sequences must be *criterion-referenced*. For each student they should tell us "The student has mastered these units but not those." The IPI placement test is this type of test. It consists of subtests for each unit designed to tell whether or not the pupil has mastered that unit. Here it is not relevant to know a student's percentile rank, grade-equivalent, or any other "norm-referenced" score. We do not wish to know where the student ranks in comparison with other students. We must know where he or she stands in relationship to a continuum of abilities or objectives, that is, to a criterion. In IPI the sequential ordering of the units over levels provides this continuum, and the "criterion-referenced" information provided by a placement test is of the type that says "This student has mastery of all addition and subtraction units up through Level C but does not have mastery of any units in these topics above that level." Information of this type would appear to be essential to the task of starting each pupil in the curriculum at that point appropriate for his or her individual abilities.

Of course, placement may also involve the use of other data. For example, the teacher may place students showing marginal mastery of a given unit in the next unit if their aptitude or intelligence test scores are relatively high but may place them in the given unit if such scores are low. That is, it is assumed that a pupil with high scholastic aptitude will be able to make progress in a unit even though his or her mastery of prerequisite skills is only marginal but that the low-aptitude student, under the same conditions, will find progress difficult. Similar decisions may also be made on the basis of knowledge of past performance at lower levels in the topic.

2. *Diagnostic Testing*—A program of individualized instruction requires the periodic diagnosis of each student's capabilities and needs. One instrument that is used for this purpose under the IPI procedure is the unit pretest. Diagnosis using this type of test is carried out whenever a student starts a new unit. As has been pointed out, the unit pretest is made up of a number of subtests, one for each objective in the unit, and the report from such testing tells which objectives the student has and has not mastered. Again, this is "criterion-referenced" information. Also, it is basic and essential diagnostic information since it says "This student needs to study these objectives but does not need to study these." In addition, within the structure of the IPI program, it is highly useful diagnostic information because a teacher who knows that, for example, a student needs to study Objective 7 in Level D addition and subtraction knows what kinds of study materials should be given to the student. This is true because all study materials are clearly and specifically referenced to the objective that they teach. Because of this provision of the system, diagnostic test results have clear-cut implications for what the student should study. In other words, diagnosis leads directly to prescription. This would seem to be an essential quality of diagnostic testing in a workable model for individualized instruction.

Present IPI pretests measure the extent to which a student already has mastery of the objectives in the unit that the student is about to enter. It might be useful to have such tests also measure the pupil's mastery of certain key abilities that are immediately prerequisite to objectives within this unit. This would be further useful diagnostic information. In the IPI program it is assumed that the organization of the curriculum into a sequence of prerequisites guarantees that a student who has mastered everything preceding a given unit will have the abilities prerequisite for studying that unit. However, this may or may not be a valid assumption, depending upon the extent to which individual students retain what they have previously learned.

Diagnosis probably should take other measures into account. Certain scores on standardized tests may yield important information concerning students studying in a program such as IPI. Knowledge of a student's reading rate and reading comprehension scores may suggest that he or she should be given lesson materials requiring less reading, for example. The student's scores on subtests of study skills may suggest other prescriptions. Personal knowledge of the individual's study habits may also result in differing prescriptions. The slow student might be given fewer practice exercises than the fast student. (Of course, there will certainly be cases in which the teacher will judge that a slow student, though thorough, needs more speed, and that a fast student, if careless or superficial, needs to slow down and be more thoughtful.)

For this reason, important pupil evaluation data for systems of individualized instruction may include anecdotal records or rating scale data that are kept in each pupil's file and updated on a regular basis.

3. *Unit Posttesting*—The IPI program uses the pupil's performance on lessons and on the CET for each objective as a check on progress, but it also uses more comprehensive tests that cover a total unit to yield another type of check on progress and to provide a basis for decisions regarding the pupil's future direction within the curriculum. In an individualized system of the type represented by IPI, the key to regular progression on the part of every student is the organization of the curriculum in terms of relatively small steps represented by the sequenced objectives. These small steps permit the pupil to move from one objective to the next with a minimum of direct teacher instruction, a necessary aspect of an efficient individualized program. However, effective learning cannot consist only of this step-by-step progression through a series of discrete skills. It also requires some organizing of these skills into more meaningful wholes. Evaluation must be carried out to determine the extent to which pupils have command of these larger segments of knowledge, the extent to which they have retained and organized what they have acquired.

In IPI the unit organization and the use of unit posttests help to serve this function of testing retention. Such tests, comparable in content and format to the unit pretests, cover all objectives in the unit. They help to answer questions regarding the extent to which the pupil has retained mastery over each skill in working through a set of related skills. Information provided by this test may cause pupils, on the basis of their own or the teacher's decision, to be cycled back through certain skills that they have not retained. A pupil who shows mastery of all skills on this posttest has reached a point where a decision must be made as to which unit he or she should move to next. The IPI program provides for a relatively standard sequence in moving from unit to unit, but it also permits enough freedom so that a student successfully completing one unit can go in more than one direction. For example, upon completion of the Level D addition and subtraction unit pupils would, most typically, move on to the Level D multiplication. However, they might easily move on to Level E addition and subtraction or Level D fractions or any of a number of other units.

An extension of the idea of unit posttesting would be the readministration of such a test several weeks after a pupil had first completed it, to see if the pupil had retained the important skills over this longer period of time. Another extension would involve the development of tests covering even larger segments of the curriculum and measuring the extent to which the student could combine and relate ideas or skills acquired in different units, at different levels, and at different times. Also, a useful aid to this more comprehensive testing would be subtests from carefully selected standardized tests. To the extent that items on such tests could be identified as measuring objectives of the individualized curriculum, pupil performance on these selected items would provide evidence of the extent to which pupils could display abilities developed by this curriculum as measured by outside item-writers.

4. *Monitoring Progress*—Effective individualized instruction requires a system for providing systematic information on pupil progress. In group instruction the teacher may choose to assume that most pupils are keeping up with the pace of presentation and may base instruction purely on this average. In individualized instruction neither the pupil nor the teacher has this rough guide to help answer the question "How am I progressing?" Some other procedure must be established for telling the student when he or she should leave one lesson and move on to the next. Of course, some indication of progress is obtained from examining pupil performance on the lesson materials themselves. This means that a procedure should be established for having each lesson scored by the pupil or by a teacher or teacher's aide. There are many reasons for having pupils do such checking themselves. In fact it is probable that individualized instruction cannot be achieved unless major reliance is placed on individual pupils' monitoring and guiding their own progress. Of course, the pupil should be given considerable assistance in this. The IPI program employs the curriculum-embedded test (CET) to provide an additional check on the pupil's mastery of each objective. In a sense, this brief quiz answers the pupil's question, "Have I really mastered this skill?"

Of course, an individualized system cannot employ its monitoring procedures with an enforced rigidity. Teachers and pupils may choose to make exceptions to the standards suggested by the system. In IPI, for example, certain pupils may sometimes progress from one objective to the next even though they have not shown mastery on the appropriate CET. Such a decision may be based on the judgment that it will be a better learning experience for the pupil or will make for quicker progress if he or she is not required to spend an extended period of time on one objective.

IMPLICATIONS FOR THE CLASSROOM TEACHER

This chapter was introduced by a description of the situation of a third-grade teacher recognizing the great differences in ability among the pupils in her classroom and determined to modify her teaching procedures to take these differences into account. Of what value can the procedures described in this chapter be to this teacher? If she were to read this chapter, she would be justified in concluding "That sounds interesting, but I have neither the time nor the resources to implement such a program." How, then, could she benefit from what she read?

First, it should be clear that individualizing instruction is not a simple matter. Teacher trainees and practicing teachers taking part in in-service training programs have long been told "You must adapt your teaching to individual differences." Testing experts have advocated "test results should be used as a basis for individualizing instruction." The difficulty of putting these maxims into practice is attested to by the fact that the persons who emphasize such statements have been unable to present workable procedures for applying them. If our third-grade teacher recognizes that individualization requires extensive planning and preparation and a considerable expenditure of time and of funds, she at least has the basis for dealing with the problem in a realistic manner.

Recognizing the difficulty of the task, this teacher could then consider what might be a reasonable goal and a reasonable approach for her situation. Of course, she might consider using some commercially available materials. If she could find some that met her needs and could convince the responsible persons in her school system that funds should be provided for purchasing these materials, this could give her many of the essential components for setting up an individualized system.

Another possibility would be to take steps to arouse the interest of fellow teachers, particularly those teaching the same grade level, in embarking on a cooperative project for developing a local program for individualizing one subject or a part of one subject. Frequently a school system has special funds for supporting such a curriculum development effort.

If the situation is such that the teacher must develop her own individualized system by herself, she should recognize the magnitude of the task and probably start with a relatively small part of the year's work in one subject area. This might be as small as one or two units of study. If this experience was successful, she could add to the program in succeeding years.

SOME SUGGESTIONS FOR DEVELOPING AN INDIVIDUALIZED SYSTEM

A number of schools and individual teachers have found it possible to develop local systems of individualized instruction using the same general model employed in IPI. A few suggestions as to how this may be done can be outlined in terms of basic components of such a system.

1. *The Structure of Units and Objectives*—As illustrated by the IPI example, organizing and managing an individualized system is easiest when it is based on specifically defined objectives grouped in meaningful units and organized in terms of prerequisite relationships. This provides a structure for systematic testing. It also is the basis for identifying and labeling specific lesson materials for teaching each objective. Help in constructing such a framework of units and objectives can be obtained by the examination of relevant textbooks, workbooks, and curriculum guides.

2. *Lesson Materials for Teaching Each Objective*—Published systems, such as IPI, use lesson materials developed specifically for that system. One school

or an individual teacher probably would find it impossible to develop their own materials. However, once objectives have been defined it should be possible to identify specific pages in available textbooks or workbooks that would be useful for helping a pupil to master each objective. This could result in a "prescription development guide" that listed every objective in the curriculum and, for each objective, noted the exact pages in one or more textbooks or workbooks that could be used in studying this skill. This guide would then be used by teacher and pupil in developing daily assignments.

3. *Placement Tests*—The most easily usable type of placement test for a given individualized program would be one developed specifically for that program. Although its development might require a considerable investment of time, it would probably be a worthwhile investment because of the pupil time that would eventually be saved in test administration and interpretation of results. However, it might be found that a certain published test provided information, in terms of available subscores and performance on specific items, that permitted placement that was sufficiently valid for program operation.

4. *Tests for Monitoring Progress*—The IPI program uses unit pretests, unit posttests, and short quizzes on each objective (CET's) to help determine pupil mastery of each objective in a unit. Such information on mastery is useful for deciding when a pupil should move on to something new and what he should study next. Individualization requires information of this type. A locally developed system might incorporate tests of the type used in IPI or it might employ some modification of this system. Some systems make greater use of teacher inspection of pupil performance on lesson materials to determine mastery. This could reduce the need for testing but might require more teacher time than is available for this aspect of classroom management. It might be useful to note here that the test development process under the IPI system is somewhat simplified because of the fact that similar items appear on all four types of tests. That is, a given objective is tested on a CET, on both the pretest and posttest for that unit, and probably on the placement test. This means that once items have been written for a CET, alternate forms of the same items can be used on the other tests measuring that objective.

5. *A Management System*—The preceding descriptions of the tests and lesson materials used in individualizing instruction provided some indication of how each would be used. However, procedures for their use must be as simple and clear-cut as possible if a teacher is going to be able to manage the system. This necessitates attention to record-keeping procedures and to rules for the use of such records. A partial example of how this might be done was provided earlier in this chapter in the case of the student profile form (Figure 9.2) used with the IPI program. Here we saw how placement test results were recorded and how the form was used to determine the unit in which the

pupil was to work. This same form can also be used to record a pupil's passing a unit posttest, and it will then indicate which unit the pupil should move to next. In other words, the form provides a continuing record of pupil progress and serves as a guide for determining a next assignment. In a similar way, other forms are used for recording mastery of CET's within units and for developing specific prescriptions as to what the pupil is to use in studying. Of course, the particular record forms used by any given individualized system must be unique to the needs of that system. They grow out of, and help to clarify, the procedures used in managing the system. With such specified procedures and record forms pupils can be given major responsibilities for helping to operate the program. This type of responsibility seems essential if an individualized system is to be manageable, and it is of great importance for pupil growth.

Summary

The individualization of classroom instruction is not a simple task. It requires that instructional decisions be made on an individual basis and that they be made as part of a continuing program for guiding pupil progress. The basis for this type of planning and guiding of pupil learning can best be provided by a structured program of testing and evaluation. This program, in turn, should be organized around a sequence of specific instructional objectives and units of study. Given this type of organization, tests can be used to provide the basis for pupil placement, for the diagnosis of specific needs, and for decisions concerning mastery of objectives and units. Under this system it is also useful to specify, in advance, what decisions are indicated by pupil mastery or non-mastery of each specific test. This latter procedure can be facilitated by the development of standard forms for recording pupil results that at the same time indicate related decisions. Programs using the foregoing components have been used quite extensively and have been found to be effective in the individualization of instruction.

SUGGESTIONS FOR CLASS DISCUSSION
AND FURTHER INVESTIGATION

1. Obtain or develop an outline for some course that is of interest to you. (If you have difficulty obtaining such an outline, you could use the science course outline presented in Chapter 10.) Develop a placement test or suggest alternative or supplementary evaluation procedures that could be used to determine where each pupil should start to study if the course were to be managed on an individualized instruction basis.

2. Outline one unit of study. This could be a unit from the course outline used in Exercise 1 above. Define all of the major objectives for this unit. Develop a unit pretest that could be used for determining exactly which of these objectives any pupil had already mastered.

SUGGESTIONS FOR FURTHER READING

Persons interested in a further description of the development of the IPI program will find this discussed in C. M. Lindvall and Richard C. Cox, *Evaluation as a Tool in Curriculum Development: The IPI Evaluation Program,* AERA Monograph Series on Curriculum Evaluation (Chicago: Rand McNally and Company, 1970). A detailed description of the management system used with IPI is presented in Research for Better Schools, *Teaching in IPI Mathematics, Vol. 1: Diagnosing and Prescribing for Individualized Instruction* (New York: New Century Education Corporation, 1972).

A discussion of a variety of specific programs for achieving individualization will be found in Weisgerber, Robert A., *Developmental Efforts in Individualized Learning* (Itasca, Ill.: F. E. Peacock Publishers, 1971).

Rather detailed suggestions for using tests in adapting instruction to individual student capabilities are found in Benjamin S. Bloom, J. Thomas Hastings, George F. Madaus, *Handbook on Formative and Summative Evaluation of Student Learning* (New York: McGraw-Hill, 1971), chapters 3, 4, 5, and 6, and in Robert Glaser and Anthony J. Nitko, "Measurement in Learning and Instruction," chapter 17 in Robert L. Thorndike, ed., *Educational Measurement* (Washington, D.C.: American Council on Education, 1971).

10

Planning and Implementing a Comprehensive Evaluation Program

In the introductory paragraphs of the first chapter of this book the reader was introduced to Jan Miller, a hypothetical third-grade teacher making plans for her first year of teaching. Jan was raising basic questions that should be of concern to every teacher. How should she plan her teaching? How could she adapt her classroom instruction to the needs and interests of her pupils? How could she identify and provide special help for those pupils who were having problems? How would she know if her teaching was effective? Answering questions such as these involves making decisions about instruction, decisions that should be made on the basis of information about pupils. In other chapters the reader was reintroduced to Jan Miller, and it was explained how evaluation procedures could be used to provide answers to the questions that were of concern to her. The purpose of all these discussions was to demonstrate that a program of testing and evaluation will be of maximum use if it is seen as a system for obtaining information for instructional decision-making. Throughout the text the effort has been to show that any component of a system of testing and evaluation will probably be of use to the teacher only if plans for the use of the data are made before the test is administered. Such careful planning was seen to be essential. In the present chapter the effort will be to show how all the components discussed in earlier chapters can be integrated into a carefully planned, comprehensive program of testing and evaluation.

The planning of a testing program for a school or for an individual classroom has usually been approached from the point of view of answering such questions as (1) What kinds of readiness tests should we use in kindergarten and first grade? (2) How often should we administer scholastic aptitude or intelligence tests? (3) What types of standardized achievement tests should we use? (4) Should we administer the latter at the start or at the end of each school year? While many programs planned on this basis have been of value to teachers and school systems, the approach advocated in this text suggests that a more appropriate point of departure for the planning of an evaluation program is identification of the major types of instructional decisions that must be made. Key decisions must be made in conjunction with the three major phases of instruction.

Phase I. Planning Instruction
   Decisions:
      What is to be studied?
      Where should instruction start?
Phase II. Guiding Instruction
   Decisions:
      How should instruction be carried out?
      When is the class (or a student) ready to move on?
Phase III. Evaluating Results of Instruction
   Decisions:
      Have pupils mastered and retained important learning outcomes?

Table 10.1 provides an outline of an evaluation program that concentrates on obtaining information for making these decisions. This outline suggests that for each decision one must (1) have a structure or plan to which to relate the decision, (2) specify the type of information required, and (3) identify the possible sources for such information. These are the essential components of an evaluation program designed to provide information for instructional decision-making. The following sections will attempt to describe a comprehensive evaluation program based on the outline presented in Table 10.1.

Phase I: Planning Instruction

OBTAINING INFORMATION FOR DETERMINING
WHAT IS TO BE STUDIED

In the typical classroom the question of what is to be studied may take the form "What should I teach?" In an individualized program it might be "What should this student study?" Of course, in classes where the pupils have a major voice in planning their own activities, the question facing each stu-

Table 10.1

OUTLINE FOR OBTAINING INFORMATION NEEDED IN AN EVALUATION PROGRAM
DESIGNED TO AID IN DECISION-MAKING IN ALL PHASES OF INSTRUCTION

	Phase I: Planning instruction	Phase II: Guiding instruction	Phase III: Evaluating results of instruction
Major questions or decisions	What is to be studied? (What are the needs of these pupils with respect to this content?) Where should instruction start?	How should instruction be carried out? When is the class (or a student) ready to move on?	Have pupils mastered and retained important learning outcomes?
Basis for planning	Course outline. Specification of units and objectives. The textbook outline. Specification of prerequisite sequences.	Diagnostic outline of units or major topics. Identification of possible instructional alternatives. Specification of mastery criteria for objectives, units, topics.	Specification of essential content and skills (especially those needed as basis for subsequent courses).
Specific types of information needed	Do students already have mastery of any of course content? What have students studied before? Do students have prerequisites for course? What is present student status in mastery within sequence? Do certain topics have special interest and meaningfulness for students?	Do students have mastery or partial mastery of some topics within units? What type of instruction is most effective for this class (or for this student)? Have students mastered what they have been studying (objective, topic, unit)?	Have students retained the essential content and skills?
Possible sources of information	Course pretest. Standardized achievement tests. Student records. Placement test. Readiness tests. Aptitude tests.	Unit pretest. Interview with student. Student records. Personal knowledge of student. Aptitude tests. Quiz covering a given objective or topic (CET). Unit posttest. Student work. Interview. Observation.	End-of-course exam. Standardized achievement test. Projects. Observation.

dent would be "What should I study?" Note then that this basic question is one that must be answered no matter what type of classroom management is used. If planned learning is to take place, someone must make the decision concerning what is to be studied.

The basis for planning for this type of decision is some description and organization of the possible content or objectives. From what body of content does the teacher or the student make the selection of what is to be studied? In many cases the answer to this question is quite simple. The course content is quite well specified by a course outline or by a textbook. Even in many so-called open classrooms or activity-centered classrooms the basic skills that students are to acquire ultimately are specified in some way.

Table 10.2 provides an example of a simple form that might be used in

Table 10.2

SUMMARY FORM FOR RECORDING INFORMATION CONCERNING
PUPIL MASTERY OF SPECIFIC CONTENT
IN A GENERAL SCIENCE COURSE

Topics	Test evidence	Other evidence	Decision
Space and Our Universe	—	NM	S
The Sun and Its Planets	—	NM	S
The Sun as a Star	—	NM	S
The Solar System	—	NM	S
The Earth as a Planet	—	NM	S
Orbit of the Earth	—	NM	S
Comparison of Earth and Other Planets	—	NM	S
The Earth	NM	NM	S
The Earth's Crust	NM	NM	S
Composition	NM	NM	S
Factors Changing the Crust	NM	NM	S
The Moon	NM	—	S
The Moon's Orbit	M	—	O
Tides	M	—	O
Eclipses	NM	—	S
Weather	M	M	O
The Earth's Atmosphere	M	M	O
Air Pressure and Winds	M	M	O
Moisture, Clouds, Water Cycle	M	M	O
Air Masses, Fronts	NM	NM	S
The Seasons	M	—	O

M   Mastery
NM   Non-mastery
—   No information
S   Study
O   Omit

summarizing information concerning pupil mastery of content to be presented in a given course. It can be seen that this is the type of outline that could be obtained easily from a course syllabus or a textbook. For purposes of illustration we will assume that this course is to be taught largely on a group-paced basis. What the teacher needs to know, then, is the extent to which the class already has mastery of these topics at the level of understanding defined for this course. Having information of this type will help the teacher plan instruction so that there is no unnecessary repetition of lessons already mastered and so that study in this course will build directly on what the pupils already know. To obtain the needed information, one or more of a variety of procedures could be used. One quite efficient procedure would be to administer some type of pretest. If the teacher already has available an end-of-course exam, a mid-term exam, or unit tests, one of these could be used as a pretest. Such tests should provide rather direct evidence concerning pupil mastery of each topic in the course outline. If tests of this type were not available, the teacher might develop a special test. This, of course, could require considerable time, and the teacher might choose to avoid this task by searching for alternative sources of data. One possibility would be to use some type of oral quiz to sample general mastery of the various topics. This could be supplemented by a study of pupil performance on relevant items on any recently administered standardized achievement test. Procedures for this type of criterion-referenced use of a standardized test are described in Chapter 6.

If it is not feasible or desirable to use any type of pretest for obtaining the data needed in conjunction with Table 10.2, other sources of information must be sought. An obvious step, but one often overlooked, would be merely to determine what these students had studied in preceding general science courses. Did they study these same topics? If they did, was it at a level of understanding that could be considered a good background for the present course or was it at such an advanced level that the present course might be largely repetitious? If there is any duplication of content, how well did these students do? One might answer the latter question by talking to those teachers or by looking at any records of performance in earlier classes.

Note that an outline such as that presented in Table 10.2 could be used to summarize data for one student (in individualized instruction) or for the entire class (in group-paced instruction). The entries made in this table under "Test Evidence" and "Other Evidence" could be quite simple. If the evidence indicates that pupils have mastered the given topic or subtopic, an M, or some other simple symbol, could be placed in the appropriate cell. Other symbols could be used to indicate "nonmastery" (NM) or "no evidence" (—). The "Decision" column provides a place for indicating whether the decision was made to "study" (S) or "omit" (O) that particular topic in the study for this term. The table has been filled out to suggest a possible summary of data for a given class.

Obviously, the information concerning mastery of various topics as summarized in Table 10.2 is information on mastery at a given level of competence and understanding as represented by course objectives and given test items. The illustration presented here has suggested that pupils would not study topics for which they showed the specified mastery but would go on to other topics. Of course, another possibility would be to have such students study these "mastered" topics at a more advanced level of understanding. The important point here is that pupil and teacher must obtain information that can be used to fit pupil study activities to pupil needs.

WHERE SHOULD INSTRUCTION START?

In a real sense this question is a part of the preceding one about what should be studied. However, answering the question of where to start involves obtaining some additional types of information. One type is that related to any prerequisite ordering of the topics and objectives of a course. This is illustrated by the plan for placement testing described in Chapter 9 as a part of a structured program for individualized instruction. Under this approach the place to start instruction is at the lowest point in the hierarchy of objectives where the student shows lack of mastery. Something like this procedure may be essential in any subject area where there is a definite prerequisite order of abilities. For this reason, Table 10.1 suggests that identifying any such prerequisite orderings is the basic step in planning a system for determining where instruction should start. In other situations different kinds of information may be taken into account. To investigate procedures for making this type of decision in a more typical group-paced classroom we can turn again to the example provided by the science course outline shown in Table 10.2. This outline, and the associated record of pupil mastery, can also provide a framework for assisting in decisions on where to start study. If the outline represents, in the judgment of the teacher, the most meaningful and effective order for presenting these topics, then study should start with the first topic for which the class (or individual student) shows nonmastery. In the case illustrated by the hypothetical mastery data shown in Table 10.2 this would mean that study would start with the first unit, covering "Space and Our Universe."

Of course, in many cases the order of topics represented by such an outline does not represent any necessary prerequisite sequence, which means that pupils can study and master the second unit without having mastered the first. In such cases other types of information can be taken into account in determining where to start. Pupil interest may be an important consideration. Pupils could be given a choice as to where they should start. Relevance of the topics to community and individual needs might be taken into account. This might be done on the assumption that establishing the meaningfulness of learning content can be an important contribution to continued motivation. Note that such decisions will probably make little use of test results or of data from other formal evaluation procedures. Nevertheless they should be based on information concerning the potential content to be presented in the course and its interest and meaningfulness to students.

USING READINESS TESTS AND SCHOLASTIC APTITUDE TESTS AS AIDS IN DETERMINING WHERE INSTRUCTION SHOULD START

As the foregoing analysis has suggested, the most useful information for helping decide where instruction should start is specific information concerning what skills and content have already been mastered by the student. This tells us what the pupil is ready to study next. To obtain this type of information, teacher-made tests and other teacher-developed evaluation procedures will probably be of most value. However, published readiness tests and scholastic aptitude tests may also be of some help. Such tests have been discussed in some detail in Chapter 8.

Readiness tests are typically used in kindergarten or first grade and are intended to yield information concerning the extent to which a pupil is ready to profit from beginning instruction in reading and other first-grade subjects. They can, then, provide this rather specific information for planning instruction at this one, rather critical, point in a child's school career. In selecting a readiness test to best serve this purpose it is desirable to find a test that not only permits the teacher to select those students who are ready to begin formal instruction but also offers guidance as to what kinds of learning experiences to provide for pupils who show a lack of given prerequisites.

Scholastic aptitude tests, or intelligence tests, can also be of some value in planning instruction. However, the information such tests provide should be looked upon largely as a supplement to specific information concerning pupil mastery level. Since scholastic aptitude scores provide some indication of a pupil's ability to profit from typical school instruction, they may be useful in planning the type of instruction and the intensity of instruction that a pupil is likely to require in studying a given topic. It might be anticipated that pupils with low-aptitude test scores would frequently require special instruction to supplement that provided for the typical class member. For example, a teacher's planning decision might take the form of the statement "On this topic I will use special small-group instruction with these particular students." Again, however, it should be emphasized that in such use, aptitude test scores serve only as a supplement to the more important information concerning what the pupil has and has not mastered.

Phase II: Guiding Instruction

HOW SHOULD INSTRUCTION BE CARRIED OUT?

Perhaps the most important determiner of the effectiveness of classroom instruction is the quality of the decisions that a teacher must make, on a daily basis, as to how instruction should be carried out. Here we are concerned with such questions as "How should I teach this lesson?" "What things should be emphasized in this unit?" "What kind of lesson materials will be most effective for this student?"

To answer some of these questions certain kinds of diagnostic information are useful. In planning for a particular unit of study it is helpful to have information concerning any partial mastery that students may already have of the various topics within the unit. It is also helpful to know if it will be necessary to review any of the essential prerequisites to this unit. These types of information may be obtained through some form of unit pretest. Such a test was described in Chapter 9 as a component of a system for individualized instruction. Since this provides a very specific example of a test designed to provide one type of information that can be important in instructional planning, it might be useful for the reader to review this instrument at this point. Comparable information could also be obtained before beginning a unit of instruction in a course organized in a more conventional fashion. To illustrate this we could return to the example of the general science course outlined in Table 10.2. Looking at the "test evidence" recorded in that table for the unit on the moon, we can see that these students show some partial mastery of this unit. Before teaching the unit, it might be quite useful to obtain additional information on the nature of that partial mastery. This could be organized through the use of a detailed outline of the unit as shown in Table 10.3. For the hypothetical information recorded in this table we have assumed that no pretest was available and that it was decided that the construction of such an instrument was not warranted. However, the teacher was aware of the importance of obtaining information as to what the pupils already knew and, in this way, being aware of pupil needs. To make the decisions of mastery and nonmastery as recorded in the "other evidence" column this teacher gave the class a simple oral quiz and checked the validity of the results by reexamining pupil performance on selected items on a recent standardized test. As a result of this analysis decisions were made that some topics could be omitted, some would merely be reviewed, and others would have to be studied.

Obviously, the decision as to how instruction should be carried out involves many considerations in addition to those of which topics to omit and which to stress. The decision may involve, for example, the question of what type of lesson should be used. Should the student be expected to do a lot of reading and independent study? Will this lesson when presented to these students require an extended oral presentation by the teacher? Is pupil activity and manipulation of materials desirable? Will laboratory activities be essential? It can be seen from these questions—and there are many similar ones that could be asked—that at least two things must be taken into consideration, (1) the nature of the content and objectives to be taught and (2) the characteristics of the pupils. The nature of the content and the considerations that serve to identify any alternative methods of teaching it are frequently built into the curriculum in some manner. Instruction in some subjects typ-

Table 10.3

SUMMARY FORM FOR RECORDING PREINSTRUCTIONAL
INFORMATION CONCERNING PUPIL MASTERY OF THE
CONTENT OF ONE UNIT OF INSTRUCTION

Topics and subtopics	Test evidence	Other evidence	Decision
Unit: The Moon			
The moon's orbit			
Path and duration	—	M	O
Phases of the moon	—	M	R
As seen from earth	—	M	R
Explanation of cause	—	NM	S
Tides			
Gravity	—	M	O
Gravity of moon, sun	—	M	O
Causal explanation of tides	—	M	R
Eclipses			
Size and position of earth, moon, sun	—	M	R
Eclipse of the moon (diagram)	—	NM	S
Eclipse of the sun (diagram)	—	NM	S

M	Mastery
NM	Non-mastery
—	No information
S	Study
O	Omit
R	Review

ically relies heavily on the use of a textbook; in some it makes extensive use of laboratory activities; in others it can be carried out quite well through teacher lecture and demonstration. Most of the possible activities and the materials needed to carry them out are a part of the tools available to the teacher. Of course, the more creative teacher or more progressive school system will supplement the traditional procedures with additional ones especially designed to foster pupil growth in such important areas as problem solving, problem analysis, evaluation, and so on. The basic decision that will be made concerns which of these various procedures should be followed in teaching this content to this class (or to this individual pupil).

What information will be helpful in making this decision? One type is information about the present capability of pupils. How well can they read? Do they have the study skills required to use a workbook? Can they follow teacher directions of the type required in carrying out laboratory or other pupil activity lessons? Answers to some of these questions will be quite obvious and are related to the grade level and age of the children and to their past school experience. Some questions will have to be answered for individual pupils. One pupil may be able to use study materials requiring extensive reading, another may not. Dealing with such a situation will require adaptation to such individual differences.

The starting point for designing an evaluation program that will aid the teacher in answering the above questions is determining what procedures and materials are feasible. It is of little value to obtain information indicating that pupils will learn best in a certain manner if no materials or procedures are available for carrying out instruction in this manner. For example, it would be of no value to know that a pupil or a class could best come to understand a given process when they saw it portrayed in a movie if such a film were not available. Similarly the decision that certain pupils could best come to grasp a given concept in arithmetic if they carried out specified manipulative exercises would be of little help if such exercises could not be made available to them. Again, the starting point for deciding what information would be useful in adapting method of instruction to pupil capabilities must be a specification of what instructional alternatives are available for practical use.

An example of a very specific procedure for providing information concerning what types of lesson materials are available for teaching each instructional objective in a unit of study is shown in Table 10.4. This presents a modification of a form used in prescribing the lesson materials to be used by a student working in a math program that the authors have helped develop. It can be seen that this form first provides space for recording pretest results on each of the five objectives (A, B, C, D, and E) in this unit. This is followed by a listing of lesson materials available for use in studying each objective. As can be seen, there are three sets of manipulative lessons (manip.), one game, and one workbook available for Objective A. For Objective B there are two sets of manipulatives, two games, and one workbook. It can be noted also that the form provides space for indicating which materials a given pupil is to use, for noting when each lesson is completed (to be indicated by placing date in "Date Started" box), and for recording pupil performance on the test for the objectives. At the bottom of the sheet is a form for recording the pupil's score for each objective on the unit posttest. As indicated above, this particular form is used in a structured program where all the materials listed are available for use in the classroom. As such, this specific form has no general application to other classroom situations. It is introduced here largely to suggest the type of exact information that must be available if the teacher is to make useful decisions as to how instruction should be carried out. When the instructional alternatives are clear to the teacher, data concerning such things as a pupil's reading ability, his or her past performance when studying with manipulatives or games, and information as to which materials are of greatest interest to the pupil can be used in prescribing the most promising lesson activities.

Something approximating the information provided in the form shown in Table 10.4 could be developed from a more traditional course outline. For example, one could take the unit outline shown in Table 10.3 and add col-

Table 10.4

PRESCRIPTION FORM FOR ASSIGNING SPECIFIC LESSON
MATERIALS IN A UNIT IN INDIVIDUALIZED MATHEMATICS

UNIT 13: GROUPS BY TENS AND ONES

Name _____

Unit	Obj. A		Obj. B		Obj. C		Obj. D		Obj. E	
Pretest	Score	M/NM	Score	M/NM	Score	M/NM	Score	M/NM	Score	M/NM
Scores										

Prescriptions

Objective A

	Date started	Date completed
13–A–1 (Manip.)		
13–A–2 (Manip.)		
13–A–3 (Manip.)		
13–A–4 (Game)		
13–A (Work Bk)		

Test: Obj. A

Date	Score	M/NM

Objective B

	Date started	Date completed
13–B–1 (Manip.)		
13–B–2 (Manip.)		
13–B–3 (Game)		
13–B (Work Bk)		

Test: Obj. B

Date	Score	M/NM

Objective C

	Date started	Date completed
13–C–1 (Manip.)		
13–C–2 (Manip.)		
13–C–3 (Work Bk)		

Test: Obj. C

Date	Score	M/NM

Objective D

	Date started	Date completed
13–D–1 (Manip.)		
13–D–2 (Manip.)		
13–D (Work Bk)		

Test: Obj. D

Date	Score	M/NM

Objective E

	Date started	Date completed
13–E–1 (Manip.)		
13–E (Work Bk)		

Test: Obj. E

Date	Score	M/NM

Unit	Obj. A		Obj. B		Obj. C		Obj. D		Obj. E	
Posttest	Score	M/NM	Score	M/NM	Score	M/NM	Score	M/NM	Score	M/NM
Scores										

umns that indicated what instructional alternatives were available for each topic and subtopic. Possible alternatives here might be such things as "textbook," "teacher demonstration," "encyclopedia article," "reference books," "laboratory activities," and "field trip to planetarium." It is important for the teacher to know exactly what is available for each topic and how effective each alternative might be. When such information is at hand the question of what to use at a given time with a given topic can be answered quite easily.

WHEN IS THE CLASS (OR STUDENT) READY
TO MOVE ON TO A NEW TOPIC OR UNIT?

In a group-paced classroom this question will be answered on the basis of information about the group as a whole. In an individualized system it will be answered on the basis of information about the individual pupil. Of course, the latter is true whether the teacher or pupil is making the decision. Either one needs information if the decision is to be an intelligent one.

The basic data needed for answering this question is that concerning the extent to which pupils have mastered the content of a unit or some given segment of instruction. In the individualized program presented in Chapter 9 information of this type was provided by curriculum-embedded tests measuring mastery of each objective and by unit posttests. Basically the two considerations involved in the decision are (1) "What skills and content was the pupil expected to acquire in this segment of instruction?" and (2) "Have they been acquired to the degree necessary for successful work in succeeding units?"

A first step in planning an evaluation program for aiding decisions concerning pupil progress is to identify "check points" where such decisions will be made. In a textbook-centered class such points may be at the end of each chapter. Where a definite course outline has been developed and is followed, such decision points may be specified in the outline. Of course, progress will have to be checked more often in some subject areas than in others. In a subject such as mathematics where a lack of understanding of one concept or operation may make it impossible for the student to understand the next, checks may have to be quite frequent. Once these "check points" have been identified, it is then necessary to determine how mastery of the goals and content of the relevant bit of instruction is to be assessed. This may require the use of special tests (such as unit posttests). In many situations it is possible to make this type of assessment without tests—by examining classwork, by interviewing students, by observation, or by any of a number of other procedures. Again, what is important is to get criterion-referenced information, specifically, information that tells whether or not the pupil has mastered the given content. This part of the evaluation program will probably not make use of standardized tests.

The Individualized Mathematics program that uses the prescription form presented in Table 10.4 provides an example of an instructional system that makes specific provisions for determining when a pupil is ready to move on. The form shown in Table 10.4 has space for recording the pupil's score on the test taken when study for one objective is completed. A passing score on such a test provides evidence that the pupil is ready to move on to the next objective. Also shown on the form is space for recording the pupil's posttest scores on each of the five objectives. Note that in the case of both of these types of tests the scores are criterion-referenced, that is, they tell exactly what behaviors the pupil has mastered.

For a class organized on the basis of an outline showing topics and subtopics, such as is the case in the general science course described in earlier sections of this chapter, a comparable organization for evaluation could be used. This could involve a record form parallel to that presented in Table 10.3 but with "postinstructional information" substituted for "preinstructional information." Such information concerning mastery of each successive topic and mastery of the total unit would be basic to the decision of when a student or a class is ready to move on.

Phase III: Evaluating Results of Instruction

HAVE PUPILS MASTERED AND RETAINED IMPORTANT LEARNING OUTCOMES?

Jan Miller, our hypothetical third-grade teacher, as well as all other class-room teachers, will find it important to determine just what pupils have learned during a given term or school year. Here the concern is what pupil changes have been produced during some extended period of instruction. What kind of learning has taken place? This is important both in assessing pupil growth and in determining the effectiveness of instruction.

In evaluating the results of instruction for an extended period of time such as a term or a school year it is particularly important to obtain a variety of types of information. We will want to know if pupils have achieved our specific course goals and objectives, but we will also want to determine what other outcomes there have been. Has the study of the specific course goals had a transfer effect that has enabled pupils to master certain related goals? Have there been changes in certain noncognitive qualities such as attitudes, interests, and pupil self-concept? Answering such questions will require many different kinds of evidence.

EVALUATING PUPIL ACHIEVEMENT OF SPECIFIC COURSE GOALS AND OBJECTIVES

Probably the most widely used procedure for carrying out this step in the evaluation program is the administration of some form of "final exam." This type of exam, whether it involves an objective test, an essay examination, an oral exam, or some other procedure, is designed to measure the specific goals of the course. Procedures for developing tests of this type were presented in earlier chapters.

Of course, with many types of learning outcomes the typical final exam is not the most valid evaluation procedure. For example, in some courses a term paper or term project of some type may provide a more direct assessment of pupil mastery of course goals. In some courses, such as a speech course or an instrumental music course, the most valid type of evaluation will require that the teacher observe pupil performance. In other cases, such as a shop course or a home economics course, evaluation will involve the examination of pupil products. A comprehensive evaluation program will employ a number of nontesting methods that are essential for providing valid information about pupil achievement of certain types of objectives. However, a major weakness of most such procedures is their lack of reliability and objectivity when they are employed in the rather casual fashion of many teachers. These deficiencies can be reduced, however, if the teacher is conscious of them and makes use of certain strategies and techniques.

Some simple nontesting procedures such as the grading of classwork and homework assignments can be made to produce more reliable information if some of the same steps are used here as are used with essay examinations. This means that great care must be employed in phrasing the assignment and in planning the scoring method. The aim should be to produce a more objective assessment of the pupils' work.

A more difficult job of evaluation is involved in cases where the desired pupil behavior does not produce a tangible product but is some performance that can be observed or listened to only at the time that the pupil is exhibiting it. Objectives of this type include the ability to give a speech, participate in a discussion, perform some type of athletic feat, sing, or play a musical instrument. When a pupil exhibits these behaviors, the performance does not result in a paper that can be scored or in some other tangible product that can be assessed and reexamined several times if necessary. The performance must be evaluated through the use of a subjective and rather instantaneous judgment of its value, making a reliable evaluation more difficult. The techniques described in the following sections may help improve the objectivity and the reliability of the assessment of pupil achievement in many situations where observational methods must be used.

1. *Rating Scales*—One of the most useful nontesting evaluation devices is the rating scale. This can be particularly helpful where the behavior being evaluated is made up of several different aspects each of which can be a dimension on the rating instrument. For example, in assessing the ability of a student to present a speech to the class, the teacher would be concerned with several separate aspects of the total performance. Some of these are suggested by the simple rating scale on page 220.

In using this device the teacher would give careful attention to the pupil's speech and then decide which descriptive category comes closest to describing the performance for each dimension. A check mark would then be placed on the scale above the pertinent description. This place on the scale or the numerical value associated with it would then represent the pupil's rating on the dimension.

RATING SCALE FOR CLASSROOM SPEECH

Pupil's name _____ *Date* _____
Speech topic _____

1. Did the speech contain content relevant to the topic?

1	2	3	4
Most of speech content not relevant	Only about 50 percent of speech relevant	Most content relevant; occasional irrelevant idea	All content obviously and clearly relevant

2. Was the delivery smooth and unhesitating?

1	2	3	4
Long pauses and groping for words in almost every sentence	Pauses and groping for words in about 50 percent of sentences	Occasional pause and groping for words	Delivery smooth; no pauses or groping for words

3. Did the speaker use correct grammar?

1	2	3	4
Errors in most sentences	Errors in about 50 percent of sentences	From 1 to 3 errors	No errors

4. Did the speaker look at the audience?

1	2	3	4
Looked away most of the time	Looked at audience only 50 percent of the time	Looked at audience most of the time	Looked continually at audience

This scale deals with four separate aspects of a speaking performance and provides for rating the student on each of the four dimensions. This division serves to call the teacher's attention to these aspects, and the scale, when marked, provides a rather descriptive but simple record of the pupil's presentation. It can serve as a basis for specific suggestions to the pupil, and, if it is filled out each time a pupil presents a speech, the series of ratings can be used to note changes in a pupil's performance.

As suggested before, a rating instrument of this type can be used in assessing many types of achievement. In some cases, the teacher may discover useful published devices. More frequently, however, it will be necessary to develop the desired scale. This may be done by one teacher or may be the cooperative venture of several teachers with a common need. In making an instrument of this type it is first necessary to decide what aspects of the total performance are to constitute dimensions. What are the important things to observe or listen for? Each such dimension may be defined by some specific question such as those used in the scale presented here. The points along each dimension are then identified by brief descriptions. One should start by describing the two extreme categories, the very best and the very poorest performances. After this one describes the intermediate points. The number of descriptive categories or points on the scale that should be used will depend to some extent on how many distinctly different performances it is possible to identify. Usually four or five such categories will be used.

In writing the descriptive categories it is important to be clear and specific. Each one should be so unambiguous that different raters observing the same performance could be expected to agree on the rating to be assigned. That is, subjectivity is to be reduced to a minimum. Scales are sometimes developed in such a way that each point on the scale is described by only one word such as "always," "frequently," "seldom," and "never." Such scales are of little value since words such as "frequently" and "seldom" do not have a specific meaning and the rating to be assigned depends too much on the subjective judgment of the rater.

Rating scales represent one of the most useful evaluation devices available to the teacher and probably should be used much more widely. Their use can introduce a degree of specificity and objectivity into the assessment of many types of achievement that are too often evaluated through highly unreliable procedures. The major advantages of rating scales may be summarized as follows.

1. They provide a uniform set of the essential aspects of a performance constituting the specific qualities to be observed.

2. The use of specific descriptive categories to identify the various points along a dimension greatly improves the objectivity and reliability of scores assigned.

3. The dimensions and descriptive categories provide a useful basis for offering suggestions for improvement.

4. The filled-in scale provides a permanent record of a given per-

formance. Such a record can be very useful in studying pupil progress. It also provides a basis for a reexamination and reappraisal of a given performance if this is needed in discussions with pupils or parents or in such decisions as determining an overall grade.

2. *Check Lists*—Another simple evaluative device that can be used as an aid to observation is the check list. This is useful where some type of desired pupil performance is made up of several steps or parts in such a way that each part can only be judged as either present or absent and cannot be given a rating. Shown below is a brief check list that might be used in observing whether a sewing student has learned all the steps necessary to set up a machine so that it is ready for sewing.

CHECK LIST FOR FIRST STEPS
IN PREPARING TO SEW ON A MACHINE

Name of student _____ *Date* _____

_____1. Wind bobbin
_____2. Thread bobbin case
_____3. Thread upper machine
_____4. Pull up bobbin thread
_____5. Set stitch length

_____6. Insert fabric under presser foot
_____7. Position needle in fabric
_____8. Lower presser foot

This instrument might be useful to teachers in assessing pupil performance and to individual pupils in analyzing their own mastery of the required steps. It can be an important aid to instruction in that it calls attention to all the essential steps in a performance. It can also be used for marking pupils merely by assigning a score representing the number of steps that the pupil has mastered and remembers to execute.

Check lists can be constructed for use in evaluating a variety of behaviors. The above example suggests that these are easily applied to the assessment of a pupil's ability to operate equipment or machines. Physical-education teachers find them useful in analyzing a pupil's ability to carry out an athletic feat that is made up of several component parts. For example, a check list for assessing a beginning performance in tennis might include such items as "hits forehand stroke," "hits backhand," "serves," and similar basic parts of the game. Similarly, woodshop teachers use such a device in connection with operations that may be considered as consisting of several component parts.

Check lists may also be useful for assessing pupil "products," that is, for checking to see whether something the pupil produces contains all the essential elements. For example, a woodshop teacher might make an evaluation of a piece of furniture built by a student more objective and reliable by employing a check list containing such items as are shown in the following example. It is clear that comparable lists could be developed for evaluating written products such as business letters, outlines, and plans for an experiment.

_____Dimensions are accurate within allowed limits
_____Parts are fitted together as per drawings
_____Joints are tight
_____Surfaces show proper sanding
_____Finish is applied evenly and smoothly
_____Surfaces are rubbed to proper finish

3. *Anecdotal Records*—Certain types of instructional objectives that must be evaluated by observation of behavior cannot be divided into dimensions and rated on scales or check lists. The behavior can only be described and given a general assessment. In the evaluation of such objectives anecdotal records may be of some use. An anecdotal record is a brief written description of some specific behavior or action that was observed by the writer. If the behavior observed and recorded represents evidence of the extent to which the pupil has mastered an objective, a series of such records can provide valuable data on pupil progress. For example, let us assume that one objective an elementary school teacher has established for science teaching is that "the pupil will develop enough interest in science to choose, during free periods, to read science books or to work with some of the science equipment." The teacher might do certain things to stimulate this interest and then observe what a pupil does during a free period. Brief anecdotal records could then be used to note any progress shown by an individual student. A series of anecdotes for one student might be something like the following.

> November 3, 10:30 A.M.
> End of arithmetic lesson
>   When Paul completed his arithmetic, I told him he could do anything he wished for the next ten minutes. He went to the reading table and looked at the covers of three or four different books. Then he returned to his seat and gazed out the window until reading period started.

> November 7, 10:30 A.M.
> End of arithmetic lesson
>   Paul completed his assignment and I told him that he could do what he wished. He went to the reading table and leafed through two books. He then went to the science shelf and played with a magnet for about two minutes. After this he returned to his seat and rested with his head on his desk.

> November 9, 10:25 A.M.
>   Since Paul had finished his arithmetic test, I told him that he would have fifteen minutes of free time. He returned to his desk and gazed out the window for two or three minutes. Then he went to the science shelf and spent about five minutes seeing how many nails he could pick up with the horseshoe magnet.

In this illustration the three anecdotes seem to show that Paul is developing some interest in using free time to work with the science equipment. The teacher might note this progress through casual and unrecorded observation, but the use of written anecdotes forces one to note and record specific evidence. The anecdotes also provide a written record that can be examined from time to time for the reassessment of progress and can be shown to another teacher, a supervisor, parents, or to the pupil.

Anecdotal records will probably not be used too widely by the classroom teacher since writing them can be time-consuming and since there are only a few types of objectives for which they are appropriate. Such records will probably be used only with selected students. In the situation described above, for example, anecdotes would not have to be written for those pupils who always displayed a great interest in working with science equipment. It could merely be noted that they had achieved the objective, and the recording effort could then be concentrated on those pupils in whom the interest had yet to be generated. Also, the teacher might find it necessary to do some time sampling by observing two or three pupils on one day, another two or three on a second day, and so on, so that the pupils first observed might not be observed a second time until four or five days later. Although this would not provide a complete record of what any pupil did, it should be sufficient to detect trends in behavior patterns.

It is generally suggested that each written anecdote should be placed on a separate small card and that such cards should be placed in the individual pupil's folder. The behavior described should be behavior that is relevant to the objective that is being evaluated. Statements should be limited to specific, factual descriptions of what took place. The anecdote should not evaluate the behavior as good or bad. Neither should the anecdote contain statements that attempt to explain the reasons for a behavior. These are separate steps to be carried out after the anecdotes have been read and studied. An anecdote is merely a "picture" of a pertinent instance of some behavior and might be considered as an economical substitute for a motion picture of what took place.

A very important caution must be observed by anyone using anecdotal records. Great care must be taken to maintain the confidentiality of such records and to see that they are not misused. They should be available to parents and to authorized school personnel but must not be open to examination by unauthorized persons. Also, when any such record has served its purpose, it should be destroyed.

THE USE OF STANDARDIZED TESTS IN EVALUATING THE RESULTS OF INSTRUCTION

Standardized achievement tests can be of some value in assessing pupil achievement of the specified goals of an instructional program. Using such a test in this way, however, requires a special analysis of the test and a determination of which items measure which specified course goals. Since this procedure will result in the identification of only a limited number of goals that can be measured by such items, it is typically much more satisfactory to develop special tests and other instruments to assess pupil mastery of all program goals.

However, end-of-year standardized testing can serve very important purposes. It can provide broadly descriptive information concerning what pupils have in fact acquired. It is to be hoped that pupils learn much more than just those abilities spelled out in the course objectives. All schooling must be built on the assumption that the specific skills the pupil studies and masters have a transfer value resulting in the mastery of certain related skills that were not studied. Measuring these possible outcomes is one of the functions served by a good standardized achievement test. Of course, when tests are used in this way, the information they provide is probably more useful for evaluating the curriculum and instruction than it is for evaluating individual pupils. These tests provide descriptive information represented by statements such as "Our pupils seem to be acquiring these kinds of skills and understandings, but they are not acquiring those." Such analyses may serve to validate the curriculum as it is presently being offered, or it may serve to identify certain learning outcomes that should be given more formal attention.

EVALUATING NONCOGNITIVE OUTCOMES

This text has been concerned largely with instruments and procedures for assessing the cognitive outcomes of instruction, outcomes such as knowledge, comprehension, and a variety of intellectual skills and abilities. The emphasis on evaluating such outcomes, however, should not be interpreted as representing a judgment by the authors that pupil growth in affective qualities is of less importance. Indeed, it is our feeling that a strong case could be made for schools' giving major attention to pupil attitudes, interests, habits, and personality traits. A comprehensive evaluation program then should provide information about these types of variables.

A major part of the program for evaluating noncognitive variables probably ought to be based on specific goals that have been established in this area. These goals should be relatively simple. They should be goals that pupils can be expected to achieve or toward which they can at least show progress. Some examples would be the following:

The pupil shows an interest in learning.
The pupil shows appropriate attention to learning tasks.
The pupil shows some degree of self-confidence about learning.
The pupil cooperates with others in appropriate ways.
The pupil shows a willingness to be of assistance to others.

Of course, when goals of this type are established, plans must be developed for helping pupils to achieve the goals. Just as specific objectives in the skills area provide direction for the selection of lesson materials and instructional activities so must goals in the noncognitive area provide direction for planning an appropriate classroom environment. For example, if pupils are to acquire an interest in learning, then learning activities must be made interesting and rewarding. If pupils are to develop a confidence in their ability to learn, then they must be given learning tasks at which they can succeed. It can be seen that the specification of goals in the noncognitive areas should influence a teacher's practices in classroom instruction and management.

A program for evaluating goals such as those listed above will probably depend largely upon teacher observation as the basic data-gathering procedure. It will be noted that each of the goals in our example describes a behavior that a pupil should display on a rather continuing and typical basis. The most direct and valid way to assess such behaviors is to observe what pupils do. An earlier section of this chapter provided an example of how anecdotal records could be used to record information concerning changes in pupil interest as this was noted through observation of the student. This same procedure, using anecdotal records, could be followed in describing pupil change with respect to a variety of types of behaviors. Rating scales could also be a useful tool in recording assessments made through observation. With certain goals check lists could be developed as a means for recording the number of instances of specified behaviors. Of course, all of these devices merely provide a means for recording those things that the teacher observes. The basic assessment procedure involved is teacher attention to those behaviors that have been specified in the noncognitive goals.

In a few limited areas, teachers may be able to find published instruments, such as attitude inventories, which can be useful in a classroom evaluation program. If such devices really measure the attitudes that are of interest, they can be incorporated into the evaluation program. Other instruments in the noncognitive area, such as personality inventories, should probably not be considered for inclusion in classroom evaluation. Their use should be left to persons having special training in their use and interpretation. It is the authors' recommendation that the assessment of noncognitive variables in the classroom be carried out almost exclusively through observation.

The foregoing discussion has dealt with the evaluation of noncognitive variables where these have been identified as specific instructional goals. It is important also that some attention be given to noncognitive variables that may represent "unintended" results of instruction. This concern is somewhat parallel to that represented in the earlier discussion of the use of standardized achievement tests to measure cognitive outcomes not specified in the objectives of a course. The difficulty in the noncognitive domain is that no comparable broad survey assessment instruments are available. Again, here, reliance must be placed principally on teacher observation. Undoubtedly this will be largely informal observation where the teacher will be alert to various types of unintended outcomes, both desirable and undesirable.

The assessment of noncognitive outcomes in an evaluation program will be carried out mainly for purposes of examining the overall results of instruction. Typically, such judgments of individual pupils are not of sufficient validity and reliability to warrant their being used in reports to parents or to the pupils. Of course, in unusual cases this may be necessary. In most cases, however, such an evaluation should be used as a basis for judging the general quality of the classroom environment and providing a basis for improvement.

Summary

The goal of this chapter has been to present an outline of an evaluation program that will provide a teacher with information that can be used in instructional decision-making. In Chapter 2 of this text, "Planning for Instruction and Evaluation," the instructional process was described as consisting of three basic steps or phases:

1. Determining what the pupil is to learn
2. Carrying out the actual instruction
3. Evaluating the change in pupil behavior

Planning and carrying out instruction require that many decisions be made with respect to each of these three phases. The present chapter has outlined an evaluation program directed toward the obtaining of information that can be useful in making such decisions. The focus of the proposed evaluation program was on the types of questions that must be answered rather than on the types of tests or instruments that should be administered. For this reason the program was outlined in terms of basic types of questions associated with each of the phases above, here identified as (1) planning, (2) guiding, and (3) evaluating instruction. In answering these basic questions, data from certain tests, both teacher-produced and standardized, will be of great value. However, a variety of other kinds of information will also be essential. In all cases the determination of what information to seek will be based on judgments as to what will be of most value in helping to answer the key questions.

SUGGESTIONS FOR CLASS DISCUSSION
AND FURTHER INVESTIGATION

1. Use Table 10.1 to develop the outline of an evaluation program for some course that is of interest to you. Identify the specific instruments and procedures that you would use as sources of information for each of the three phases of instruction. You should be able to use some of the instruments developed in exercises for earlier chapters.

2. For the course identified in Suggestion 1 above (or for some other course) develop a content outline such as that used in Table 10.2 of this chapter. For each topic in the outline, identify the type of evidence (test, nontest) that you would use to determine present pupil mastery of that topic.

3. Using the outline developed in Suggestion 2 above, list the possible instructional alternatives (textbook, reference book, teacher demonstration, etc.) that might be used in helping pupils master each topic. Develop procedures that would be useful in determining which alternatives to use with a given student.

4. Develop a check list of the type shown on page 223 that could be used for rating the quality of a teacher-made objective test. Items in the list might include such things as "adequate instructions," "specific provisions for marking answers," and so on. Use the check list to assess a test you developed for this course. What important qualities of a test cannot be assessed by a check list?

SUGGESTIONS FOR FURTHER READING

A further discussion of the use of a testing program for instructional decision-making is presented in Benjamin S. Bloom, J. Thomas Hastings, and George F. Madaus, *Handbook on Formative and Summative Evaluation of Student Learning* (New York: McGraw-Hill, 1971), section 2, "Using Evaluation for Instructional Decisions," and in Robert Glaser and Anthony J. Nitko, "Measurement in Learning and Instruction," in Robert L. Thorndike, ed., *Educational Measurement, Second Edition* (Washington, D.C.: American Council on Education, 1971), pp. 625–70.

The description of a total program of testing and evaluation as presented in this chapter is that of a program oriented to the purpose of guiding classroom instruction. This type of program can be compared with a more typical program that endeavors to serve a broader variety of needs of a school system by examining such sources as Robert L. Thorndike and Elizabeth Hagan, *Measurement and Evaluation in Psychology and Education, Third Edition* (New York: John Wiley, 1969), chapter 16, and in Julian C. Stanley and Kenneth D. Hopkins, *Educational and Psychological Measurement and Evaluation* (Englewood Cliffs, N.J.: Prentice-Hall, 1972), chapter 17.

Index

of noncognitive outcomes, 225–26

objectivity, 24–25

planning for, 30–34, 206–28

reliability, 23–24

testing for, as a *Taxonomy* level. *See* essay test items

validity, 21–23

experimental studies in construct validation, 114

extrapolation:

as a *Taxonomy* category, 31

in deriving grade-equivalents, 96

F

Feldt, Leonard S., 148

fixed instruction, 169

French, Will, 11

frequency distributions, grouped, 80

G

Gagné, Robert M., 28, 74, 169

Glaser, Robert, 74, 75, 102, 169, 205, 228

Glass, Gene V., 102, 132

Goslin, David A., 67, 68

grade-equivalent scores, 92–98, 99, 150–52

Griffiths, Nellie L., 183, 184

Gronlund, Norman E., 27

grouped frequency distributions, 80

grouping by ability, 181–82

growth, measuring, 97–98

H

Hagen, Elizabeth, 166, 169, 228

Harvard Committee on the Objectives of Education in a Free Society, 11

Hastings, J. Thomas, 35, 46, 64, 67, 205, 228

Hieronymus, Albert N., 138, 150, 161

Hildreth, Gertrude H., 183, 184

Hills, John R., 133, 189

Hopkins, Kenneth D., 9, 64, 228

I

individualized instruction, 18, 190–205:

framework for, 191–92

suggestions for development, 202–04

See also Individually Prescribed Instruction

Individually Prescribed Instruction (IPI), 76–78, 100, 192–202:

implications for classroom teachers, 201–02

management system for, 193–98, 205

procedures used in classroom, 193–98

role of testing and evaluation in, 198–201

student profile used with, 196

information:

as need of teacher, 4

as purpose of testing, 4

obtaining needed, 19

instruction:

decisions to be made in, 18, 207

evaluating results of, 218–27

guiding, 212–18

how carried out, 212–16

planning, 10–28, 207–12

instructional decision-making, 8, 18, 20:

and criterion-referenced *vs* norm-referenced scores, 78, 103

decisions to be made, 19

obtaining needed information for, 19–20

Prescott, George A., 142, 149
prescriptions for learning, 197, 215–16
pretests, unit, 78, 195
principles, testing for knowledge of, 36
profile, student, 196
Project TALENT, 86

Q

Quantitative measurement, 65–102:
  benefits of, 65–66
  cautions for use of, 67–68
  need for, 65–67
  See also scores

R

rating scales, 219–22
raw scores. *See* scores
readiness tests, 6, 169, 183–85, 212
reliability:
  alternate forms:
    delayed administration, 127
    immediate administration, 123–24
  coefficient, 123, 125, 128
  of an evaluation procedure, 23–24
  improving, of essay test scoring, 50–52
  internal consistency, 124–26
  Kuder-Richardson formula, 20, 125
  odd-even split, 125
  on a single occasion, 123–26
  over a time period, 126–27
  of a published achievement test, 157
  Spearman-Brown formula, 125
  split-halves, 124–25
  summary of types of, 128
  test, 120–29

test-retest, 126–27

S

sample:
  standardization, 141–43
  test items as a, 111–12
Sapon, Stanley M., 185, 186
Scannel, Dale P., 166
scholastic aptitude. *See* standardized scholastic aptitude tests
Schumaker, John A., 102, 132
Schwarz, Paul A., 133, 189
scores:
  basal age, 170, 171
  criterion-referenced, 74–78
  DIQ, 175, 179
  grade-equivalent, 93–98, 99, 150–52
  IQ, 170–73
  mental age, 171, 172
  normalized standard, 87
  norm-referenced, 78–100
  percentage score, 81
  percentile rank, 79–81, 90, 99, 146–48, 179
  raw, 68–74
  SS-score, 85–86, 99
  standard, 81, 84–86, 99, 144–46, 171, 175
  stanine, 91–93, 99, 144, 148–50, 179
  test, 65
  z-score, 84–85, 90, 91, 92, 99, 104–06
scoring key, use with essay tests, 50–51
Seashore, Harold G., 176, 177
selection-type items, 117–19
Simon, Theodore, 170
sorting procedure, in scoring essay tests, 51
Spearman-Brown formula, 125

specific objectives. *See* objectives, specific behavioral

specimen sets of tests, 152, 165

SS-score. *See* scores

standard deviation, 81–84, 86

standard error of measurement, 128–29

standard scores. *See* scores

standardized achievement tests, 134–65:

    administering, 160–61

    development of, 135–52:

        planning, 136

        scaling phase, 143–44

        standardization phase, 141–43, 157

        tryout and item analysis, 136–40

    manual for, 152

    norm-referenced, definition of, 135

    obtaining criterion-referenced information from, 161–63

    publishers of, 166

    selecting a published test, 157–58

    in specific subject areas, 155–56

    survey batteries, 153–55

    types of, 153–56

    using results of, 158–60, 224–25

standardized scholastic aptitude tests, 167–89:

    and adaptive instructional procedures, 168

    contrasted with achievement tests, 168

    cultural-fair, 178

    group tests, 173–77

    major categories of, 169

    meaning of scores from, 178–80

    as measures of innate capacity, 168–69, 177

    as measures of general scholastic aptitude or intelligence, 169–82:

        history of, 169–70, 173–74

        role of Alfred Binet, 170

    multiple aptitude batteries, 176–77

    nonverbal, 176

    omnibus type of, 174–76

    readiness tests, 183–85

    in specific subjects, 185–87

    stability of scores from, 180–81

    using results of, 177–78, 181–83, 212

    verbal, 176

Standards for Educational and Psychological Tests, 178–80, 189

Stanford Achievement Test:

    description of, 155

    items from, 36, 37, 38, 40, 42, 43

    percentile rank norms table, 147

    stanine interpretations, 149

    subtest intercorrelations, 130–31

Stanford-Binet Test, 170–75

Stanley, Julian C., 9, 64, 102, 132, 133, 228

stanine scores. *See* scores

Sterrett, Barbara G., 161, 162, 163

supply-type items, 48, 52–54

synthesis:

    as a *Taxonomy* category, 32, 33

    evaluating, 43–44

T

Taxonomy of Educational Objectives, 30–33, 35, 40, 42–43

teacher-made tests, 5, 47–64

"teaching for the test," 160

Terman, Louis M., 170, 172, 173

test appraisal, technical concepts, 134–66

Test Collection Bulletin, 156, 157

testing:

    for application, 39–43

    categories of, 5

    for comprehension, 37–39

Weinberg, George H., 102, 132
Weisgerber, Robert A., 102, 205
Wesman, Alexander G., 64, 176, 177
Wolf, Richard M., 181, 182

Z

zero as a meaningful score, 70, 72, 73
z-scores. *See* scores